SOCIETY OF ILLUSTRATORS
53RD ANNUAL OF AMERICAN ILLUSTRATION

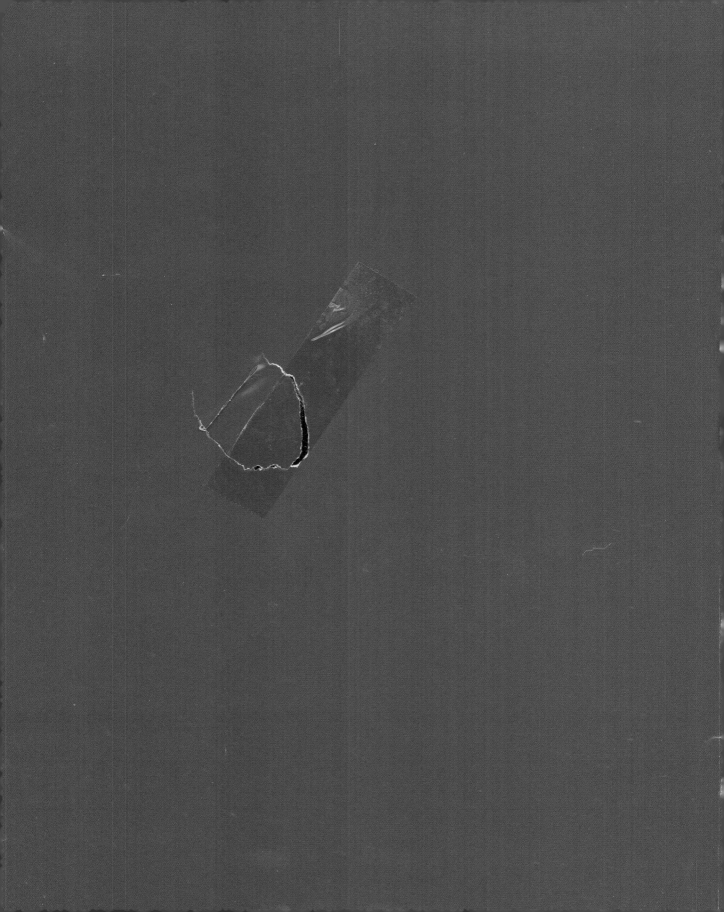

SOCIETY OF ILLUSTRATORS
53RD ANNUAL OF AMERICAN ILLUSTRATION

SI
53

FROM THE EXHIBITION HELD IN THE GALLERIES OF THE
MUSEUM OF AMERICAN ILLUSTRATION AT THE SOCIETY OF ILLUSTRATORS
128 EAST 63RD STREET, NEW YORK CITY
JANUARY 5 – MARCH 19, 2011

PUBLISHED BY SOCIETY OF ILLUSTRATORS AND HARPER DESIGN

HARPER DESIGN
An Imprint of HarperCollins Publishers

ILLUSTRATORS 53

Society of Illustrators, Inc.
128 East 63rd Street, New York, NY 10065-7392
www.societyillustrators.org

PUBLISHED BY:
Harper Design
An Imprint of HarperCollins*Publishers*
10 East 53rd Street
New York, NY 10022
Tel:(212) 207-7000
Fax:(212) 207-7654
harperdesign@harpercollins.com
www.harpercollins.com

LIBRARY OF CONGRESS CONTROL NUMBER: 2011934725
ISBN: 978-0-06-212336-7

DISTRIBUTED THROUGHOUT THE WORLD BY:
HarperCollins Publishers
10 East 53rd Street
New York, NY 10022
Fax: (212) 207-7654

EDITOR, Jill Bossert
BOOK AND JACKET DESIGN BY Erin Mayes and Simon Renwick, EmDash, Austin
JACKET COVER ILLUSTRATIONS BY Yuko Shimizu (front), Eddie Guy (back)

PHOTO CREDITS: Jury photos by Jessica Yoemans

PRINTED IN CHINA
First printing 2011

S153
TABLE OF CONTENTS

PAGE 2
President's Message

PAGE 4
Chair's Message

PAGE 6
2011 Hall of Fame

PAGE 28
Hall of Fame Laureates

PAGE 30
2011 Hamilton King Award and
Richard Gangel Art Director Award

PAGE 36
Editorial

PAGE 200
Advertising and Institutional

PAGE 364
Book

PAGE 440
Uncommissioned

PAGE 516
Sequential

PAGE 558
Zankel Scholar
Distinguished Educators of the Arts
Student Scholarship Award Winners

PAGE 574
Index

I'm looking at a beautifully drawn scratchboard illustration of Homer by Mark Summers. Homer's writings are about 3,000 years old, and Mark's technique is probably as old as Homer. The image I'm looking at is a screen saver on my e-reader. It's ironic that this cutting edge (the day I got it, anyway) electronic device displays pictures created using a method that's as old as wood. The best art is the art that's bought, no matter what the delivery system. Out where the shortcuts end, trained artists will continue to make pictures that illuminate, entertain, and sell. By way of evidence, we offer *Illustrators 53* as a sample portfolio of the year in American illustration. Unlike my e-reader, it has pages, and they are filled with a variety of wonderful and exciting images created by artists who gave the pictures everything they had, using every available tool.

My thanks goes to this year's annual chair, Edel Rodriguez, to assistant chair, Yuko Shimizu, and to the jurors for the careful choices they made for inclusion in the exhibition and this book. To our director, Anelle Miller, for making the show and all the related events appear seamless, and to the Society's staff, who worked very hard to make it look as though it's not hard work. Thanks to our member volunteers, who generously gave their time to hang these exhibits. And to you, the illustration community, for keeping it all alive with your continued participation.

We hope you will enjoy the Annual and appreciate the artists who cared enough to give us their best.

Facing page: Portrait by Joe Ciardiello.

Sometimes, I am asked by students whether a career in illustration is viable. With all the changes that are happening in the industry, some wonder whether they should be doing something else. I tell them that if they ask that question, they should probably be doing something else. Art is not something one opts out of. You either have to do it, or you don't. Artists have work inside of them and they have a drive that makes them want to share that work. This drive, desire, and excitement to share what's inside of them is what makes an artist. Everything else follows. When I was 18 and struggling to figure out how I was going to make a living, my college mentor, Ms. Mary Buckley, said these words: "Do the work, everything else follows." I needed career advice, information, details, but all I got was "Do the work, everything else follows." I felt frustrated, but I continued on, with those words as my guide.

I had my first introduction to the Society of Illustrators while I was a young art student at Pratt Institute. The work in the Society's galleries and annual books gave me a peek into the illustration world and helped me understand the work of many of its artists. I'm very thankful for everything the Society has given me over the years and am very honored to have been selected as chairperson for this year's annual. I would like to thank Nora Krug for nominating me, and Yuko Shimizu for her work as my co-chair this year.

Early on in the process, I worked with past chairs to choose this year's stellar jury. All of us brought names to the table and spent a day balancing and considering the entirety of the jury to assure that all aspects of the field were well represented. The selected juries met over a span of a week in the fall of 2010 and brought an inspiring amount of talent and observational skills to the proceedings. A big note of thanks goes out to all the judges for their input and for the time they gave to the Society. It was a real pleasure to get to know all of them.

I was given the exciting task of choosing a poster artist and designer for the annual's call for entries. I chose Sam Weber to create the artwork and Kim Bost to design the poster. They both did a wonderful job to promote the competition and my thanks go out to them for their time and generosity. Many of the details of this year's annual were handled by the Society's Kate Feirtag and Anelle Miller. I would like to thank them and the rest of the SI staff and volunteers for the hard work they put into installing the exhibitions, organizing the juries, and hosting the various opening nights.

Finally, there would not have been a show without the great work that was submitted by all the artists—over 4,000 entries from all over the world. I am always inspired by illustrators' capacity to innovate and come up with new ways to tell stories that help define the culture around us. This year was no exception. Thanks to all the artists who submitted their work this year and congratulations to all of the award winners.

My mentor, Ms. Buckley, passed away last year, but as I sat down to write this chair's message, her words came into my thoughts once again. Twenty years later, I still remember them. They're simple words, but when there is so much information, business advice, statistics, and issues to process, they've kept me focused. I wanted to share them and hope they continue to inspire. Do the work, everything else follows.

Facing page: Portrait by Gérard DuBois.

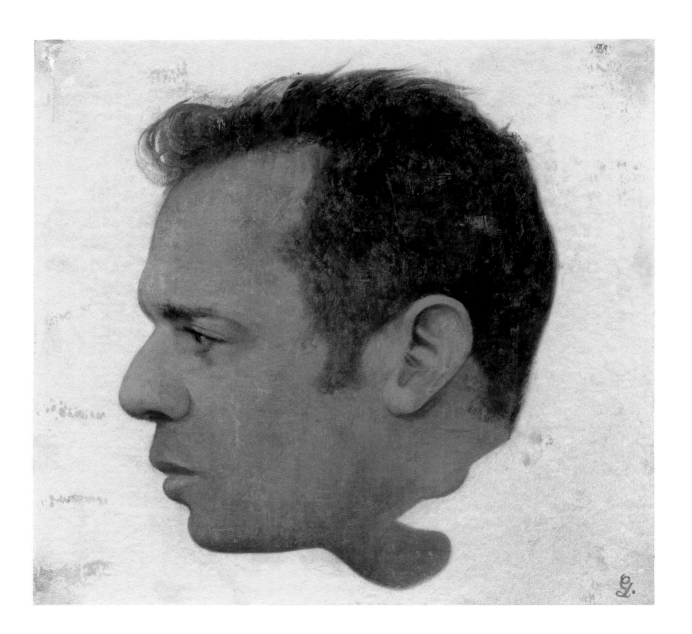

HALL OF FAME 2011

Since 1958, the Society of Illustrators has elected to its Hall of Fame artists
recognized for their distinguished achievement in the art of illustration.
Artists are elected by former presidents of the Society and are chosen based on
their body of work and the impact it has made on the field of illustration.

Howard Pyle, Father of American Illustration. Poster illustration celebrating the Society of Illustrators' 75th Anniversary. Published 1976. Assemblage of printing plates depicting Howard Pyle and some of his illustrations, type, woodblocks, and found objects. Courtesy of the Museum of American Illustration at the Society of Illustrators.

FRED OTNES

[b. 1930]

The art of collage, for which Fred Otnes is best known, relies on chance—the seemingly random arrangement of disparate elements from unrelated sources. The skill, taste, and experience of this consummate practitioner controls chance to such felicitous ends that they appear to be inevitable.

Otnes was born in Junction City, Kansas, and raised in the Midwest, where his family frequently moved because of his father's work. His peripatetic youth made socializing difficult, but it also resulted in Otnes's strong sense of independence. His artistic ability was evident from an early age, when he imitated his favorite cartoonists and comic book artists. His skill, which was encouraged by his father, was also recognized by his high school art teacher, who arranged for him to visit *The Lincoln Journal*, where he was hired to work when he was not attending school. Various jobs led to an apprenticeship in the engraving department. Working at the paper enabled him to imagine a future in art for himself.

In 1947 Otnes joined the Marine Corps, where he produced illustrations for brochures and other printed materials. Two years later, after a short time back at *The Journal*, he enrolled at the Art Institute of Chicago, where exposure to its fine art collection was more important to his art education than his classes. To support himself he worked at the Illustrators Studio and found it, too, to be more meaningful than his formal education, which he discontinued after a year. Though appreciative of the Old Masters, he found himself drawn to modern artists, especially Braque and Picasso. Cubism, with its pictorial flatness, was to have a lasting impact on him; it instilled in him a love of Modernism with its commitment to form without the illusion of depth.

While taking night classes at the Academy of Art, he worked at Whitaker-Guernsey, one of Chicago's top studios, where he turned out illustrations for major advertising clients such as Abbott Laboratories and United Airlines. At the time, his work reflected the influence of illustrators he admired—expert draftsmen Al Parker, Robert Fawcett, and Austin Briggs, among others.

In 1953 Otnes met and married Fran McCaughan, who created order out of the chaos of his bachelor life, and with whom he had a uniquely close and equal partnership. That same year, after having conquered Chicago, Otnes moved to New York to work at the prestigious Rahl Studios. He rented a house in Westport, Connecticut, and became close friends to many of the famous illustrators who lived in the area. For more than ten years he worked successfully in a representational style for such clients as *The Saturday Evening Post*, *True*, and *Collier's*, specializing in masculine themes. In 1962, Otnes signed with the highly respected art representative Bill Erlacher, of Artists Associates, beginning a strong relationship that lasted more than 30 years.

In the early 1960s, the Otneses built and decorated their International style dream house—a Modernist gem that he credits, in part, with his development as an artist. At that time, the publishing world was in a state of flux due to the influences of photography and television on the marketplace. Otnes could see that a change had to be made to the narrative approach to illustration. To that end, he added a spacious studio to his home, where he learned a variety of printing techniques. What has been called his "metamorphosis" was abrupt. Robert Hallock, art director of *Lithopinion*, responded by frequently publishing the artist's new work, to which Otnes soon added collage elements. He then employed photographic images within the collage, using his own photography or adapting imagery from other sources, such as old family photos. General acceptance of his new style quickly followed and assignments came from *The Saturday Evening Post* and the Franklin Library, the publisher of finely made illustrated books for whom he worked for many years.

The late 1960s and 1970s was a period of political and social turbulence—fertile ground for editorial debate and deliberation. The complex and abstract nature of such debate was difficult to render in traditional, narrative methods but was very well served by Otnes's collages. He strongly related his artistic explorations to the work of Robert Rauschenberg, with its crowded juxtaposition of silk-screened images. Also, Otnes felt his audience, by way of television, had grown accustomed to repeated images and had the ability to take in large amounts of visual information. His illustrations, with their numerous and varied elements, encompassed entire events and atmospheres.

For three decades, Otnes's illustrations appeared in *Penthouse*, where his technique was ideally suited for wide-ranging or abstract features on current affairs. In the same vein, his series on the historical life of Christ appeared in *The Atlantic Monthly*. For assignments with less pointed agendas, Otnes produced many works with a nostalgic, dreamy

atmosphere, combining old photographs rendered with the photo-transfer technique, paint, antique collage elements, and even flowers that his wife had pressed. Attracted by the work of Louise Nevelson, with the overarching precedent of Joseph Cornell's boxes, Otnes began constructing assemblages for illustration assignments.

In the early days of the personal computer and other emerging technologies, Otnes's work was sought after by companies desperate for symbolic visuals to project a high-tech look for their products and services. Influenced by the work of Eduardo Paolozzi, Otnes photographed the programming symbols off the screen of a small computer he used primarily for playing chess. This look was also effective for a variety of pharmaceutical giants and large conglomerates—companies with no single product to represent—who wished to express the intangible benefits of their holdings. Otnes enjoyed extraordinary success working with editorial and advertising clients, designing stamps for the U.S. Postal Service, and creating posters for 34 movies and a mural for the Ronald Reagan Library.

His poster for the Smithsonian National Air and Space Museum was also enlarged to a dramatic wall-size mural. The clean design and sheer beauty of Otnes's multilayered work belied its difficulty. The complexity required that the artist think "like a three-dimensional chess game." After

careful research to get the appropriate elements, he set up each layer and transferred it, one color at a time, requiring that he visualize in advance how every shape and value would relate to all the others in the completed piece.

By the mid-1980s the sophistication of graphic design software, as well as a proliferation of stock illustration and photography, caught up with advertisers' needs and Otnes saw it was time to consider another change. He felt that, "something created by hand was going to be the way to go." This transition came at a time when he was showing his work at universities and colleges where he lectured, and in galleries nationwide, as well as in Paris, Japan and Korea.

With his unique approach, Otnes, as an agent of change in the field of illustration, was among the forces that moved illustration away from the traditional, representational narrative, providing clients an alternative interpretation of text or concept. His beautifully elegant solutions to countless illustration problems garnered Otnes more than 200 awards from prestigious arts organizations. The Society of Illustrators, which awarded him many Gold and Silver Medals and its Hamilton King Award, now has the honor of including him, most deservedly, in its Hall of Fame.

JILL BOSSERT
author, Fred Otnes: Collage Paintings

CLOCKWISE FROM TOP: Illustration for *Sports Illustrated*, c. 1970s. Mixed media; Illustration for *Penthouse* magazine, c.1980s. Mixed media; Cover, *The Washington Post Magazine*, c. 1970s. Mixed media; *Robber Barons*. Mixed media. All art courtesy of the artist.

Jerry Pinkney's icons of living culture have, since 1960, been an important part of the American visual landscape. Created for the covers and pages of periodicals and picture books, postage stamps, greeting cards, advertisements, and well-traveled historic sites, his art is intimately encountered by a vast and eager audience seeking meaning in the stories he has chosen to tell. Intricately conceived, his narratives imbue ordinary activities with a sense of historical importance, and his exquisite characters and meticulously researched details inspire belief by millions in the vision that he continues to refine.

Born on December 22, 1939, and raised in Philadelphia, Pinkney never imagined that a career in art might be possible. In his modest but loving home, his creativity was encouraged by his mother Willie Mae, a homemaker, and his father James, a craftsman with a flair for style. "I was drawing to learn," Pinkney later reflected, "but no one was able to point me to a way of making a living in art."

At home, storytelling was a treasured oral tradition. Pinkney's parents, who migrated from the South, retold classic folk tales in rhythmic cadences that captured his imagination, providing a sense of cultural belonging. The legend of John Henry, the adventures of Uncle Remus, and *The Ugly Duckling*, all illustrated by the artist later in life, were among his favorites.

While working at a local newspaper stand, sketching whenever he could, Pinkney met cartoonist John J. Liney, known for his work on the comic strip *Henry*. Liney offered Pinkney a glimpse into the professional world of art. At Dobbins Vocational High School, Pinkney immersed himself in the commercial art program, taking courses in calligraphy, drafting, and graphic design, and drawing regularly from the live model. Determined to succeed, he entered the Philadelphia School of Art as a design student and scholarship recipient, the first in his family to achieve higher education.

Taking his first professional step in 1960, at The Rust Craft Greeting Card Company in Dedham, Massachusetts, Pinkney entered the field as a designer with an emerging interest in the art of illustration. Boston's publishing industry proved supportive of his work, and in 1964, while at Barker-Black Studio, he produced *The Adventures of Spider: West African Folk Tales* by Joyce Cooper Arkhurst—the first of more than 100 picture books to come. As co-founder of Kaleidoscope, an independent

art studio, Pinkney deepened his commitment to illustration, and in 1965, made the bold decision to launch a career as a freelance artist.

As he and wife Gloria Jean Pinkney raised their young family, opportunities to create culturally-themed picture books emerged. During the 1960s, the unwritten mid-century conventions that avoided depictions of ethnicity in published art began to fall away, inspired by the demand for more inclusive representations. Pinkney's art reflected his own compassionate nature, and his desire to be "a strong role model for my family and other African Americans" was becoming a reality.

By the time he moved to the New York area in 1970, he had already received professional accolades and public recognition. Book publishers engaged him to illustrate stories inspired by the realities of the African American experience, and corporations offered high-profile commissions, carrying historical conscience more deeply into popular culture. A lover of music—from jazz and blues to classical—Pinkney enjoyed the chance to illustrate album covers for RCA Records, and calendars honoring jazz greats of the Harlem Renaissance for Smirnoff. Distributed widely by Seagram Distillers in the mid 1970s, *African American Journey to Freedom* looks back on history, from the Great Migration to the Voting Rights Act of 1965—a series of 35 paintings that are now among the collections of the Schomburg Center for Research in Black Culture.

In the 1970s, Pinkney's art for contemporary fiction referenced the real-life experiences of people of color. Book jackets for the Newbery Medal winner, *Roll of Thunder, Hear My Cry* by Mildred Taylor, and many others, became the face of living, breathing characters that readers could believe in. His commissions included powerful, carefully researched art for *National Geographic* and the National Guard, significant visual documents. "These addressed the experience of being African American, and the importance of African American contributions to society," he said. "I wanted to be a strong role model, and to show my children the possibilities that lay ahead for them. That was very important."

Family loomed large in Pinkney's important mid-career works that opened a window onto the everyday lives of African Americans. Pivotal were his 1985 illustrations for *The Patchwork Quilt*, Valerie Flournoy's reflection on the intergenerational bonds within an African American family. The book's appearance on PBS television's *Reading Rainbow* brought its message to a broad audience, and signified success.

The Lion. Cover illustration for Caldecott Medal winner *The Lion & the Mouse*, by Jerry Pinkney. Little, Brown Books for Young Readers, 2009. Photo of artist by Myles Pinkney. All art courtesy of the artist.

Pinkney's warm, humanizing portrayals of people from the past in books like *Back Home* and *The Sunday Outing*, written by Gloria Jean Pinkney, were replete with images recalled from childhood, establishing a positive, empathetic view.

In 1987, an enduring collaboration was launched when Pinkney was invited to illustrate *The Tales of Uncle Remus*, retold by author Julius Lester. Working to capture the spirit of these stories, Pinkney and Lester left stereotypes behind and explored new cultural narratives. *John Henry* offered the opportunity, in 1994, to "create an African American hero that would inspire all." Familiar, too, was the story of Ybo Landing, the subject of Lester's masterpiece, *The Old African*, a stirring legend infused with magical realism, brought to life by the artist in 2005.

Published in 1998, *Black Cowboys, Wild Horses: A True Story* shed light on the contributions of people of color on the frontier. The artist's dynamic, textural paintings provide sensory depictions of Bob Lemmons' struggle and triumph over the unforgiving plains. "As a boy growing up in the 1940s, Westerns were huge," remembered the artist. "I found out later that many cowboys were black and Mexican, as were stagecoach drivers, saloon proprietors, laborers, and explorers."

In other books like *Minty: A Story of Young Harriet Tubman* by Alan Schroeder, Pinkney pieced together historical facts to construct visual realities—a skill that he has brought to several site-specific commissions. In 2008, he gave voice to documented northern slaves in a series of powerful works for the African American Burial Ground Interpretive

CLOCKWISE FROM ABOVE: *Her Little Hands and Feet Were Almost Stiff With Cold*. Illustration for *The Little Match Girl* by Hans Christian Anderson. Puffin, 1999; *The Old African*. Cover illustration for *The Old African*, by Julius Lester and Jerry Pinkney. Dial, 2005; *Escape at Night*. Illustration for *The Underground Railroad Handbook*, National Parks Service, 1997.

Center in New York. "My role was to individualize the people who were buried there," he said, "to give a face to history." Installations for the National Parks Service at Arlington House, the Booker T. Washington National Historic Site, and the George Washington Carver National Monument, are stunning recreations based in fact.

The recipient of the 2010 Caldecott Medal, as well as five Caldecott Honor Medals, five Coretta Scott King Awards, and four Coretta Scott King Honor Awards, Pinkney has received many commendations for his outstanding body of work, including the Original Art's Lifetime Achievement Award from the Society of Illustrators in 2006. Always wishing to give back, he served on the United States Postal Service Citizens Stamp Advisory Committee for 10 years, from 1982 to 1992, and in 2003 was appointed to the National Council on the Arts/NEA, where he became an influential advocate for arts funding.

"I am a storyteller at heart," Jerry Pinkney reminds us after a half century of image making. "There is something special about knowing that your stories can alter the way people see the world, and their place within it." Always rooting for the underdog, he continues to make images that bear witness to an underlying belief that all things are possible. Reaching beyond their aesthetic and conceptual underpinnings, his vibrant illustrations reveal larger truths about who we are and who we might become.

STEPHANIE HABOUSH PLUNKETT
Deputy Director/Chief Curator
Norman Rockwell Museum

KENNETH PAUL BLOCK

[1924–2009]

Kenneth Paul Block decided as a child what his profession would be and never wavered from his choice. Fashion illustration caught his imagination in the 1930s as he flipped through his mother's copies of *Harper's Bazaar* at the family home in Larchmont, New York. The stylish world depicted in the magazine and the "glamorous women in beautiful clothes" who inhabited it became his ideal, he said. Kenneth wanted to draw them and did. His single-minded focus resulted in a body of work generally considered the most influential fashion art of the postwar era.

Kenneth could be deliberate about more than art. When he and I collaborated on a monograph of his work, *Drawing Fashion*, I would sometimes go to him for help with specific words. For one description of a group of fashions worn by society women, I asked if I should call the garments *chic* or maybe something grander—*magnificent*? But no, said Kenneth, "the word you want is *splendid*." Which of course was just right.

Kenneth's enduring importance and renown is due in part to his extraordinary artistic abilities. Another factor is the publication that was his primary platform—*Women's Wear Daily*, where he worked from the mid-1950s until the disbanding of the fashion art department in 1992. As chief features artist, he was also a major contributor to *WWD*'s sister publication, *W*, which launched in 1972.

Although *Women's Wear Daily*, owned by Fairchild Publications, began in 1910 as a traditional trade paper, it expanded its reach in the early 1960s by altering its tone and outlook. The staid garment-industry publication suddenly became irreverent, newsworthy, and fun. Attention from *WWD* could make or break a designer. It could also launch, or derail, a socialite's career. By the time John F. Kennedy and his fashionable wife, Jacqueline, had settled into the White House, *WWD* had become a must-read for anyone interested in society, celebrity, or fashion.

Through Kenneth's incisive eye, mere dresses and coats became works of art, as did the women wearing them. Babe Paley, the Duchess of Windsor, and Gloria Vanderbilt were among those Kenneth drew, helping to define their status as 20th-century style icons. As Isaac

Mizrahi has noted, many legends of New York's fashionable society in the 1960s and '70s grew into Kenneth's vision of them.

Born in Larchmont, New York, on July 26, 1924, Kenneth Paul Block, the youngest of three boys, showed an early interest in the arts. His mother, Elizabeth, a gifted amateur pianist, and his father, Goodman, a lawyer, encouraged his interest. He regularly visited museums and attended dance and music concerts, all of which influenced his work. He was not especially encouraged in his career choice of fashion illustration, however. His aunt by marriage, Elsie Dick, an editor at *Harper's Bazaar,* told his mother to keep him away from the field; she did not think fashion art an appropriate profession for a man. Though Kenneth admired his aunt a great deal, both for her intelligence and her sense of style, he ignored her advice and studied fashion art at Parsons School of Design.

After graduating from Parsons in the late 1940s, Kenneth paid his dues for several years as an artist for McCall's Patterns, an experience he later described as tedious. Because the drawings had to be meticulous in their depiction of garment detail, Kenneth found little room for personal expression. He was far happier in his personal life; in the late 1940s, Kenneth met Morton Ribyat, also an artist and an accomplished textile designer, who remained his companion until Kenneth's death in 2009.

Even during Kenneth's first few years at Fairchild Publications, he drew what was expected of him—competent but somewhat sedate fashion illustrations. It was not until his personal style began to emerge, and he started to inject his drawings with movement and light, that his superiors took note. He still depicted detail in his drawings, as during his days at McCall's, but instead of a seam or a buttonhole, his specialty became gesture—how a woman held her cigarette, looked over her shoulder, or picked up a cocktail glass. The women in his drawings—this being fashion illustration, he mostly drew women—had a distinctive posture, too, one that reflected both elegance and élan. He also gave his women a sense of command; they clearly could do as they pleased.

By the mid-1960s, Kenneth had become, and remained throughout his tenure with Fairchild Publications, the most prominent figure in the company's art department, a considerable achievement given the many talented fashion artists who were his colleagues—Steven Stipelman,

LEFT: *Woman in Pink and Gray.* Gouache. *Women's Wear Daily*, Fairchild Publications. Courtesy of the Museum of American Illustration at the Society of Illustrators. Photo of the artist courtesy of Susan Mulcahy.

CLOCKWISE FROM ABOVE: *Gertrude Stein and Alice B. Toklas.* Ink, watercolor, and pencil on paper, 1980s; *Trio in Black Hats.* Ink and pencil on paper, 1991; *Redhead in Green Negligee.* Watercolor and charcoal on paper, 1991; *Cocktails with Christian (Bébé) Bérard.* Oil on canvas. All art courtesy of Morton Ribyat.

Anneliese Kapp, and Robert Melendez among them. His drawings regularly appeared on *WWD*'s front page, and he received the choice assignments, including coverage of the Paris couture and portrait sessions with well-known society women. He was so well regarded that he arranged to work at Fairchild only three days a week, using the other two days to fulfill contracts for freelance clients, including such major department stores as Bergdorf Goodman, Lord & Taylor, and Bonwit Teller.

Fairchild was the last media company to employ an entire department of fashion artists. Even as Kenneth was beginning his career in the 1940s, photography was replacing illustration as the dominant means to convey the latest styles. Kenneth's artistry, and his success, helped keep his profession alive. During more than forty years as an illustrator, he was able to capture the tumultuous changes in fashion without ever abandoning his vision; his art recognized trends without ever being trendy.

As prolific as he was in the field of fashion art—Kenneth created thousands of fashion drawings throughout his career, 2,000 of which are now part of the collection of the Museum of Fine Arts in Boston—he made another large group of drawings that was wholly invented. The figures in them appear to be from the 1920s or '30s. They are often in evening clothes, and though always stylish, not necessarily attractive in the conventional sense. Kenneth said they might have been characters invented by Ronald Firbank, the eccentric British novelist who was one of Kenneth's favorite writers. They also could have existed in an issue of *Harper's Bazaar* from Kenneth's childhood. Early on, Kenneth discovered a world that captivated him, and he never tired of re-creating it through his art.

SUSAN MULCAHY
Author, *Drawing Fashion: The Art of Kenneth Paul Block*

Cover for the catalogue *Alan E. Cober: A Retrospective Afterlife*, an exhibition organized by the Selby Gallery at the Ringling School of Art and Design which traveled throughout the United States. This was one of the artist's last drawings. All art courtesy of Leslie Cober-Gentry.

ALAN E. COBER

[1935–1998]

Alan Edwin Cober was a part of his time, yet ahead of his moment. He was an expressionist and satirist while other illustrators of his generation were realists and romanticists. He was a journalist while other illustrators in his circle were drawing entirely from the imagination. His practice often contradicted his affiliation. He was one with the Rockwell milieu but a pioneer of the anti-Rockwellian evolution. He made it possible for gritty graphic commentary to flourish in the rigid precincts of American illustration—and even the Society of Illustrators in the late sixties.

Cober was one of a small group of American illustrators who injected the precepts of modern art into commercial art, which, after World War II, was mired in overly rendered sentimentality. In the early sixties, when he began, illustration was at the proverbial crossroads, between mimicry and expression. A few progressive art directors, notably Cipe Pineles at *Seventeen*, Richard Gangel at *Sports Illustrated*, and Henry Wolf at *Esquire*, introduced young illustrators, many who were previously unwelcome in the illustration brotherhood. Cober broke through.

Rejecting realistic narrative painting for expressive and symbolic drawing, and watercolor rendering, his illustrations did not slavishly mimic a passage of a text, as was the convention, but complemented the story with an alternative vision and interpretation. Such work is commonplace now but Cober was among those who fought for its acceptance. His editorial art appeared in numerous publications, among them *TIME*, *Newsweek*, *Rolling Stone*, *Life*, *Look*, *The Atlantic Monthly*, and *The New York Times*.

Cober's loose, expressive, deceptively primitive linear style owed a debt to the economical line of Ben Shahn and the conceptual acuity of George Grosz. He often included scrawled texts on his pictures. Among his many credits were his coverage of the shuttle liftoffs from Cape Canaveral for NASA, the 1980 presidential campaign for *TIME*, and Pope John Paul's 1987 visit to the United States for *Rolling Stone*.

ABOVE: *A Figure Upon The Stage*. A mural of George Washington's birthplace, in honor of the first president's 250th birthday. February 1982. The Smithsonian Institution, Washington, D.C.; RIGHT: *Robert McNamara*. Portrait for *TIME*, April 12, 1995.

For most of his professional life he compulsively filled hundreds of sketchbooks with everything from simple notations to fully realized paintings. From these sketches he would complete drawings, watercolors, and prints. His work on the mentally retarded, prisons, and the aged were compiled in a book of drawings, *The Forgotten Society*, for Dover Books in 1972, a volume that has been reprinted in 2011. And it is this investigative illustration that stands as testament to Cober's life and career. He believed that narrative art could influence and inform public opinion. Yet he was a commentator without a specific agenda.

Sure, he was politically left of center, but his drawings, in the tradition of, but not the style of the 1930s Social Realists, was more humanist than polemical. One cannot view his drawings of Sing Sing prison's moth-balled electric chair without emotionally experiencing the violent surge of electricity that Cober described as passing through his own body when he saw this instrument of "justice" upon entering the death chamber. Nor is it possible to look at Cober's etchings of mammoth industrial turbines without knowing how totally fascinated he found these monuments of the Machine Age.

As a visual commentator, Cober responded to three stimuli: manuscripts, social and political events, and his environment. Sometimes all three fused into one. As a traditional illustrator, Cober never mimicked the texts, as many were commanded to do. He routinely injected his own symbolic commentary (even if it was not quite comprehensible). When he was commissioned to cover events, like a Pope's visit to the

United States or Jimmy Carter's unsuccessful second-term presidential campaign, he transcribed reality, yet translated it into his own visual language. When he interpreted his surroundings, he replaced discipline with free-form expression.

The man loved, loved, loved to draw—anything and everything. And his journals were fanatically filled with everything from outtakes of assignments to a series of portraits at his local swimming pool. He enjoyed the act of capturing friends and acquaintances, not as caricatures, but as characters.

Cober was a descendant of the 19th and early 20th century artist-journalists, and one of its foremost torch-bearers. However, it wasn't easy keeping the flame burning. Through the force of his will and ego (with a mild or intense touch of arrogance—he enjoyed the well-placed curse word), he could usually make art directors and editors bend to his desires. Yet that could not stop the inevitable shifts in media and method. At the time when he most actively practiced illustration, many of the traditional outlets for such work had cut their budgets and slashed their interests. Cober continually pitched his stories to deaf ears. And as young art directors took veterans' places and the institutional memory of his achievements faded, he was forced to pitch even harder. So he found alternative methods—books and exhibitions. Just think what he would have accomplished had he lived long enough to embrace the Internet.

Cober was also an influential and beloved illustration teacher. He was a professor of art and distinguished visiting artist at the University of Buffalo,

Ruby Shoots Oswald. Illustration for the article *150 Moments That Made Texas, Texas,* for *Texas Monthly,* November 11, 1985.

State University of New York. He also held the Lamar Dodd Professorial Chair at the University of Georgia, and, at the time of his death, was teaching at the Ringling School of Art in Sarasota, Florida, where the Ringling Brothers circus, which he loved to draw, retired for the winter. His work is held in the collections of the Library of Congress, the Smithsonian Institution, and the New Britain Museum. During his last two years he was exploring the medium of clay as an extension of his drawing.

Before passing in 1998 at age 63, he was firmly entrenched in the netherworld—which for some is a black hole—between "fine" art and illustration. He was a maverick in the truest sense: at times quite or-

nery, as mavericks tend to be, other times entirely sanguine about everything around him. By example he showed that illustrators needn't be schizophrenic in their creative or professional lives; rather, they can have multiple personalities. Cober didn't abide roadblocks or stop signs. He enjoyed the status of hybrid, yet pushed the concept of illustrator as "author" as far as he could take it. And today, in large part owing to Cober's tenacity, illustrators can do anything, as he might say, "they fuckin' well please."

STEVEN HELLER

Co-chair, MFA Design Department, School of Visual Arts, New York

Sleeping Woman. Cover illustration for *Sleep & Cardiovascular Disease* for Roche Products Inc., c. mid-1980s. Design director, John deCesare. Mixed media on linen canvas. Courtesy of the Estate of Robert Heindel.

ROBERT HEINDEL

[1938–2005]

This is a difficult assignment for me—writing an essay on Bob Heindel. How should I approach this? As a close business and personal friend of almost 40 years? As a designer who commissioned illustrations from him in the 1970s? Or, as his business partner in The Illustrators Workshop in the 1980s? Then again, perhaps I should simply describe and applaud his enormous talent and creativity as an artist.

Bob was born in Toledo, Ohio, and his career was a truly creative journey. By the age of 16 he knew he wanted to be an artist and boldly enrolled in The Famous Artists School, eventually to become its most heralded graduate. While still studying at FAS, he was hired as a staff artist at Coen & Foger in Toledo. He married Rose Petres, whom he'd known since high school, and together they had three sons, Toby, Troy, and Todd. Bob often said that from the start Rose had a major effect on his work, for which she often posed. In the late 1970s he would acknowledge her contribution in a beautiful suite of work entitled *Notes to a Flower*.

His journey continued when he moved to Akron, where he drew automotive parts, then to Denver, where he started an art studio, and subsequently to Detroit, where he illustrated cars and backgrounds at New Center Studio. It was an exciting time in his emerging career. He completed the FAS course and made a short trip to New York City to see what some of the top agencies and publishers thought of his work. Bingo! Assignments came from advertising agencies and magazines such as *The Saturday Evening Post*, *TIME*, *Redbook*, and *Sports Illustrated*. He loved having his work seen by the millions of people who read the popular magazines of the day. His confidence growing, it was time to move again. This time, close to New York City—where the action was.

The Heindels bought a 100-year-old farmhouse in Easton, Connecticut, in the early 1970s. The artist found himself among the legendary illustrators who lived in the Westport area, including Bernie Fuchs, Mark English, Fred Otnes, and Bob Peak. Frequent luncheon meetings with some of these artists at Chez Pierre in Westport were analogous to the gatherings of artists at Le Dome in Paris at the turn of the 20th century. The level of creativity in the area enlivened Bob's creative juices.

Artists Associates in New York, a major firm representing top illustrators, asked him to join their ranks and his star continued to rise. Assignments broadened and included jobs from major pharmaceutical companies such as Ciba-Geigy and Roche Labs, and limited edition books for the Franklin Library including *The Grapes of Wrath*, plus a host of advertising campaigns and editorial assignments. He worked in oil, conté crayon, collage—whatever suited his mood.

The 1980s were an exciting and extremely busy time for Bob. He pursued three creative fronts simultaneously: First, he continued to attract interesting and lucrative assignments as an illustrator. Second, he continued, along with Alan E. Cober, Mark English, Bernie Fuchs, Fred Otnes, and Bob Peak, as a core member of The Illustrators Workshop. The headline for the workshops was "Come Study with Six of the World's Greatest Illustrators." Bob had clearly joined the ranks of the elite American illustrators of the day. Young and emerging artists from all over the world came to study with these great talents. The programs were held in cities across

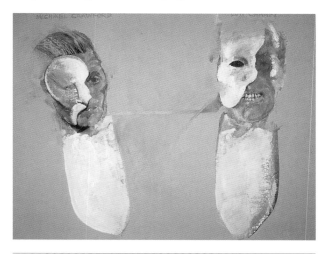

Michael Crawford as the Phantom for *The Phantom of the Opera* by Andrew Lloyd Weber, c. mid-1980s. Oil on panel. Courtesy of the Estate of Robert Heindel/R.U.G.

Cover illustration for *Family in Distress*. Ciba-Geigy promotion. Design director, John deCesare. Mixed media, including photos of the artist's three sons. Courtesy of John deCesare.

Sleeping Man. Illustration for a series, *Sleep & Cardiovascular Disease*, for Roche Products Inc., c. mid-1980s. Art director, John deCesare. Oil. Courtesy of John deCesare.

the country—from New York to Monterey, California, and abroad in Paris and St. Maarten. Bob's interest in teaching flourished in this environment and he once said he didn't know who benefited the most from the workshops, the attendees or the faculty.

Third, he became interested in dance—especially ballet. Never one to rest on his laurels, he began working with various ballet companies, exhibiting his paintings at the opening of their ballet season. Interestingly, his drawings and paintings focused on rehearsal rather than performance. In 1985 his works were shown at the Royal Festival Hall in London, with HRH The Princess Margaret attending the opening. A giant banner hung outside the hall, "*The Obsession of Dance by Robert Heindel*" announcing the show. A new creative world was in the making.

He garnered awards from the major graphic arts competitions and many medals from the Society of Illustrators, as well as its prestigious Hamilton King Award in 1982 for a painting for The Dallas Ballet Company. At this time he met Andrew Lloyd Weber, for whom he created iconic images for the musical spectaculars *The Phantom of the Opera* and *Cats*. He followed those commissions with set and costume designs for the folk ballet *Still Life at the Penguin Café*.

He focused more and more on paintings of the ballet, and mounted major shows of his work in America, Europe, and Japan. Art Gallery International stated "Heindel has become 'the Degas of our time'." His work is held in many private and public collections, including the National Portrait Gallery in London and the Smithsonian Institution in Washington, D.C.

On his blog, *American Illustration*, David Apatoff quoted Bob as saying, "When you do really terrific work, you know that you've done it. You can tell. I know who I compare myself against, who I've been up against. And it starts all the way back with the cave paintings in France. You start out thinking your competition is the guy you want to get a job away from that day. Then you gradually realize that you are your competition. The job is your competition."

Throughout Bob's career he tried to see things through fresh eyes. His color palate was broad and what he left out of his illustrations and paintings was as important as what he included. He wanted the viewer to discover something that possibly he or she had not anticipated seeing.

Lest one think he was overly serious, let me correct that thought. He was a brilliantly informed conversationalist, argumentative to a fault, salty in his use of the language, very funny, and as warm and friendly as anyone I have ever met. He loved to cause tongue-in-cheek angst whenever possible. For instance, at one of the Illustrators Workshops, he surprised me one day in front of a live audience of aspiring illustrators. He delivered a finished illustration assignment I had given him and asked for a critique of his painting on the spot, then proceeded to argue every criticism I made—with a big smile on his face.

Bob leaves a legacy of creativity, risk-taking vision, and achievement. Election into the Society of Illustrators Hall of Fame, in recognition of his extraordinary career, is a fitting honor for this remarkable artist.

JOHN A. DeCESARE

Mother and Baby. Woman's Day, 1975. Acrylic and pastel on board. Courtesy of the Museum of American Illustration at the Society of Illustrators.

1958 Norman Rockwell
1959 Dean Cornwell
       Harold Von Schmidt
1960 Fred Cooper
1961 Floyd Davis
1962 Edward Wilson
1963 Walter Biggs
1964 Arthur William Brown
1965 Al Parker
1966 Al Dorne
1967 Robert Fawcett
1968 Peter Helck
1969 Austin Briggs
1970 Rube Goldberg
1971 Stevan Dohanos
1972 Ray Prohaska
1973 Jon Whitcomb
1974 Tom Lovell
       Charles Dana Gibson*
       N.C. Wyeth*
1975 Bernie Fuchs
       Maxfield Parrish*
       Howard Pyle*
1976 John Falter
       Winslow Homer*
       Harvey Dunn*
1977 Robert Peak
       Wallace Morgan*
       J.C. Leyendecker*
1978 Coby Whitmore
       Norman Price*
       Frederic Remington*
1979 Ben Stahl
       Edwin Austin Abbey*
       Lorraine Fox*
1980 Saul Tepper
       Howard Chandler Christy*
       James Montgomery Flagg*

1981 Stan Galli
       Frederic R. Gruger*
       John Gannam*
1982 John Clymer
       Henry P. Raleigh*
       Eric (Carl Erickson)*
1983 Mark English
       Noel Sickles*
       Franklin Booth*
1984 Neysa Moran McMein*
       John LaGatta*
       James Williamson*
1985 Robert Weaver
       Charles Marion Russell*
       Arthur Burdett Frost*
1986 Al Hirschfeld
       Rockwell Kent*
1987 Maurice Sendak
       Haddon Sundblom*
1988 Robert T. McCall
       René Bouché*
       Pruett Carter*
1989 Erté
       John Held Jr.*
       Arthur Ignatius Keller*
1990 Burt Silverman
       Robert Riggs*
       Morton Roberts*
1991 Donald Teague
       Jessie Willcox Smith*
       William A. Smith*

1992 Joe Bowler
       Edwin A. Georgi*
       Dorothy Hood*
1993 Robert McGinnis
       Thomas Nast*
       Coles Phillips*
1994 Harry Anderson
       Elizabeth Shippen Green*
       Ben Shahn*
1995 James Avati
       McClelland Barclay*
       Joseph Clement Coll*
       Frank E. Schoonover*
1996 Herb Tauss
       Anton Otto Fischer*
       Winsor McCay*
       Violet Oakley*
       Mead Schaeffer*
1997 Diane and Leo Dillon
       Frank McCarthy
       Chesley Bonestell*
       Joe DeMers*
       Maynard Dixon*
       Harrison Fisher*
1998 Robert M. Cunningham
       Frank Frazetta
       Boris Artzybasheff*
       Kerr Eby*
       Edward Penfield*
       Martha Sawyers*
1999 Mitchell Hooks
       Stanley Meltzoff
       Andrew Loomis*
       Antonio Lopez*
       Thomas Moran*
       Rose O'Neill*
       Adolph Treidler*

2000 James Bama
       Alice and Martin* Provensen
       Nell Brinkley*
       Charles Livingston Bull*
       David Stone Martin*
       J. Allen St. John*
2001 Howard Brodie
       Franklin McMahon
       John James Audubon*
       William H. Bradley*
       Felix Octavius Carr Darley*
       Charles R. Knight*
2002 Milton Glaser
       Daniel Schwartz
       Elmer Simms Campbell*
       Jean Leon Huens*
2003 Elaine Duillo
       David Levine
       Bill Mauldin*
       Jack Potter*
2004 John Berkey
       Robert Andrew Parker
       John Groth*
       Saul Steinberg*
2005 Jack Davis
       Brad Holland
       Albert Beck Wenzell*
       Herbert Paus*

2006 Keith Ferris
Alvin J. Pimsler
Jack Unruh
Gilbert Bundy*
Bradshaw Crandall*
Hal Foster*
Frank H. Netter, M.D.*
2007 David Grove
Gary Kelley
Edward Windsor Kemble*
Russell Patterson*
George Stavrinos*
2008 Kinuko Y. Craft
Naiad Einsel
Walter Einsel*
Benton Clark*
Matt Clark*
2009 Paul Davis
Arnold Roth
Mario Cooper*
Laurence Fellows*
Herbert Morton Stoops*
2010 Wilson McLean
Chris Van Allsburg
Charles Edward Chambers*
Earl Oliver Hurst*
Orson Lowell*
2011 Fred Otnes
Jerry Pinkney
Kenneth Paul Block*
Alan E. Cober*
Robert Heindel*

**HALL OF FAME
COMMITTEE 2011**

Chairman
Murray Tinkelman

Chairman Emeritus
Willis Pyle

Former Presidents
Richard Berenson
Vincent Di Fate
Diane Dillon
Judy Francis Zankel
Al Lorenz
Charles McVicker
Wendell Minor
Howard Munce
Alvin J. Pimsler
Shannon Stirnweis
Steven Stroud
John Witt

*Presented posthumously

2011 HAMILTON KING AWARD
AND
RICHARD GANGEL ART DIRECTOR AWARD

The Hamilton King Award, created by Mrs. Hamilton King in memory of her husband through a bequest, is presented annually for the best illustration of the year by a member of the Society. The selection is made by former recipients of this award and may be won only once.

The Richard Gangel Art Director Award was established in 2005 to honor art directors currently working in the field who have supported and advanced the art of illustration. This award is named in honor of Richard Gangel (1918 – 2002), the influential art director at *Sports Illustrated* from 1960 to 1981, whose collaboration with illustrators during that period was exceptional.

MARC BURCKHARDT

[b. 1962]

What does it take to be an illustrator and artist who will be remembered as one of the greats? We all know that there is a steady winnowing down from the great pool of little artists who begin making art as children. Some continue through art school, even fewer finally make it into the highly selective and rarified world that combines art and commerce. It takes inner drive, character, and taste to succeed. Marc Burckhardt is one who has what it takes. He is an artist of unequalled talent and skill, who follows his own path and, in his own way, is redefining what an illustrator can be.

Marc grew up in Waco, Texas, and spent his summers in Germany. He drew inspiration from the refinement of Flemish painters and folk art—a unique pairing he alone would combine. Over his career he has received numerous awards from *Communication Arts*, *American Illustration*, *Print*, *Graphis* and several Gold and Silver Medals from the Society of Illustrators. Clients are all top notch and include *Rolling Stone*, *TIME*, Sony Records, the Rock and Roll Hall of Fame, and many others. In 2010, Marc was named the official state artist by the Texas State Legislature and the Texas Commission on the Arts. He served as the president of ICON, and is on the advisory board of *3X3*. The chairman of the Society of Illustrators Annual Exhibition, *Illustrators 47*, he is also on the Society's museum committee.

The art that Marc creates is both unique and ubiquitous, simultaneously new and old. He makes ideas you've never seen before look as though they've always been on earth. Marc loves museums, and somewhere in his formation, his admiration for vintage set in. Perhaps it's not only that his work would hang in galleries and museums, but that it would appear as if the work had hung there for ages. Marc's illustrations convey many things, but one overriding element is that each piece of art is important, iconic and a solid part of history.

To me, Marc as a person is a masterpiece. It's widely understood in our industry that Marc is thought of as a sage and that he charts a course for many artists, both artistically and professionally. He is an independent thinker who makes reasoned and measure decisions. I don't think a week goes by when someone is not contacting him with a career question. All of this lays out a case for an illustrator of substance, a man who is admired and whose career is one for the record books. Still, it is in an even more rarified group that he's now in: a Hamilton King Award recipient. Although the award is for a single illustration, it is understood that it also represents an appreciation for a career of meaningful art. Marc could have won this award for at least a decade, and if this were an award that could be won more than once, he would soon be building a shelf in his Austin home.

Marc does not work alone, however. Beside him is his wife Janice, who cares for him in the most loving way. They work and dream together, and when Marc tells a story, it's not "I" but "Janice and I." They are truly a well-knit couple. I celebrate Marc's successes, but in one way I find myself feeling a tinge of jealousy. Every morning, Janice takes Gertie, their beloved schnauzer, outside, and makes coffee. Gertie grabs the newspaper and together they walk to Marc's bedside to present him his cup and paper to start the day. It's the kind of advantage that seems unfair, but Marc is my friend and I'm learning to celebrate this particular success.

So now, on behalf of so many fellow illustrators who love and admire Marc, let me congratulate him on the Hamilton King Award. He inspires us and raises the bar for everyone.

TIM O'BRIEN
Hamilton King Award Winner, 2009

Himmelblick, created for the *BLAB!* exhibition.

A BRIEF, FAIRLY UNRELIABLE, VISUAL BIOGRAPHY OF FRANÇOISE
[part 1]

HER PARENTS

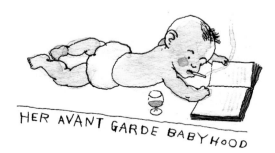

HER AVANT GARDE BABYHOOD

SCORNFULLY REJECTING CONVENTION AT AGE EIGHT

QUITS STUDYING ARCHITECTURE
(OVER THE LACK OF WORD BALLOONS)

FIRST DATE WITH SPIEGELMAN; THEY DINE ON GAULOISES

A SERIES OF ODD JOBS ANTICIPATE HER FUTURE TRIUMPHS...

SUSHI CHEF ("RAW")

JUGGLER ("THE NEW YORKER")

Biography by Barry Blitt.

HAMILTON KING AWARD

[1965–2011]

1965	Paul Calle	1974	Fred Otnes	1984	Braldt Bralds	1992	Gary Kelley	2003	Anita Kunz
1966	Bernie Fuchs	1975	Carol Anthony	1985	Attila Hejja	1993	Jerry Pinkney	2004	Michael Deas
1967	Mark English	1976	Judith Jampel	1986	Doug Johnson	1994	John Collier	2005	Steve Brodner
1968	Robert Peak	1977	Leo & Diane Dillon	1987	Kinuko Y. Craft	1995	C.F. Payne	2006	John Thompson
1969	Alan E. Cober	1978	Daniel Schwartz	1988	James McMullan	1996	Etienne Delessert	2007	Ted Lewin
1970	Ray Ameijide	1979	William Teason	1989	Guy Billout	1997	Marshall Arisman	2008	Donato Giancola
1971	Miriam Schottland	1980	Wilson McLean	1990	Edward Sorel	1998	Jack Unruh	2009	Tim O'Brien
1972	Charles Santore	1981	Gerald McConnell	1991	Brad Holland	1999	Gregory Manchess	2010	John Jude Palencar
1973	Dave Blossom	1982	Robert Heindel			2000	Mark Summers	2011	Marc Burckhardt
		1983	Robert M. Cunningham			2001	James Bennett		
						2002	Peter de Sève		

RICHARD GANGEL ART DIRECTOR AWARD

[2005-2011]

2005 Steven Heller

2006 Fred Woodward

2007 Rita Marshall

2008 Patrick J.B. Flynn

2009 Gail Anderson

2010 DJ Stout

2011 Françoise Mouly

Editorial

PHILIP BURKE
ILLUSTRATOR

Born in Buffalo, NY, Philip moved to NYC in 1977 at the age of 21 and immediately was given drawing assignments from the *New York Times*, *TIME*, and *FORTUNE*, as well as becoming a regular in the *Village Voice*, and experiencing a musical awakening as punk flourished in the East Village. In 1983 Philip started painting, signed an exclusive contract with *Vanity Fair* at its rebirth, and returned upstate to start a family. From early 1989 to the end of 1995, his paintings appeared as a regular feature on the contents page of *Rolling Stone*. His work has appeared monthly on the cover of the *New York Observer* for the past 15 years. Philip's original paintings were featured in a one-man show at the Rock and Roll Hall of Fame in 2006.

STEVEN CHARNY
SENIOR ART DIRECTOR, *ROLLING STONE*

Steven Charny is senior art director at *Rolling Stone*. Besides hanging out with Ke$ha and Justin Bieber, his favorite task at the magazine is assigning illustration, especially the lead record review, for every issue. In over 20 years in the publishing business, he has held various art director positions at magazines such as *Sports Illustrated* and *Food & Wine*. In the years prior to becoming a magazine art director he was a failed illustrator/bartender. He graduated from Syracuse University as an illustration major. He lives in a small town in New Jersey (although he would like everyone to know that he is not actually *from* New Jersey) with his wife and two teenage children who are constantly pestering him for concert tickets.

ROBERT HUNT
ILLUSTRATOR

Robert Hunt received a bachelor's degree in art history and a masters degree in Illustration. As described by Walt Reed in the 2003 edition of *The Illustrator in America*, "His work reflects his classical training, but with a contemporary take." His work has appeared on the covers of hundreds of books by many leading authors, and his clients include every major American publisher. He has also created illustrations for a wide variety of projects, including editorial illustrations, animated motion logos, advertisements, and annual reports. In addition to his assigned illustration work, he does personal experimental paintings, including documentary projects and landscape paintings. A member of the Society of Illustrators in New York, Robert is a past president of the San Francisco Society of Illustrators.

KORY KENNEDY
DESIGN DIRECTOR, *RUNNER'S WORLD*

Kory Kennedy studied Communication Design at Parsons School of Design in New York City. After graduation, he accepted a position as designer for *Interview* magazine and has excelled in publishing ever since. He trotted over to the American Kennel Club for a few twirls around the ring, then got called up to the big leagues at *Sports Illustrated* for a couple of seasons. He then dissected and experimented on *Discover* magazine, before returning to *Sports Illustrated* as deputy art director. From there, he crowd-surfed his way to become senior art director of *Rolling Stone* before tearing up the main stage as design director of *SPIN*. He is currently the award-winning design director of *Runner's World* and resides in Allentown, PA, with his wife, two sons, and cat. His website is www.korykennedy.com.

JOHN KORPICS
CREATIVE DIRECTOR, *FORTUNE*

John Korpics has been a publication designer and art director for over 20 years. He has worked at *Esquire*, *Entertainment Weekly*, *GQ*, *InStyle*, *Premiere*, *Musician*, *Regardie's*, and *Philadelphia* magazine. John has won the national magazine award for design twice, as well as the magazine of the year, and numerous Gold and Silver Medals from the Society of Publication Designers. You can see his work at www.johnkorpics.com. John currently lives in Waccabuc, NY, with his wife and two daughters, a dog (which he loves), and two cats (which he tolerates).

ANITA KUNZ
ILLUSTRATOR

Anita Kunz, OC, DFA, has worked internationally as an artist and illustrator for 30 years for magazines, book publishers, and advertising agencies. Her works have been shown in numerous galleries and museums. She has won many awards for her work, including the Hamilton King Award from the Society of Illustrators in 2003. She has received the highest Canadian civilian honor, The Order of Canada, for her work as an artist. She has also received an honorary doctorate from the Ontario College of Art and Design University. She lives in Toronto where she continues to work and teach.

SCOTT MENCHIN
ILLUSTRATOR

Scott Menchin worked for *How* magazine and *Seven Days* before running his own design studio. He began illustrating in 1989 and has worked for Ford, Intel, Pfizer, Toyota, *TIME*, *Newsweek*, *Esquire*, *Wired*, *Sports Illustrated*, *Smart Money*, *Bloomberg*, *Saveur*, *Rolling Stone*, the *New York Times*, and the *Washington Post*. His work has appeared in *American Illustration*, *Print*, *Communication Arts*, the Society of Illustrators, and the Society of Publication Designers. His children's books include *Man Gave Names to All the Animals* with text by Bob Dylan, a series by Doreen Cronin, and *Riding in My Car*, based on the famous Woody Guthrie children's song. *Taking a Bath With the Dog and Other Things That Make Me Happy*, which Scott wrote and illustrated, won the Christopher Award and was cited by the Bank Street College.

JANET MICHAUD
DESIGN DIRECTOR, *THE WASHINGTON POST*

A graduate of Syracuse's Newhouse School of Public Communications, Janet Michaud began her career as a graphic artist at a newspaper in upstate New York, then moved to the Jersey Shore to design *Sports* for the Asbury Park Press. In 1996, Janet went to the *Boston Globe*, her hometown newspaper, to create the sports art director position, and to design projects. After orbiting New York City for 10 years, Janet moved to Brooklyn in 2001 to become an art director at *TIME*, where she art directed many special sections and cover stories. She moved to Washington, DC, in 2008 to create the features design director position at the *Washington Post*. She has also been on a team to redesign the newspaper and the magazine, which she has also art directed.

BRIAN STAUFFER
ILLUSTRATOR

Brian Stauffer's illustrations, which are best known for their conceptual take on social issues, have appeared in the *New York Times*, *TIME*, the *New Yorker*, the *Nation*, the *Village Voice*, *Rolling Stone*, *Esquire*, *GQ*, and over 300 other publications worldwide. Through a unique combination of hand-drawn sketches, painted elements, and scanned found objects, Brian's work bridges both the traditional and digital realms. His images are in the permanent collections of The Wolfsonian, the Museum of American Illustration at the Society of Illustrators in New York, the American Institute of Graphics Artists, The Newseum of Washington, DC, and the Art Directors Club of New York. Born and raised in Arizona, Brian graduated from The University of Arizona in 1989 with a BFA emphasizing graphic design. He received an Editorial Gold Medal in the Society of Illustrators 52nd Annual, and his work was featured in the March/April issue of *Communication Arts*. He now lives in San Rafael, California.

GOLD MEDAL WINNER
STEVE BRODNER

Reservoir Runners
This was a standalone piece for the *New Yorker*. The art directors, Chris Curry and Caroline Mailhot, wanted a portrait of the unique kind of New York athlete who will carry on no matter what. So I arrived early one morning at the Central Park Reservoir track and faithfully recorded the scene. Essentially the piece painted itself. It's always great when that happens.

GOLD MEDAL WINNER
Gérard DuBois

Sacred Space
I've been working for *TIME* on Nancy Gibbs's essays for two years now; her articles are always great, and it's always a challenge to do them justice with my images. The subject of this one was rather delicate, not only because of the controversy that was going on at the time, but also because Nancy's text was subtle and all but Manichean. I came up with the sketch pretty fast. Though I had other ideas, this one seemed the strongest, as was its impact. I cannot say a lot about the illustration itself; I guess its strength has much more to do with the subject than with my idea or technical skills. Often less is better and sometimes, less is gold.

GOLD MEDAL WINNER
Eddie Guy

Open Heart
The assignment was to illustrate a series of essays on people who have returned to some kind of spirituality in their lives. This image explores the idea of re-inhabiting the heart or opening the heart up to new life. The heart was built, textured, and rendered in Modo 401 software.

MGMT
The editor had a vision of the band "in kind of hipster version of astronaut uniforms." This naturally led me to *Yellow Submarine* (the animated Beatles movie from the '60s), trying to find a way to correspond with that trippy psychedelic palette, and the life-embracing curves.

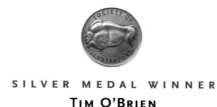

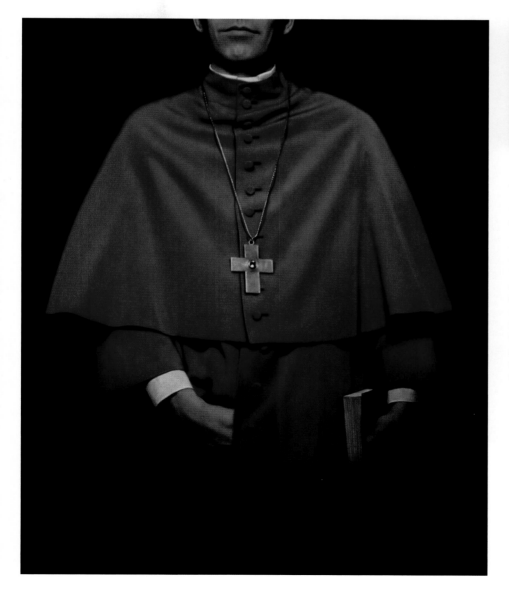

Catholic Church Abuse
All the scandals that have rocked the Catholic Church have been well earned. Abuse of children at the hands of priests is one of those horrible topics that most turn away from, but *Der Spiegel* is not that kind of magazine, and with art director Stefan Kiefer, the artwork attacks this subject. This illustration was a complete collaboration between art director and artist and I share this award with Stefan. Powerful topics need powerful illustrations. I think we did that here.

Woman, Fire, and the Sea
I had originally started to make the piece the way you might a model car kit—having all the parts laid out in front of you, and then slowly piece-by-piece snapping it together. But then, like a model car kit, you apply too much pressure and break something, and then you freak out and try haphazardly gluing stuff back together, but then the glue is all blobby and makes other things fit weird, and it's just a mess. So that happened first. Then I picked up a piece of board I had lying around, angrily scribbled what I thought I wanted—and suddenly there she was.

DANIEL ADEL
The Union Jack Is Back

DANIEL ADEL
Sir Thomas Brokaw

DANIEL ADEL
Farmer Renzo

JONATHAN BARTLETT

Tension

This was an illustration for a book review about two different novels that share similar themes: family struggle, love, and tragedy, to name a few. The image was inspired by one of the book's main characters, a young woman who struggles with life's challenges while growing up in a cotton mill town during the Industrial Revolution. Published by the *New York Times Book Review*, it was art directed by Nicholas Blechman.

JONATHAN BARTLETT

Mutual Self-Deception

Using visual metaphor and unusual juxtaposition, *Mutual Self-Deception* pokes fun at the concept of perfection by telling the story of a character whose only true enemy is his own conscience. The image was originally part of a personal body of work, which explores the themes of absurdity and society's questionable characters, but was later published in the "Gallery" section of the *Atlantic*.

JONATHAN BARTLETT

The Fox Trap

While the prescribed concept of a dandy lifestyle may be noble, the irony of striving for perfection in an imperfect world is worth exposing. With *The Fox Trap*, I intended to build an alternate world, playing off nostalgia and putting to use the archetype of the Gentleman Dandy. Lifting the shroud of the proper world, we find a reality of tongue-in-cheek criticism, filled with incapable fools—the punch line to the joke that they are ignorantly incapable of recognizing: themselves.

JONATHAN BARTLETT

Fear the Unknown

Sometimes it is what we don't see that has the biggest impact. Such is the case with this piece, the opening image for a report about haunted locations around America. While the other illustrations showcase actual locations, this image serves to set the mood. My goal is for the view-ers to see themselves within the lonesome character–apprehensive, but prepared to embark on a journey into the supernatural. Published by *Spirit* magazine, it was art directed by Emily Kimbro.

JONATHAN BARTLETT
Small Business Big Success
As the economy crumbled, small businesses saw a surge of success, while in contrast big business was not doing very well. Published by *Plansponsor* magazine, it was art directed by SooJin Buzelli.

LOU BEACH
AfterLife

LOUISA BERTMAN
Happy Holidays

GUY BILLOUT
The Sound of Virtue

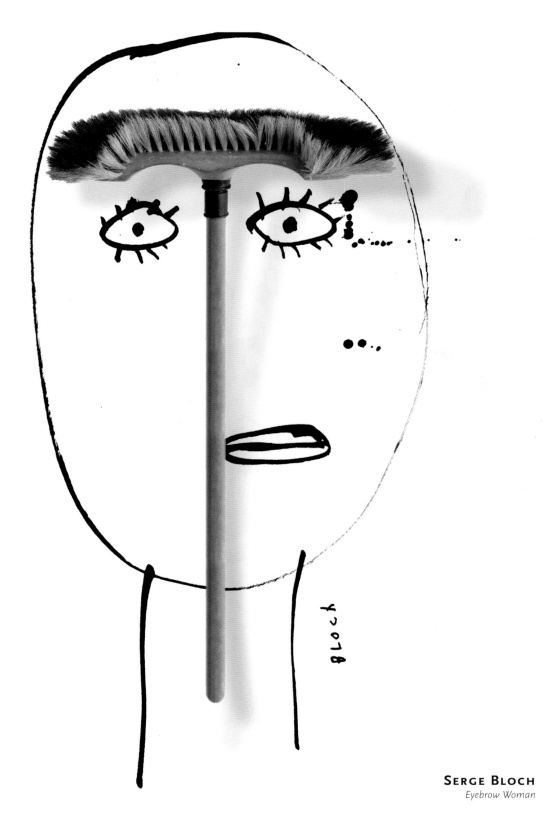

SERGE BLOCH
Eyebrow Woman

RICHARD BORGE

Knot

This piece was for an article describing the bottlenecks and obstacles that still remain in the lending sector of banking. The idea was to show a tangled mess of pipes, with the pipeline being extremely complex and cutting off the supply of funds. The art was created by using a combination of sculpture, photography, drawing, and Photoshop.

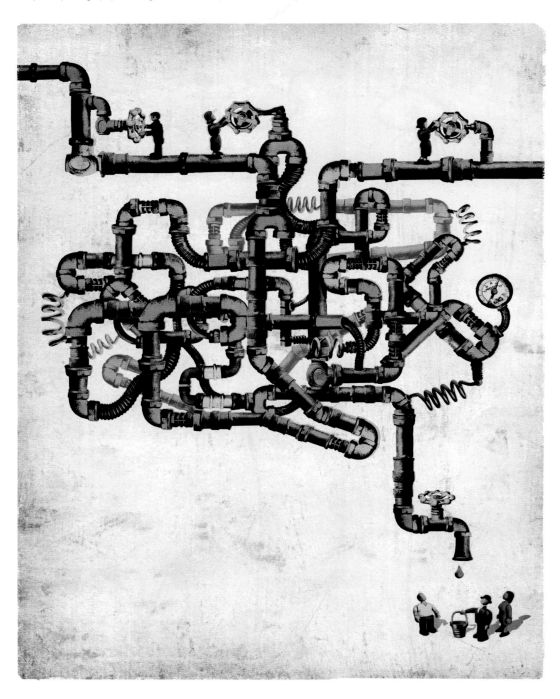

RICHARD BORGE

Sarge

This piece was for an article about the proliferation of military spending in the state of New Mexico. Art director Angela Moore was looking for a simple, striking image that combined money and military equipment. The art was created by using a combination of sculpture, photography, drawing, and Photoshop.

SAM BOSMA
Naming Names

This cover, and several accompanying spots, illustrated an article about the impact of names on their bearers. The art director wanted a cover with a lot of faces, and some way in which the young readers of the magazine could create and attribute names to each person. We landed on a yearbook-style image with the names crossed out.

SAM BOSMA
Transferring Risk

This piece ran alongside an article about the pros and cons of transferring out of defined benefit pensions, but the art director simply gave me the prompt, "Transferring risk," and told me to go from there. I was thinking about the film version of Frankenstein, where the villagers form a posse to roust out the monster. I worked with that idea on a larger scale, where the villagers decide to clean house entirely and anything dangerous is trussed up and moved out.

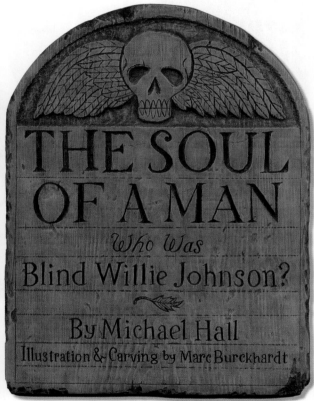

MARC BURCKHARDT
Blind Willie Johnson Spread

This spread was for a *Texas Monthly* article on legendary blues musician Blind Willie Johnson, and the search for his gravesite. Because few biographical details are known about Johnson, I chose to depict him as a ghost-like figure against a great Texas sky. The "shooting star" references the Voyager spacecraft, which carries a Johnson song in its hold. I designed and carved the tombstone as well—a first for me!

MARC BURCKHARDT

Selena

This portrait was commissioned for the cover of *Texas Monthly* to mark the 15th anniversary of the murder of Mexican-American singer and "Queen of Tejano," Selena Quintanilla. Selena's rise from humble roots to international fame inspired a generation of Latinos in Texas, her home state, and I wanted to capture the iconic status she achieved among her fans.

PHILIP BURKE
Jay Leno

Philip Burke
George Stephanopolous

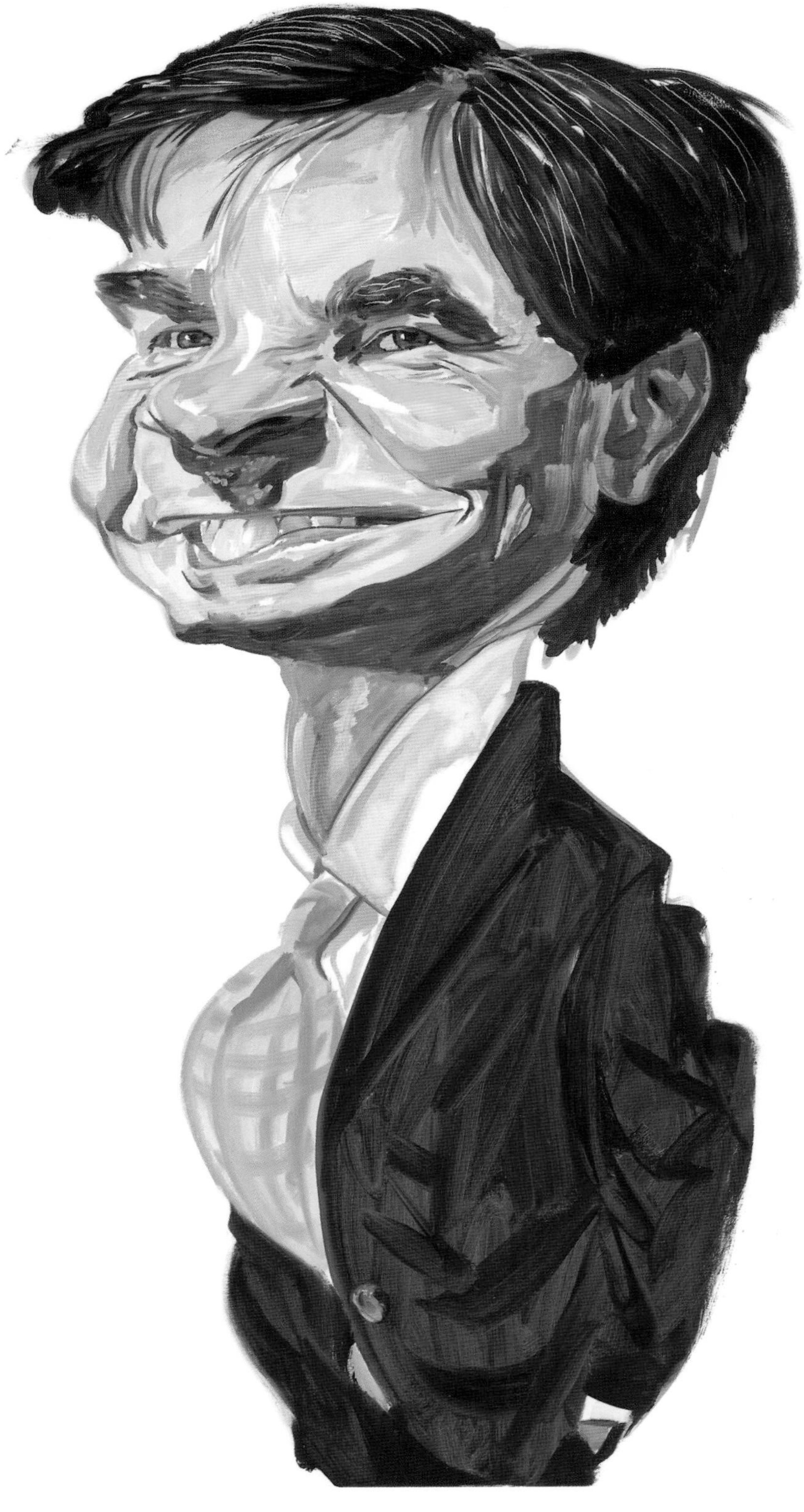

CHRIS BUZELLI
Aging Tiger
This painting for *ai5000* magazine was for an article about Singapore's crumbling economy. Lately I've been working larger than usual, and using board instead of paper. The larger scale allowed for more detail and some extra freedom with my brushstrokes. Every once in a while I find myself in a bit of a creative slump and it helps to change things up a little.

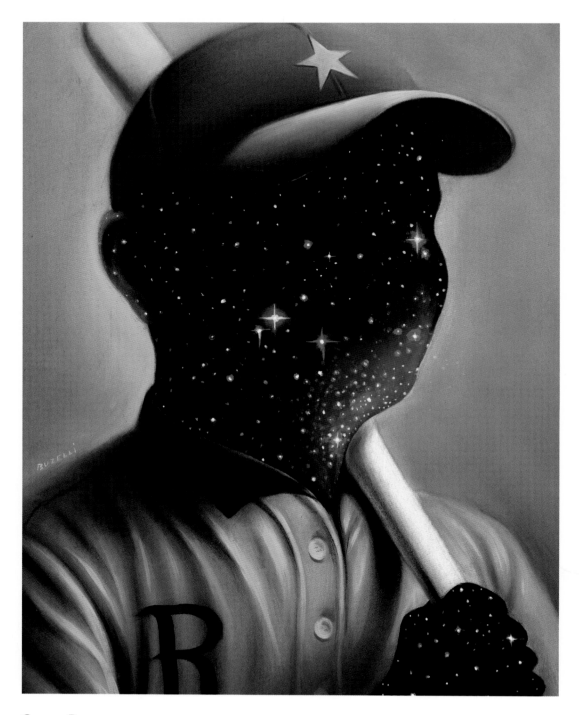

CHRIS BUZELLI

Roswell Rockets

This painting was for a historical fiction piece called "The Star and Rockets" for Tor.com. The short story is about Joe Bauman who played for the minor league team, the Roswell Rockets, throughout the 1950s. His stats magically jumped right after the supposed alien landing in Roswell. In 1954, he had that one freak, break-out year when, in 138 games, he hit 35 doubles, three triples, and 72 home runs, the latter being a record that stood throughout pro ball until 2001, when it was topped by Barry Bonds.

CHRIS BUZELLI
Ice-Skating Lessons

This painting was for the *Santa Fe Reporter's Winter Guide 2009*. I was given a list of local events which included ice-skating, back-country skiing, and hanging lights in the plaza. This soon turned into a little girl teaching the Abominable Snowman how to ice-skate. It's always a blast working with Angela Moore on these covers, especially with the rare art direction of complete creative freedom.

HARRY CAMPBELL
Global Warming Elephant
This piece was done for the *New Republic* for an article on global warming
and the Republican party.

André Carrilho
Barbarians at the Shore

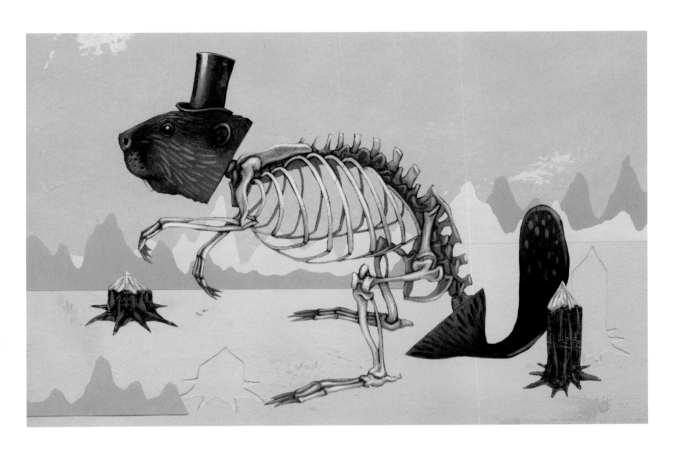

DANIEL CHANG

Fur Love and Money

This illustration was for a book review on the fur trade and its historical impact on wildlife. The beaver, whose fur was extensively used in the making of hats, was, among other animals, near extinction.

Doug Chayka

R.A.F.

As stated in the *Nation*, "The past was one single catastrophe to the Baader-Meinhof Gang, and acts of violence the only perceived exit." In this illustration I wanted to reference the diverse imagery related to the mythical media image of the German R.A.F. (Baader-Meinhof) terror organization and contrast it with their "real" appearance in infamous wanted posters from that time.

MARCOS CHIN
A Death on Facebook

MARCOS CHIN
A Portrait of Calvin Ayre

MARCOS CHIN
Soccer Is Silly

Marcos Chin

Autism

TAVIS COBURN

The Greening of the Supercar

The creative team at IEEE Spectrum asked me to produce a series depicting near-future hybrid super cars in the style of vintage mid-century car ads, juxtaposing retro and high-tech to underscore how cutting edge the cars are. Several of the cars are indistinguishable from their non-hybrid versions, so we incorporated green glows and trails to tie the pieces together.

JOSEPH CIARDIELLO
Nadine Gordimer

JOSEPH CIARDIELLO
Jonathan Franzen

JOHN CUNEO

Art or Junk?
For a (short) article regarding women's opinions on the aesthetic merits
of the male sex organ.

JOHN CUNEO

City Dog

For a first–person essay about the author's Irish Setter and his struggle to adapt to urban life.

JEFFREY DECOSTER
Running Stretch

JEFFREY DECOSTER
Flying Room

JEFFREY DECOSTER
Portrait of Anna Wintour

JEFFREY DECOSTER
Running Chain

Jeffrey Decoster
Andrew Lloyd Weber

NICK DEWAR

3x3 Cover #13

Charles Hively, Publisher and Design Director of *3x3*, wrote this commentary regarding the late Nick Dewar's work:

This is the cover for *3x3* magazine's Issue 13; Nick was one of our featured artists. We always ask artists to incorporate the issue number somehow into the cover art. I knew for this particular issue we could use a concept—superstition. My initial thought was to have someone walking under a ladder and a paint can falling off the ladder. Nick came up with this beautiful, simplistic cover that has the added shock-value of the mirror not cracking. After looking at several different directions, we returned to this one. We've entered this cover in every show imaginable and it has gotten in every show. It's the perfect demonstration of how powerful illustration can be, especially in the hands of a very talented illustrator. Nick will be greatly missed.

BYRON EGGENSCHWILER

Showing Someone You Love Them

GÜRBÜZ DOĞAN EKŞIOĞLU

Kurdish Books
The Turkish newspaper, *Milliyet*, asked me to illustrate a piece about Kurdish books, which were not being printed and published freely because of censorship and many political obstacles. I wanted to harmonize sky, book, freedom, and wire netting in this illustration.

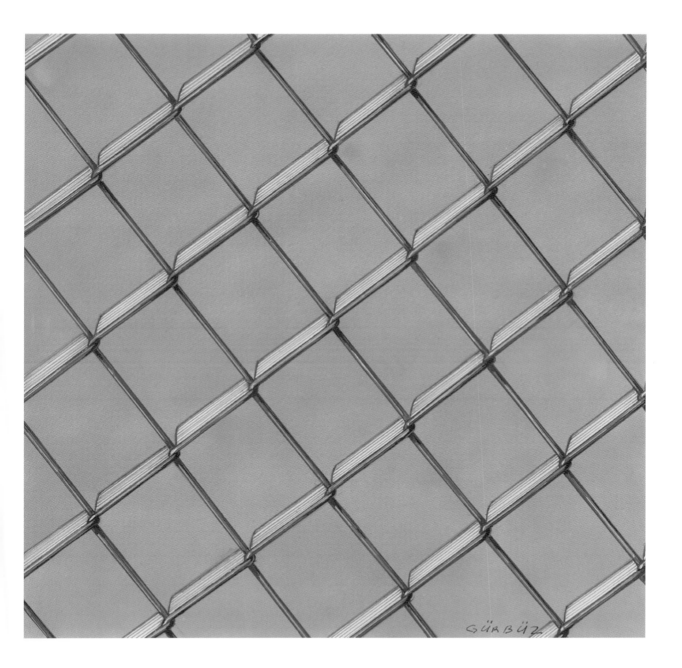

JOSEPH FIEDLER
Ina Coolbrith

This piece was commissioned for a special California author's issue of *California*, the magazine of the University of California, Berkeley. The principle narrative was an 1870 incident wherein Ina Coolbrith and poet Joaquin Miller sent a laurel wreath to London for Lord Bryon's tomb. It is the first major digital image I have made, containing over 40 layers of scanned drawings and textures! My goal was to evoke a sense of California, as I know it. The incredible, indescribable scent of California Bay Laurel, however, could not be replicated.

VIVIENNE FLESHER

Papa and Baby Doc
This is a pair of portraits of the former dictators of Haiti, a father-son horror, created for the *New York Times Week in Review*, art direction by Aviva Michaelov. As usual with this section of the paper, the sketch had to be delivered the day the assignment was given; the sketch was okayed by eleven the next morning, and final art had to be delivered four hours later.

VIVIENNE FLESHER

John Brown
This was the last image I created for Leanne Shapton before she left the *New York Times*—a portrait of the great abolitionist, John Brown, on the anniversary of his hanging. I will miss Leanne's superb art direction and eye. My husband, Ward Schumaker, created the calligraphy, which enhanced the image.

ANTHONY FREDA

Don't Tase Me, Bro

I was asked to submit images to an issue of the South African design magazine *Migrate*. Art director Roanna Williams thought my politically charged art would be a good fit for an issue titled "Signs of the Times." I chose this piece painted on a vintage wood cut-out of a duck to express my concern over the use of Tasers against unarmed civilians by law enforcement. Amnesty International alleges that 344 people have been killed by these "pain compliance" devises, including children. The words of the unarmed, restrained college student, Andrew Meyer, who was stunned with an x-26 Taser, inspired this painting.

JAMES FRYER
Economic Outrage

In the two years I've worked with Chris Barber, the designer on the Times Higher Educational (THE), I've completed about 50 illustrations. I am very lucky to have a client who allows me a great deal of freedom. The concept for *Economic Outrage* had been in my sketchbooks, in one form or another, for a few years. The article was about the public outrage toward high, overindulgent pay packets within public sector jobs, whilst in an economic downturn. I liked the idea of an old-style witch-hunt with burning torches and pitchforks. All I had to do was to put a clever twist on it with regards to finances and monetary values. The artwork was produced in acrylics on hardboard prepared with gesso. Sometimes I will paint directly onto the gesso board, but for other commissions, where a tighter finish is required, I will transfer a drawn-up sketch onto the board first and then start the painting.

BEPPE GIACOBBE
N'Drangheta

ALESSANDRO GOTTARDO
Rabenmutter

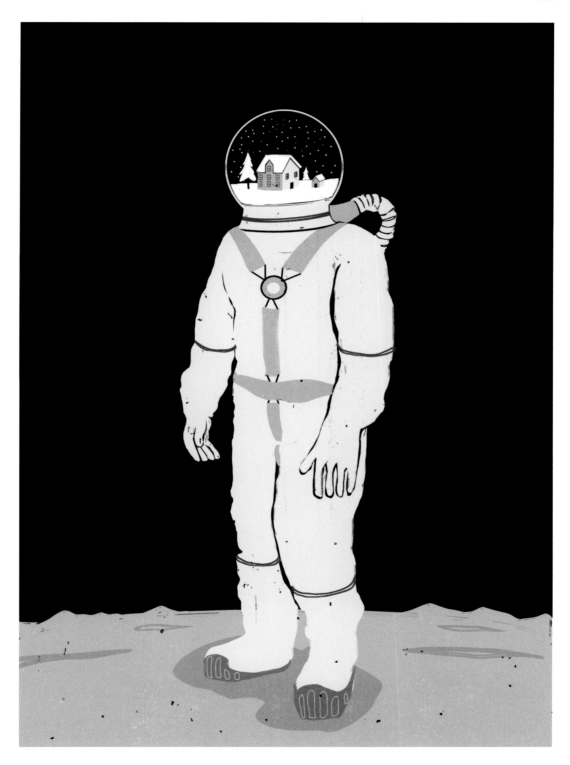

EXTINCTION OF THE MIDDLE CLASS

THE AMERICAN MIDDLE CLASS IS ON THE VERGE OF EXTINCTION. THE COST OF A MIDDLE CLASS LIFE — A HOME, HEALTHCARE, A COLLEGE EDUCATION — HAS SOARED... OUTPACING INCOMES.

IT IS BECOMING INCREASINGLY DIFFICULT TO ENTER + REMAIN IN THE MIDDLE CLASS. FORECLOSURES + PERSONAL BANKRUPTCIES ARE RISING, HEALTH-CARE COSTS ARE SOARING, EMPLOYEE BENEFITS ARE BEING CUT, SOCIAL SECURITY BENEFITS ARE UNDER ATTACK, HOME VALUES — THE MIDDLE CLASS'S MEASURE OF WEALTH — HAVE PLUMMETED.

AS OF 2007 THE TOP 1% (THE UPPER CLASS) OWNED 34.6% OF THE WEALTH. THE NEXT 19% (MANAGERIAL PROFESSIONAL SMALL BUSINESS CLASS) OWNED 50.5% LEAVING ONLY 15% FOR THE BOTTOM 80% (WAGE + SALARY WORKERS).

m.glenwood

MICHAEL GLENWOOD
White Picket Fence

EDDIE GUY

John Boehner

The assignment—illustrate a portrait of the current Speaker of the United States House of Representatives. Inspiration for the image came from the television series *Mad Men*. The photo collage was made in Photoshop Cs5.

EDDIE GUY
Bionic Tiger Woods
The assignment was to illustrate a portrait of Tiger Woods. The story explained how Tiger's perfect public persona was managed and how, due to recent events, it was over, dead. The inspiration came from English beheadings and robots. This photo collage was made in Photoshop Cs5.

EDDIE GUY
Life

The assignment was to illustrate a series of essays on people who have returned to some kind of spirituality in their lives. This particular image deals with a near-death experience where a woman hears the voice of her deceased father saying, "Choose Life." All elements of the image were built, textured, and rendered in Modo 401 software.

JODY HEWGILL
Robert Plant
Portrait of Robert Plant for the review of his Americana-influenced album, *Band of Joy*. My thanks to art director Steven Charny for encouraging and embracing the unfinished quality of this painting.

JODY HEWGILL

Death of An Addict
Portrait of Michael Jackson for an article that brings to light the many indications of his addiction to prescription drugs. I wanted to depict Michael in a somewhat sympathetic light, drawing a connection between the complexities of fame and his attempts to cope. It is acrylic on gessoed illustration board.

STERLING HUNDLEY
Lou Gehrig

Time and flooding have all but eroded the memories of Richmond's Mayo Island, and what remains is little more than a swath of earth that holds up the halfway point of Mayo Bridge. Surrounded on all sides by the James River, few stop to enjoy the island these days. There was a time when Mayo Island served as the home of Richmond's minor league baseball team, the Richmond Colts, the farm team for the Philadelphia Athletics.

Periodically, from 1894-1941, Tate Field, as it was called, was used for home and exhibition games against league rivals and professional teams. Babe Ruth and Lou Gehrig played a bit of hardball there. Frequent flooding, and a fire in 1941 eventually forced the Colts to relocate to Shepherd Stadium in Colonial Heights, Virginia.

STERLING HUNDLEY
Blessing of the Hounds

This illustration lies somewhere between my commercial work, which bears the burden of communication, and my personal work, which has teetered just this side of abstraction. This image plots the course for future work that bridges the gap between the two approaches, and marks my final collaboration with Tyler Darden at *Virginia Living* magazine. I thank Tyler for all of the opportunities and trust he put in me over the years, and I wish him all the best in his future endeavors.

STERLING HUNDLEY

Secretariat

There is no greater symbol of speed in my mind that Secretariat. The solution was simply to communicate speed.

STERLING HUNDLEY
Sheep Dung Tea

I struggled to find a palatable solution for this assignment. The accompanying story centered on an Old World remedy of sheep dung tea for a young boy's ailment. Swearing up and down that he would never drink such a foul elixir, his state gradually declined, along with his resolve. By the third day, the young boy was begging for a hot cup of sheep dung tea. I focused on the idea of eating your words and locked onto the metaphors of eating humble pie, crow, and drinking sheep dung tea.

JEREMY HOLMES
Men Caregivers
An illustration for an article about men who take on the weighty responsibility of physically caring for a terminally ill loved one. The main challenge was to create an image that reflected the story in a positive light—a difficult task when the subject matter is terminal illness.

ROBERT HUNT

Trial by Fire

I was asked by Christine Car and Joe Heroun to create a cover illustration for the *New Republic* showing Barack Obama confronting (or turning away from) the problematic second year of his presidency. Through the sketch process, the depiction of Obama was distilled to the minimum while retaining a somewhat traditional likeness. Turning him away from the viewer seemed to solve the problem on a pictorial and conceptual level, leaving the viewer some psychological wiggle room to interpret the finished art in their own way.

VICTOR JUHASZ
Your Ad Here

Victor Juhasz
Athlete Arrest Manual

TOM JELLETT
Hitchens

KAKO

The New Super Spy

Illustration for an article about the new generation of spies recruited from native target countries, rather than from U.S. or British headquarters. *Playboy* wanted an action-packed illustration, even though we know today it's more about information gathering than guns and rockets. We thought that this information gathering could involve a spy outside the balcony on the ledge of a building several stories up, spying on his targets and using technology devices, such as satellite phone or GPS devices, rather than guns. We wanted to indicate that he was either giving a location to his counterparts somewhere away from his location, or that he was recording his targets' conversation.

Edward Kinsella
Zombie Economics

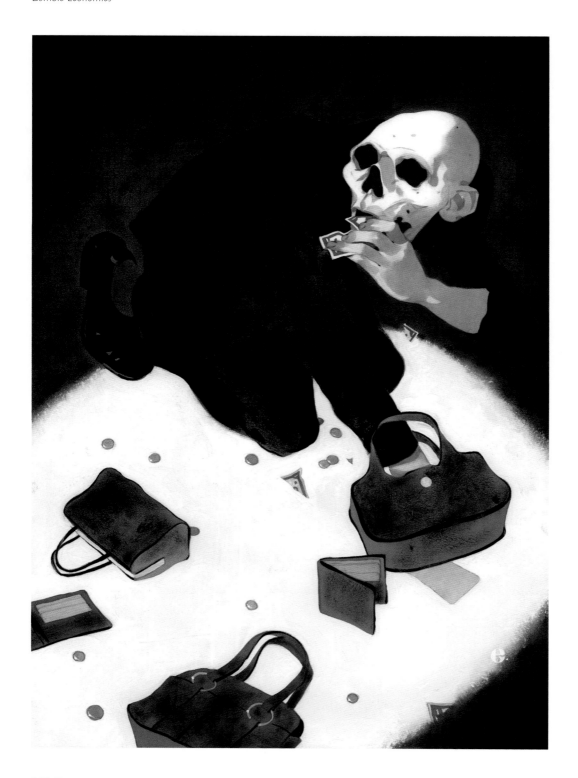

JON KRAUSE
Summer

JON KRAUSE
Medusa

JON KRAUSE
Fall

JON KRAUSE
A Relaxation Plan

NORA KRUG

Downturn in Advertising
This piece about the advertising industry's economic downturn was created for the *Deal* magazine. The art director, Larry Gendron, encouraged me to explore the theme in as open a way as possible, for which I was very grateful.

CAITLIN KUHWALD

Subway Zen

This was for an article about how religious (or spiritual) people are able to achieve peace in the midst of chaos. Putting my heroine on the subway seemed the perfect way to show someone completely blissed-out while surrounded by extreme tumult. My meditating woman is also a self portrait!

ANITA KUNZ

Human Trafficking
This was commissioned by *Mother Jones* for a story about human trafficking. It's a story that's shocking in its scope. In particular, the article mentioned one man who brought unwilling people in through Los Angeles.

ANITA KUNZ

Justin Bieber
This was a commission by *Rolling Stone*—a portrait of the singer. I've tried to make him look like a tough guy despite his little-boy appearance.

ZOHAR LAZAR
Tales of Hippie Crack

ZOHAR LAZAR
Political Orgy (Alice Roosevelt Longworth)

MICAH LIDBERG
Our Native Flora

In the opening illustration for *Proto* magazine's story on intestinal flora, a playful, decorative style lent a much-needed positive PR spin in favor of the little microbes that reside within every human body—those proponents of proper digestion and fighters of invasive bacteria.

Unpleasant physiological realities are commonplace within our daily lives as human beings. This piece shows us that there are friendly little creatures fighting the good fight deep within the darkest corners of our own anatomy.

MATT MAHURIN
Elvis at 75

BILL MAYER
10 Things You're Probably Doing Wrong

MARK McGINNIS

Turkey

This was accompanying a collection of poems. The editor hadn't picked the poems, and I figured there would be various perspectives on Thanksgiving Day. I felt like it was important to use the symbols that are associated with the holiday because it would help link the collection together. Of course, the turkey was a natural choice, but I also wanted to find a way to combine it with another image that would talk about why the turkey was so important a symbol in the first place.

GONI MONTES
Rebirth Brass

ALEX NABAUM

Memphis to Boston

For an autobiographical essay in the *Boston Globe* magazine. The author moved from her home in the South for a scholarship in the North. She remained for a career and marriage, yet never quite felt at home. She compared her experience to the Great Migration of African-Americans North after the Civil War, so I felt the piece had to have both a personal and broad feel.

BILL NELSON
What, Me Worry? . . . Worry!

With the recession, one of our main sources for work, editorial illustration, and magazines in general are hemorrhaging money. *U.S. News and World Report* has closed its doors, as have many others. But that *Mad* magazine went quarterly was a shock heard round the world. Hence, my sculpture of the venerable Alfred E. Neuman with a slight change in his famous quote, "What, me worry? . . . Worry!"

ROBERT NEUBECKER
Bound, a Novel

This illustration was done for an *L.A. Times* review of a book called *Bound, a Novel*. It used bondage as a metaphor for an enmeshed relationship between three people. Not the pervy fun kind of bondage, or the "let my people go" kind, but the sicko serial killer kind. Great assignment, but I don't read anything that has to do with serial killers, with the possible exception of historical figures, i.e., politicians.

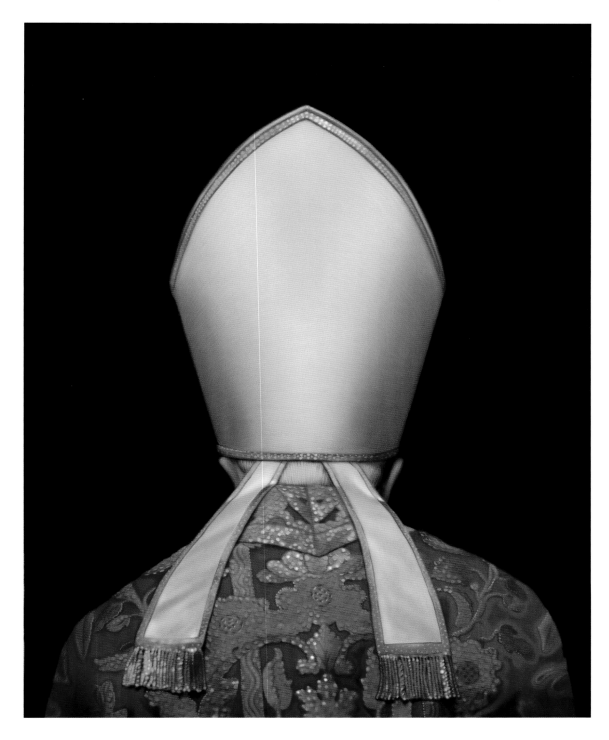

TIM O'BRIEN
Pope
Cover of *TIME*. I learned how to paint the Pope's sequins by painting Judy Garland's dress years earlier. I'll say no more.

TIM O'BRIEN

Matt Long

Illustration for *Runner's World*. Matt Long, a NYC firefighter, was biking on the morning of December 23, 2005, when he was crushed by a charter bus. His injuries were catastrophic and it took nearly a month for him to regain consciousness. A lifelong athlete, he was determined to run again, though his doctors doubted he would ever walk without a cane. A mere three years later, he ran in the 2008 New York City Marathon. Being asked to paint someone's portrait is always fun and interesting, but when I find myself attached to the subject in some way I can get stuck. Design director, Kory Kennedy, asked me to try to incorporate the stretching device Matt used to get back to running. The rack uses various levels of bars to gain a greater range of movement out of tight muscles. The device is called "the cage." I thought about that but knew if I were to come in close for a portrait it would not work well. It reminded me of scaffolding and that is where the idea was born.

TIM O'BRIEN

Neil Young
Illustration for *Record Review*. I could have just painted his ear and sideburn and it would have looked like Neil Young. It's always great to paint an icon.

YUTA ONODA

Exploring the Void
The article was about the extreme environments lab at the University of Minnesota. The knowledge may be used to select a perfect, psychologically sound crew for a mission to Mars.

YUTA ONODA

Shadowed by Coyotes
The article was about urban and rural coyotes, and the dangers they pose to dogs. Menacing coyotes are silently approaching the woman and the dog, waiting for an opportunity to strike.

KEN ORVIDAS
Child Safety

DAVID PLUNKERT

C

Cover illustration created for the *New York Times Book Review* of Tom McCarthy's novel *C*. The main character, a WWI soldier, prefers patterns over people, and likens the men he shoots from the air to singed insects.

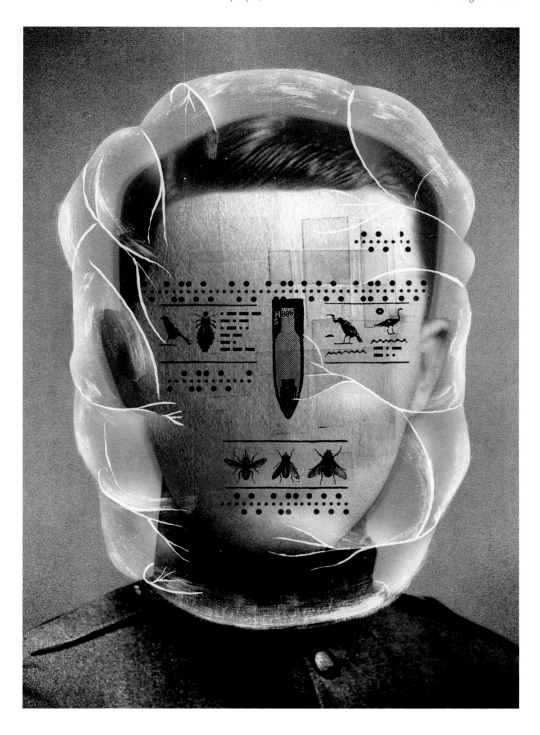

EMILIANO PONZI

Cultivation

EMILIANO PONZI
Packing for Mars

EMILIANO PONZI
Butterfly

EMILIANO PONZI
God/Darwin

EMILIANO PONZI

Arms Control

RED NOSE STUDIO
Peacock

EDEL RODRIGUEZ
History of Human Rights
For an article in the *New York Times Book Review* chronicling the history
of human rights.

EDEL RODRIGUEZ
American Politics
For a magazine article about the state of American politics today.

EDEL RODRIGUEZ
The Oath
Published in the *New Yorker* magazine, featuring a documentary film about
Osama Bin Laden's personal driver.

PETE RYAN
Has Nevada Lost its Edge

This was for a piece in *Las Vegas Weekly* regarding how the state (and city) were slowly becoming less wild and dangerous. I tried numerous solutions to show Nevada and iconic elements of Vegas being broken in one way or another. In the end, I realized that a guillotine blade with a broken edge looks *exactly* like the state of Nevada and would be a clear concept. A fortunate coincidence. It was silk-screened and painted with acrylic.

JASON SEILER
Blow Hard

The art director for the *Miami New Times* called and asked, "Do you want to paint a guy sitting on a toilet?" Well, yeah, sure I do. At first the idea was to paint record producer Scott Storch as a king sitting upon his throne, which would be a toilet. The idea evolved after I read the article and realized what a jerk Storch was. I submitted my revised idea and was told to "go for it!" I posed a friend of mine in a public bathroom, beat him to a bloody pulp and took several pictures for reference. I love my job!

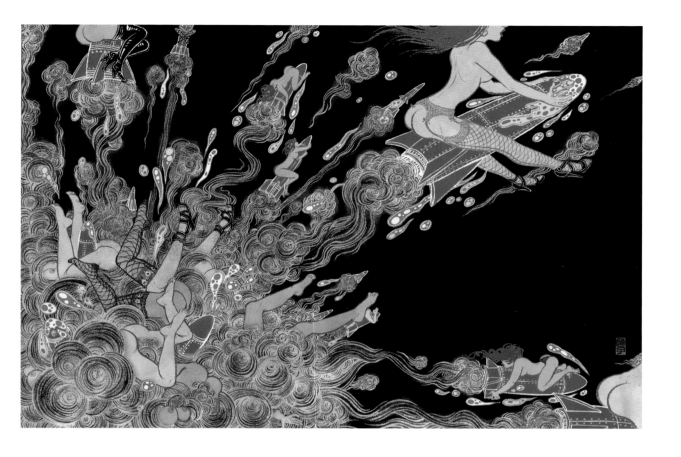

YUKO SHIMIZU
Playboy

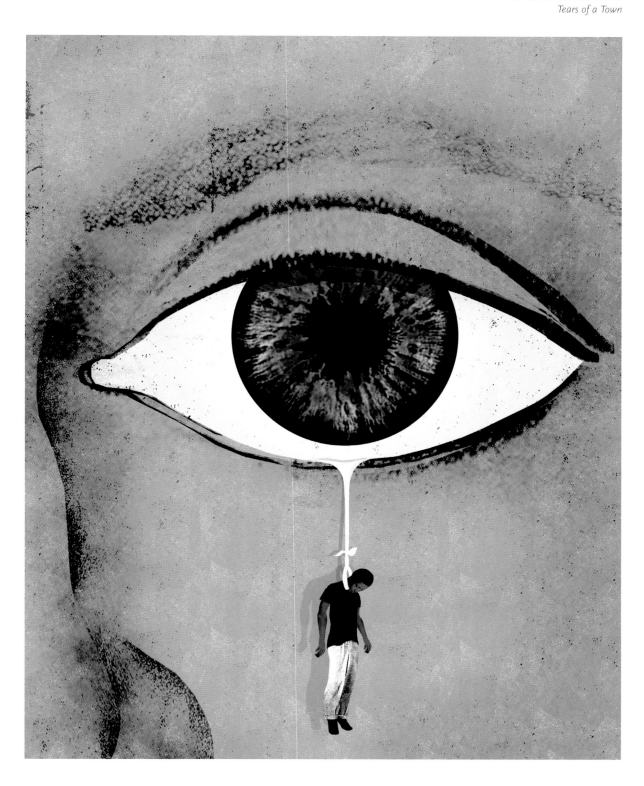

OTTO STEININGER
Pearl Diver

Gary Taxali
Circumcision

GARY TAXALI
The Ask

GARY TAXALI
Yup Sir
Cover for *Taddle Creek*.

THE HEADS OF STATE

Shopping Cart
For an *Op-Ed* piece in the *New York Times* about the mistreatment of
homeless people as criminals.

The Heads of State

Cross Bones
Technology playing a more dangerous role in modern combat; for the *New York Times*.

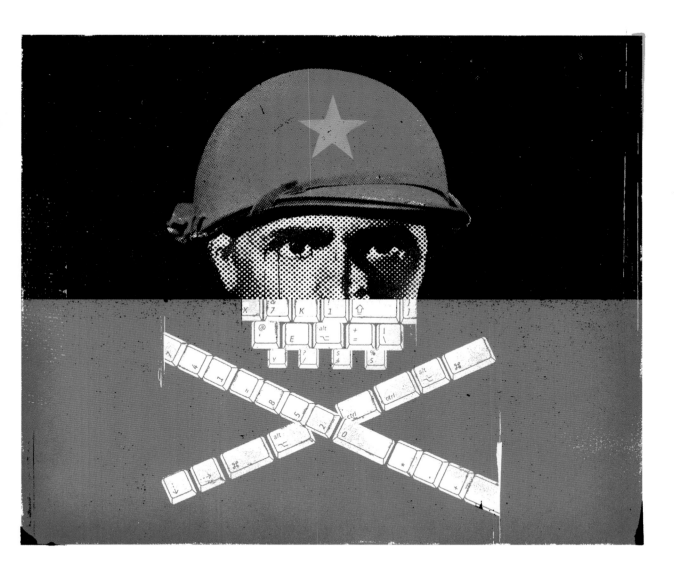

THE HEADS OF STATE

LMU magazine

Teachers are under close scrutiny after the recent public release of test scores, for *LMU* magazine.

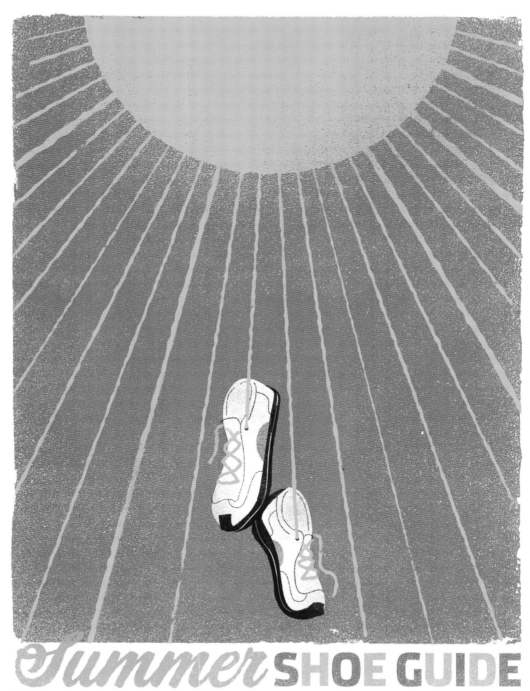

JACOB THOMAS
Comic-Con
This was the cover of the *Los Angeles Times Sunday Calendar* section and
they wanted to highlight the popular comic book convention Comic-Con,
which was happening in San Diego. Their idea was to represent a comic
book-looking character racing to San Diego for the convention. I drew out
each layer of detail in ink, scanned it in, and collaged in Photoshop.

Jacob Thomas
Baked

This was for a short essay by Mark Haskell Smith describing how he immersed himself in the research for his new book called *Baked*, a story about a botanist who wins the Cannabis Cup and the trouble that follows. Mark describes traveling to Amsterdam and trying out several different types of marijuana, detailing the effects. I concentrated on show-

ing Mark in the middle of the subtle details and differences of each new strand of weed he tried, using his eyes as a metaphor for clarity on the subject. All layers were drawn in ink, scanned in, and collaged in Photoshop.

POL TURGEON

Bike2

I got a call from *Bicycling* magazine to do a piece showing the insides of a person riding a bike. It was for a story on how to avoid numbness while riding. I told the art director that I was not a medical illustrator and if I had to do this piece, the inside view of the biker would be as far from reality as one can imagine. He said that it was quite all right, that he had seen a series of anatomical pieces that had nothing to do with reality that I'd done as personnel work so he knew what to expect. It was the first time I got an actual illustration job from that weird series! At first the biker had a biker's helmet on with no face, but I thought that taking the whole thing off and just showing the nerves coming out of the neck would be much more ... artistic.

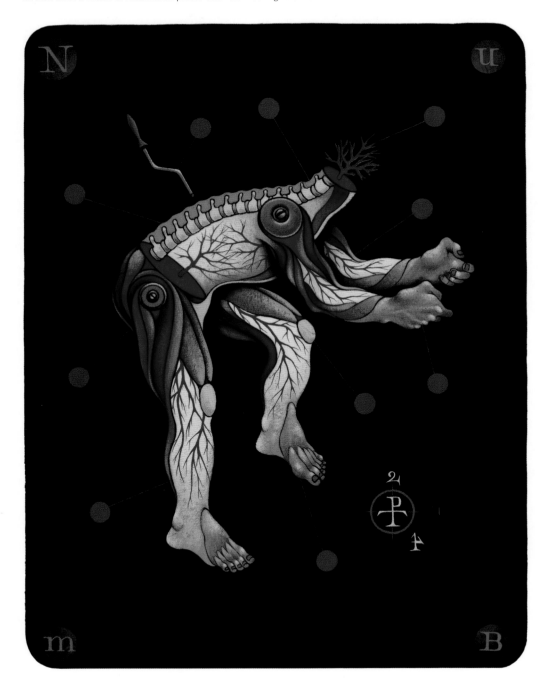

MARK ULRIKSEN
Rod Blagojevich

This portrait of embattled former Illinois Governor Rod Blagojevich was the second piece I did for this profile in the *New Yorker*. Art director Jordan Awan asked me to do a straightforward bust of Blagojevich. While reading the text about him I was reminded of Michael Scott, the charac-ter Steve Carell plays on the TV show, *The Office*. I was trying to capture that cockiness, sense of entitlement, and great hair, mingled with the mediocrity that this politician so well embodies.

JACK UNRUH

Angola Prison Warden

This is one mean motor scooter. The Warden of Angola Prison—a very evil man. I won't be going to Louisiana any time soon!

JACK UNRUH

Bill, Chainsaw
Bill just over thought the problem. This is a monthly column for *Field and Stream*.

JACK UNRUH
George Soros
A great head to work with. For an illustrator it was a gift.

JACK UNRUH
Khalid Sheikh Mohammed
Thanks, Milton! It just seemed appropriate for a visitor to NYC.

Jack Unruh

Hydroponic Gardening
A very complicated magazine. *Rosebud* promotes the high tech growing of "weed," but they use tomatoes as a euphemism to replace their product.

Sam Weber
Bone Hinge

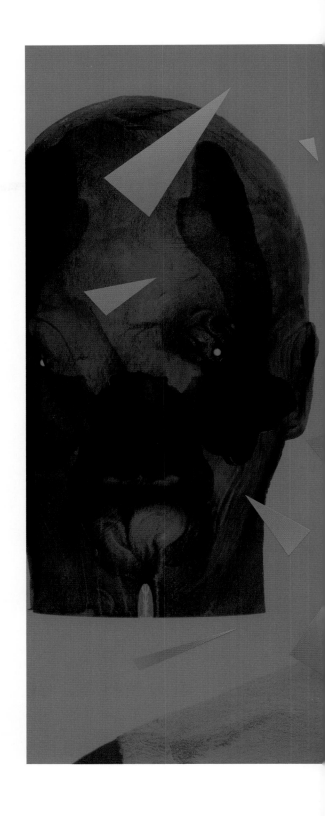

SAM WEBER
The Monster's Million Faces

ADVERTISING/INSTITUTIONAL

OKSANA BADRAK
ILLUSTRATOR

Oksana Badrak was born in 1978 in Moscow, Russia. She received a BFA in illustration from Art Center College of Design in Pasadena. Using a combination of digital and traditional mediums, Oksana's work presents an intricate and often fantastical visual experience. She has received multiple awards and recognitions from the Society of Illustrators, *American Illustration*, Society of Publication Designers and other prestigious organizations, and has had numerous exhibitions in the United States and internationally. Her work has appeared in publications such as *Oprah*, the *New Yorker*, *Rolling Stone*, *Entertainment Weekly*, *Playboy*, *Esquire*, *Nickelodeon*, *Wired*, and *Newsweek*, to name a few. The list of Oksana's diverse clientele includes Nike, Hewlett Packard, Coca-Cola, Nokia, Warner Brothers, Bourjois, and Target. Presently, she lives in Los Angeles with a pomeranian pup named Lola by her side.

MARCOS CHIN
ILLUSTRATOR

Marcos Chin graduated from the Ontario College of Art and Design, in Toronto, Canada. Since then, his work has appeared on book and CD covers, advertisements, fashion catalogues, and magazines such as *TIME*, *Rolling Stone*, and the *New Yorker*. He has received innumerable awards within the illustration industry, and has given lectures throughout North America and abroad. This April he will be hosting a workshop and exhibition at "Amarillo Centro de Diseño" in Xalapa, Mexico. Perhaps the most recognizable works in his portfolio are the illustrations for Lavalife's international advertising campaign which have appeared on subways, billboards, print, and online. Marcos currently lives in New York City, where he teaches illustration at the School of Visual Arts.

FANNY GOTSCHALL
CREATIVE DIRECTOR,
DECCA LABEL GROUP

For over 10 years Fanny Chiari Gotschall has been a creative director for Decca Label Group, a Division of Universal Music Group. She has created package campaigns for entertainers such as Liza Minnelli, Clay Aiken, David Sanborn, and Deborah Cox, among others. Fanny is also an art director and designer for Decca's advertising campaigns, which include Andrea Bocelli, Sting, Charlie Haden, Wicked Original Cast, Hillary Hahn, Renée Fleming, and Sonny Rollins. She has earned the respect of artists, and has a reputation for having a superb eye. Fanny came from Panama at the age of 17, and earned a Bachelor of Fine Arts and Business Marketing from Marian University in Indiana. She is now a resident of Park Slope, Brooklyn, where she lives with her husband, Ken, and her two lovely kids, Sophie and Elliot.

ETHEL KESSLER
CREATIVE DIRECTOR,
DESIGN CONSULTANT

Ethel Kessler is a nationally recognized design leader and art director with over 30 years of experience in the creation of communications materials. She is on the U.S. Postal Service's art director team to develop stamp designs. The Breast Cancer Semi-Postal Stamp, her first stamp design, has raised $72.2 million for breast cancer research. Over 250 additional stamps for the Postal Service have been issued under her art direction, including the Library of Congress, Frederick Law Olmsted, Louise Nevelson, 50 Year Celebration of Civil Rights, Alzheimer's, the 12-year Nature of America series, Abstract Expressionists, Latin Dance, Latin Music Legends, American Scientists, and many more. The firm focuses on underserved and multi-cultural populations, book design, and issues related to the environment. She is a graduate of Maryland Institute College of Art and an AIGA Fellow of the Washington, DC, chapter.

GAIL MAROWITZ
CREATIVE DIRECTOR,
ROADRUNNER RECORDS

Gail Marowitz has been art directing and designing music packaging for more than 20 years. In 2005, she won a Grammy® award for "Best Recording Package" for Aimee Mann's *The Forgotten Arm* and was nominated again in 2008 for Mann's *@#$%@*!* *Smilers*. She has worked with illustrators Gary Taxali, Owen Smith, Anthony Ausgang, and Maira Kalman, among others, for projects as varied as Aerosmith, Aimee Mann, Jill Sobule, and Branford Marsalis. Her recent work has been featured in *Print's Regional Design Annual* and *Varoom!* magazine. She is currently the creative director at Roadrunner Records in New York City and has a lifetime gig renovating a 145-year-old church on the Hudson River in upstate New York.

BILL MAYER

ILLUSTRATOR

In 2010 Bill Mayer won an Editorial Gold Medal from the Society of Illustrators in New York for a stamp drawing used in *Revista Piaui* magazine. The same year, he won Gold Medals from the Society of Illustrators of Los Angeles for an IBM editorial piece and an NPR calendar, as well as a "Best of Show" award for a poster for Hartford Stage. This award is presented to the best of all the Gold Award Winners. Bill received a Silver Medal from *3x3* for his comic "Bebo" and several other Awards of Merit for published and unpublished work. Bill had two pieces accepted in *American Illustration 2010*. On the personal side, this year Bill compiled an 82.5-foot, accordion-fold book of letters, which he'd sent to his wife, Lee, for a rather extravagant Valentine's present.

ADAM MCCAULEY

ILLUSTRATOR

Adam McCauley is a San Francisco-based illustrator who has been creating illustrations for clients (editorial, publishing, institutional, and advertising) nationally and worldwide since 1988. He has illustrated countless book covers, as well as 22 children's books, including his most recent, *The Monsterologist*, by Bobbi Katz, for which he won the Society of Illustrators Gold Medal. Adam's personal sketchbook work has been featured in *American Illustration*, *Print*, and *An Illustrated Life* by Danny Gregory. He is currently an adjunct professor at CCA in San Francisco. Adam's animation, *Fast Food*, is in the permanent new-media collection at SFMOMA.

TIM O'BRIEN

ILLUSTRATOR

Tim O'Brien has received awards and recognitions from the Society of Illustrators in New York and Los Angeles, *Graphis*, *Print*, *Communication Arts*, the Society of Publication Designers, *American Illustration*, and the Art Directors Club. Tim has over a dozen paintings in the National Gallery, Washington, DC, and is a winner of the 2009 Hamilton King Award from the Society of Illustrators, where he serves as the executive VP and the museum chairman. His numerous speaking engagements include The Norman Rockwell Museum, the Society of Illustrators, Syracuse University, SVA, Pratt, RISD, CCA, and the University of the Arts. Tim is a professor at the University of the Arts in Philadelphia and Pratt Institute in Brooklyn, and lectures frequently across the country.

FELIX SOCKWELL

ILLUSTRATOR, IDENTITY CONSULTANT

Felix is an avid futboler and ornery Texan who honed his skill as a promotional and advertising art director before moving from Texas to San Francisco in early 1997, and later co-founded B.I.G., Ogilvy's Brand Integration Group in NYC. In 1999, Sockwell forged his own practice, concentrating solely on the art and science of identity design and illustration. His clients include LeParker Meridian Hotel, Herman Miller, Sony, Amex, hotels. com, the *New York Times*, and Apple. He works in New York City and Maplewood, NJ, where he lives with his wife, two kids, and dog named Kitty.

GOLD MEDAL WINNER
CHRIS BUZELLI

Mirage Cartography
Wraparound CD cover for Paul
Mark's acoustical guitar album
"Mirage Cartography."

GOLD MEDAL WINNER
Brad Yeo

Founders' Gallery
Illustration created to promote The Founders' Gallery at The Military Museums in Calgary, Canada. The gallery was formed as a public exhibition space to contribute to our understanding of military experience in the field of human conflict by displaying historic and contemporary works of art and related artifacts. The theme represents the Founders' Gallery as a repository of personal stories: the many individual stories told through artifacts, letters, or artworks that collectively serve to inform and preserve our historical memory. It was necessary that the illustration be unique enough to stand apart visually, to draw attention to the gallery and define it as a particularly unique entity within the Museums.

GOLD MEDAL WINNER
GIANNI DE CONNO

Black and White
"Let's Make Peace" is the subject of the 2011 Emergency calendar. Emergency, the independent Italian NGO, asked 14 artists to develop this topic by representing opposing historians, hard-bitten enemies, contrarians, and those in opposition who are finally making peace. My concept was to show how when one player paints the other using his own color, as in a children's game, black and white rub off on each other. The artists for this project donated their images to support Emergency, which provides healthcare to victims of war and poverty, and promotes peace and respect for human rights. Since 1994 it has assisted over four-and-a-half million people. Its website is www.emergency.it.

GOLD MEDAL WINNER
TATSURO KIUCHI

Not So Polar Bear
I thought it would be striking to show a polar bear in the forest. He is now forced to live in the mountains because there are no ice floes left for him to hunt for seals in the Arctic. There he is, standing with his hands and mouth soaking in blood. I presented the bear as being rather cute, not at all menacing looking, to imply that this is reality, and this is nature. He doesn't have to be angry. He is just doing what he has to do to stay alive. The earth will keep rotating whether the natural environment is being destroyed or not.

USA 44

2010

NEGRO LEAGUES BASEBALL

44 USA

RUBE FOSTER

2010

NEGRO LEAGUES BASEBALL

Negro Leagues Stamp
This is probably the most challenging stamp I've ever worked on. The art director and I worked for weeks on end, conjuring up numerous ideas for the image. I sketched to the point of exhaustion and finally came upon the solution of using a close-up of Rube Foster on one side of the image and on-field action on the other. The only issue was that the umpire is conspicuously out of place and should more accurately be shown facing the other way, but we were reminded that no stamp collector wants to see an umpire's rear end on a stamp, so the license was granted.

FLIP 8
Poster for Festa Literaria Internacionale de Paraty (FLIP) in Brazil. Each year I produce an image long before any program is finalized. I discuss it with no one and show no preliminary sketches. Uncannily, it always mirrors exactly that year's theme. It's spooky.

I thank Liz, Mauro, and Belita for their confidence.

Swimming Pool
It's an image I did for the advertising campaign of Seac-Sub, a scuba diving brand. The campaign was focused on the safety of the company's swimming pool product. I did a diver jumping from a trampoline and passing through a cloud—a ring of the cloud remained around his chest as a life buoy. The technique is a mix: digital, drawing on paper, and textures.

La Donna Di Lago
The libretto of Rossini's opera, *La Donna Di Lago*, is based on the 19th-century Sir Walter Scott poem, "The Lady of the Lake," which draws on the romance of an Arthurian legend. I was trying to find a metaphor which could capture this dark, mythical story in a strong, disturbing image—like a haunting dream. Did I succeed in doing so? Only the viewer can judge.

To Absent Friends
Denizens of the KitKat Klub for the A.R.T.'s production of *Cabaret*, starring Amanda Palmer.

Victoria Symphony
Winter Season
Part of a series of posters/brochures for the Victoria Symphony, this was for the winter season. I played with several musical elements on the picture: the skates are the notes, the line on the ice is a violin key, the fence is a pentagram. The technique is a mix of digital, drawing on paper, and textures.

Save the Gulf
The TEDxOilSpill Conference was held in order to raise awareness of the issues surrounding the Gulf Oil Spill in 2010. The goal of the illustration was to visually interpret the disaster and its immediate impact on the region's wildlife. I wanted to simplify the concept as much as possible in order to create the most impact. I therefore chose to use images of a brown pelican, a red snapper, and an oil rig. The scribble overlaying the oil rig draws the viewer in and a simple black dotted line leads him or her down to the oil-covered fish and the simple message of "Save the Gulf."

LOU BEACH
Sunset

CONTENTS: 4 L/1.1 gal (6 kg/13.2 lbs.)

PART A 4.9-0-3.6

"Thirstin Howl III"

Advanced Nutrients

CONNOISSEUR

pH PERFECT TECHNOLOGY

MARC BURCKHARDT

Connoisseur
This label is one of approximately 50 that Pentagram asked me to illustrate for Advanced Nutrients branding redesign—each one a pre-existing product used in hydroponic farming to enhance different qualities of the plants. Using a character-driven approach, each creature embodies some trait that aligns with the product's qualities.

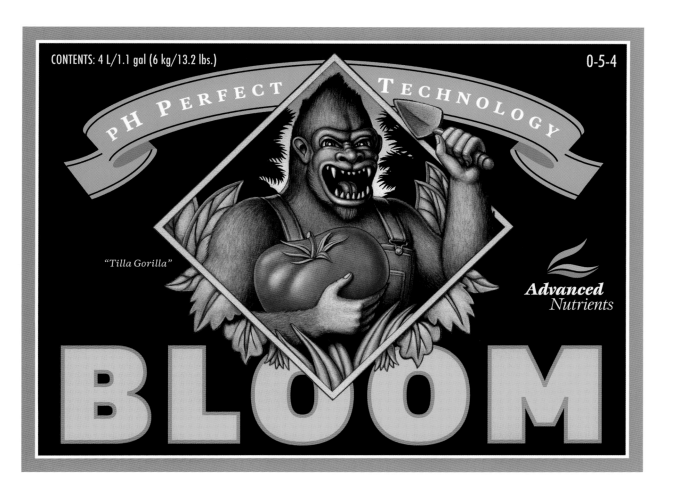

MARC BURCKHARDT
Bloom
Another label for Advanced Nutrients.

MARC BURCKHARDT

Hop Czar Label

For Bridgeport Brewing's new, extra-hoppy beer, I was asked to create a portrait of the Hop Czar, which was to be used on the labels and throughout the product line and advertising. It was great fun imagining this character, and coming up with ways to work hops into as many accoutrements as possible. Sampling the beer when it was complete was another bonus!

CASEY BURNS

Spoon and Jay Reatard

The original art for this poster was drawn on separate sheets of 14" x 17" Bristol board in sumi ink with a pen and brush—a separate drawing for each color. The gray color is actually an overprint of the transparent blue ink on top of the orange ink. The finished piece is a three-color screenprint in an edition of 200. I incorporated motifs from Spoon's songwriting with my own interesting relationship experiences. This was a fun challenge and it led to several more projects with Spoon throughout 2010. Sadly, this was Jay Reatard's final show before he died in early 2010.

CHRIS BUZELLI
Macy's Flower Show

CHRIS BUZELLI
Mariachi, MGM VIVA Festival
This painting was commissioned by MGM Resorts for their annual VIVA Festival. The five-day event included comedy shows, concerts, happy hours, tequila tasting, and more. It took place across all 10 Las Vegas MGM Resorts to celebrate the bicentennial anniversary of Mexican Independence Day.

MICHAEL BYERS

Common Grackle
Well. The man I did the poster for really loves boats. So I wanted to create
a scene that makes you feel a little sorry for the person in the water.

Q. CASSETTI
Banana Belt Wine, Watkins Glen, NY

The Banana Belt is a climate zone on Seneca Lake, tempered by the lake effects, which benefit grape growing. Atwater Winery produces a popular line of red, white, and blush wines under the Banana Belt name. I wanted to create an illustration that speaks to the banana belt, selecting a monkey that would have direct eye contact with the viewer. I wanted to focus the interest on the monkey's face, particularly the eyes, and allow the rest of the art to be very simple and graphic.

JOSH COCHRAN
Times Square

JOSH COCHRAN
The Setup

JOSH COCHRAN
Tribeca

TIMOTHY COOK

Teen Tones Hamlet Poster

I started with a very unoriginal idea of creating a skull image to advertise a rock concert. I sketched the skull, duplicated and flipped it. The mirrored shapes suggested a Hamlet scene to me, so I built the drawing from that notion.

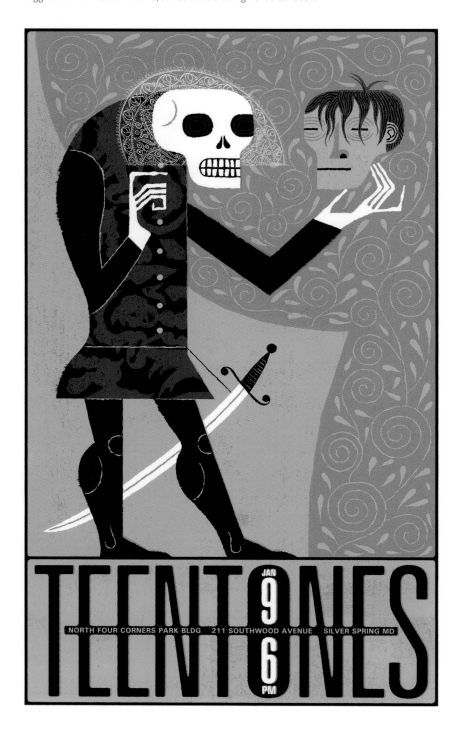

JOHN CUNEO
Mr. Bojangles, Jerry Jeff Walker

BIL DONOVAN

Buddha Couture

I was fortunate to spend a week at the designer and artist Ralph Rucci's salon during his Spring 2011 Couture Collection. I documented the experience on site through brush and ink. Time was of the essence and I quickly had to capture the fluidity of the models as they glided past my workstation—it was an incredible experience. His salon is filled with his creations and art, as well as his collection of Antique Buddha Sculptures. To capture this ambiance I used the static images of the Buddhas as a backdrop for Ruccis's sublime creations.

BIL DONOVAN

Chado Ralph Rucci

The visionary fashion designer and artist Ralph Rucci invited me to document his spring collection at his salon. I brought my brushes and paints and Ralph provided the inspiration. I utilized all of my observational skills to capture the spirit and essence of his collection worn by ethereal creatures who glided through the salon. It was challenging and exhilarating to attempt to capture so much in so little time.

HUGH D'ANDRADE

Anarchist Bookfair

I've done the poster for the Bay Area Anarchist Bookfair every year, going on eight years now. Each year, I try to do something new—each poster is an opportunity for me to experiment. For the 2010 poster I wanted to try using one of my pencil drawings, and to add the color digitally, something I rarely do in my regular work. I also wanted to capture some of the feeling of wonder and amazement I sometimes felt when I was a young radical encountering a rare, anarchist gem in an old, dusty bookshop. That can be very exciting when you're 21 and eager to change the world—like discovering your ancestors.

GÜRBÜZ DOĞAN EKŞIOĞLU

Istanbul Dance

I wanted to use the cat figure to illustrate the idea of the International Dance Festival held in Istanbul. Cats are very flexible and use their bodies instinctively and naturally. Half of the cat is twisted 180 degrees in this poster. And I added a silhouette of Istanbul in the background.

LEO EPSINOSA

WOK Characters
Originally designed for take-out sushi packaging, these characters and their quirky personalities and made-up language sparked a variety of ideas for different graphic applications, such as placemats, kids' menus, and promotional material.

BRENDON FLYNN
All Hail the End
Given apocalyptic criteria for a concept metal album, I tapped into my own knowledge and love of the genre. With this piece I paid homage to what I felt was classic metal imagery. So ... I thought that a Chimera vomiting snakes did the job.

BART J. FORBES

Bison in the Snow

The client wanted to depict their symbol, the bison, as a solitary animal in a natural environment. I decided to show the bison in the snow and cold, creating a silhouette against an almost all-white background. The elongated composition was required because the image would be used in several different ways.

Bart J. Forbes

Stan Getz CD Cover
I was given a good deal of freedom in depicting the great jazz saxophonist Stan Getz. The initial idea was to show him with a cigarette in his mouth instead of the sax. But since he struggled with drug addiction throughout his career, this seemed to be a better solution: in profile with a dark background and the suggestion of skyline to lend the dramatic effect that was always evident in the sound of his tenor sax.

BART J. FORBES

Nat King Cole CD Cover

Many people remember Nat King Cole as one of the great pop singers of our time, but he was also an accomplished musician, having begun his career leading a jazz trio and playing piano. I chose to portray him at the keyboard, as well as singing for an album featuring his collaboration with other jazz greats.

Thomas Fuchs
Tausche

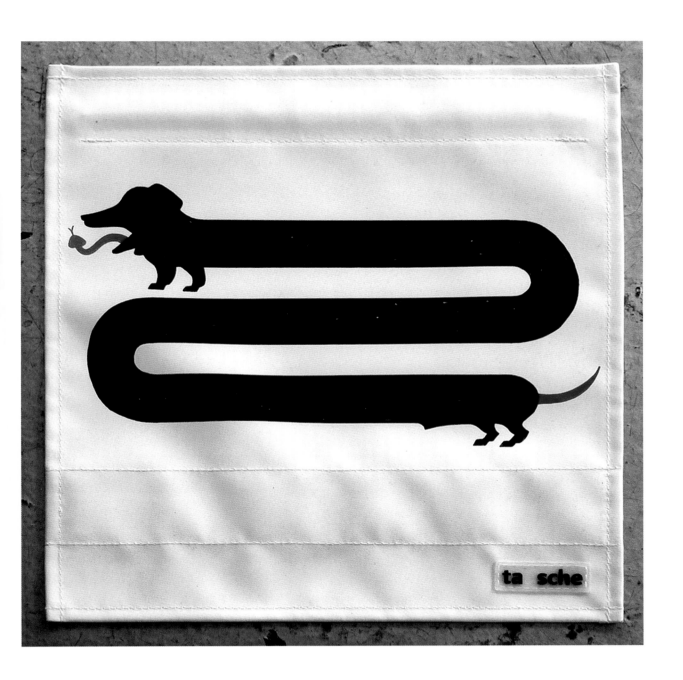

THOMAS FUCHS
Tausche

THOMAS FUCHS
Tausche

DONATO GIANCOLA

The Mechanic

This was created as a work of art for a demonstration video illuminating the entire creative process of producing an image of a science fiction concept—from abstract drawings, to reference gathering, to portrait painting, to rendering imaginary objects such as the suit, architecture, and starfield. My growth and continued development as an artist is due to teachers and professionals who took the time to reach out to those eager to learn and embrace art in all its varied complexities. I could not be the artist I am today without standing on the shoulders of those before me. I hope this image provides other artists with the joy, knowledge, and inspiration to take their art to another level.

PETER GOOD

Phillipe for Dinners at the Farm

I determined that the textures of natural fabrics were an appropriate corollary to the locally grown organic foods, and the mission of the Dinners at the Farm initiative. The selected fabrics were loosely based on the anatomy of the Golden Wyandotte Male fowl, referencing feathers, plumage, cartilage, and bone. The fabric pieces were then composed and sewn with varying thicknesses of zigzag stitching. Finally, some minimal use of ink over thread to finish the detail.

STEVEN GUARNACCIA

Mr. Brown in the City

For the annual calendar for his design agency, Vue Sur La Ville, Alain Lachartre gathers 12 artists to illustrate the theme of Mr. Brown in the City. How they do it is up to each individual artist. We're asked to invent Mr. Brown and the city he's in. For December, I chose the Paris metro at Christmas time, and decided Mr. Brown was a French Scrooge who wasn't enjoying the season much. He's easy to pick out—he's the only person on the metro platform with a scowl. Plus, just to be sure, I made him brown. And, because the colors of Christmas (and of all of the other characters in the scene) are red and green, Mr. Brown gets his color from combining the reds and greens of the holiday-spirited people around him.

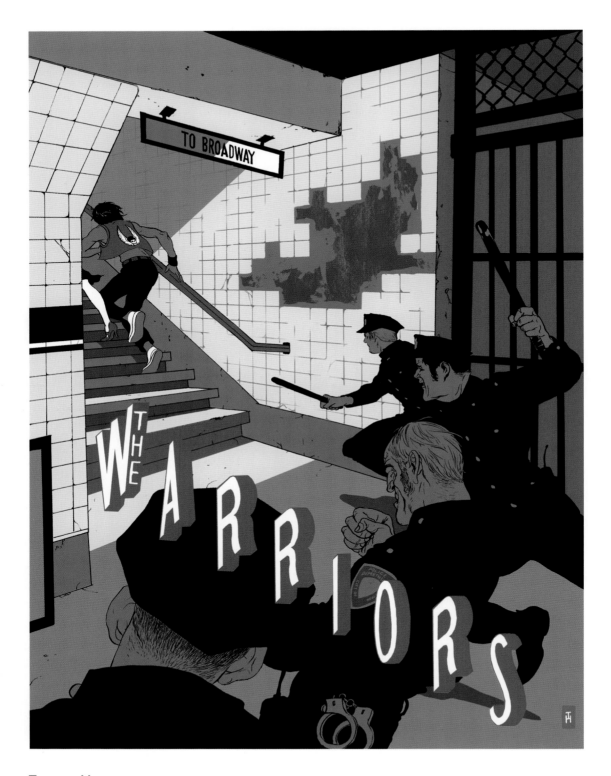

TOMER HANUKA
The Warriors

JODY HEWGILL
Every Tongue Confess

HADLEY HOOPER
Norma

PAUL HOPPE

Rabid Rabbits Over Brooklyn

Once a year I challenge myself to create a large-scale, hyper-detailed illustration inspired by my interest in atmosphere, architecture, and perspective, rendered in pen and ink. When the Rabid Rabbit Comics Collective was looking for a visual to advertise their upcoming art show in the depths of Brooklyn, I knew I had found that year's assignment.

IC4 Design

You Have Less Than a Second to See the Biker
The purpose of this advertisement was to show that it is difficult to see
the biker on the road. The client gave us a lot of freedom to illustrate this
point, so we created many interesting situations, such as a wanted thief in
hiding, and Ninjas chasing a Samurai. Our aim was to draw attention to
the picture, but at the same time to distract people from the biker.

GWENDA KACZOR

Honua Honey
This was a dream job; I was simply asked to illustrate a bee that "really looks Hawaiian" for a label for a new brand of honey. Leis and ukuleles were involved in the sketching process but happily the straw hat won out in the end.

HONUA HONEY

MACADAMIA BLOSSOM

Pure Hawaiian Honey

8 OZ

ANITA KUNZ
Hybrid
This illustration was for a German ad agency and had to do with an old folktale about specialization vs. general knowledge. The farm animals to the right all look on in wonder as the strange hybrid creature is able to accomplish by itself all they do singularly.

The Pauses contacted me about doing this cover for their CD, *A Cautionary Tale*, well ahead of their release date, and indicated they had little money to spend—two things that are unusual in my dealings with bands. I liked the music, and they agreed to let me "do whatever I wanted," which sealed it. I showed them several ideas based on a storybook angle we had agreed on, and they were drawn to the one with the arsonist kids. I think they made the right choice.

MARK LEWIS
DeVotchKa
I was asked to create a flyer/handbill to promote DeVotchKa's Valentine's Day show in Boulder. The digital collage was created using Dover clip art and Adobe Illustrator and Photoshop.

JOSÉE MASSE
Lire C'est Géant
The title for this poster, *Lire c'est géant*, means "Reading is Gigantic." The illustration portrays a friendly monster to show how books can make you enter a fantastic universe.

BILL MAYER
EvenFlo Cow

ADAM McCAULEY
Local Green Sierra

SCOTT MCKOWEN
Rosmersholm

The characters in Henrik Ibsen's haunting play, *Rosmersholm*, have a passionate faith in a bright future. Two of them share a passion for each other. But all this idealism is shot down as dark family secrets are uncovered. This poster for The Pearl Theatre Company shows a figure "gazing into an existential abyss." She could be either of two characters in the story who decide to drown themselves in the millpond—one before the play starts, the other in the final scene.

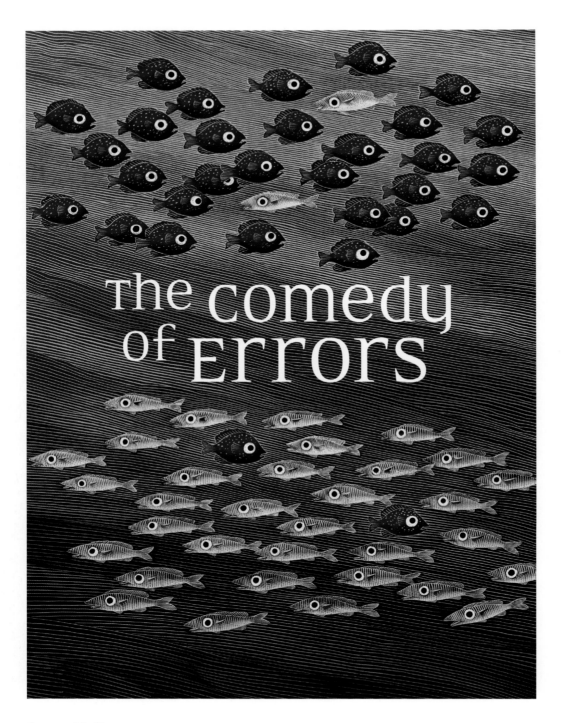

SCOTT MCKOWEN
Comedy of Errors

Shakespeare's comedy of mistaken identities involves two sets of identical twins, accidentally separated at birth. Antipholus of Syracuse and his servant, Dromio of Syracuse, arrive in Ephesus, which turns out to be the home of their "lost" twin brothers. This poster for The Acting Company summarizes the plot with a school of Syracuse fish swimming in one direction, a school of Ephesus fish swimming in the opposite direction, and a pair of lost outsiders within each group, swimming in the wrong direction.

RENÉ MILOT
Secret Sherry Society
Poster for the Secret Sherry Society: The goal was to promote an event for a secret society without divulging the identity of their members!

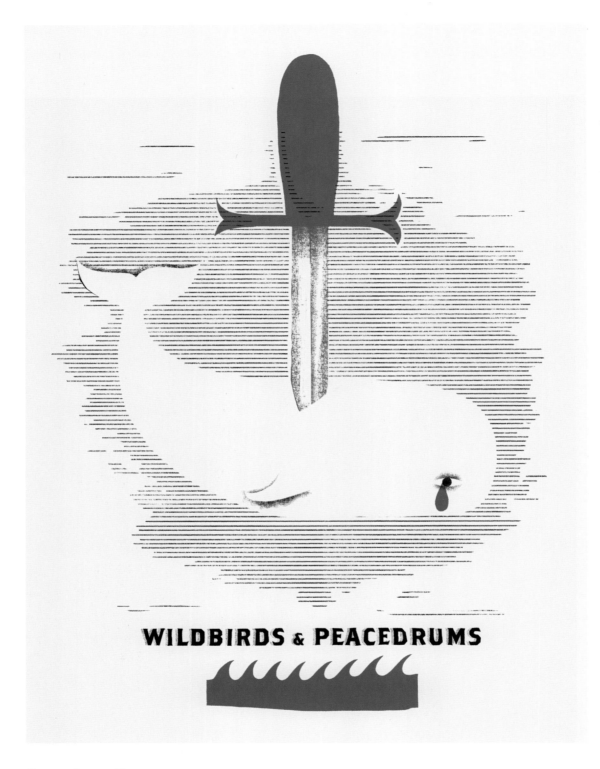

CHRIS SILAS NEAL
Wildbirds

Chris Silas Neal
Shout Out Louds

KADIR NELSON

Coke-Essence

Here's the challenge: Create an image that celebrates women of a certain age, one that they will love (and men will, too). It's summertime, she must be enjoying music, Coca-Cola; and somehow there needs to be branding of the company's anniversary and its partnership with *Essence* magazine. And add some New Orleans imagery, too. And we need it by the end of the week. Fortunately, I had an older sketch that fit the bill that needed only a bit of adjustment. Sometimes I'm just lucky.

CLIFF NIELSEN
Sparta Insurance

Mill Valley Fall
Arts Festival
September 25 & 26, 2010
Old Mill Park

MICHAEL OSBORNE
Mill Valley Fall Arts Festival Poster

DAVID PLUNKERT
The Kinks Do It Again
This two-color, screen-printed poster was created for the rock documentary *Do It Again*, a Robert Patton-Spruill film about music writer Geoff Edgers's attempt to reunite The Kinks.

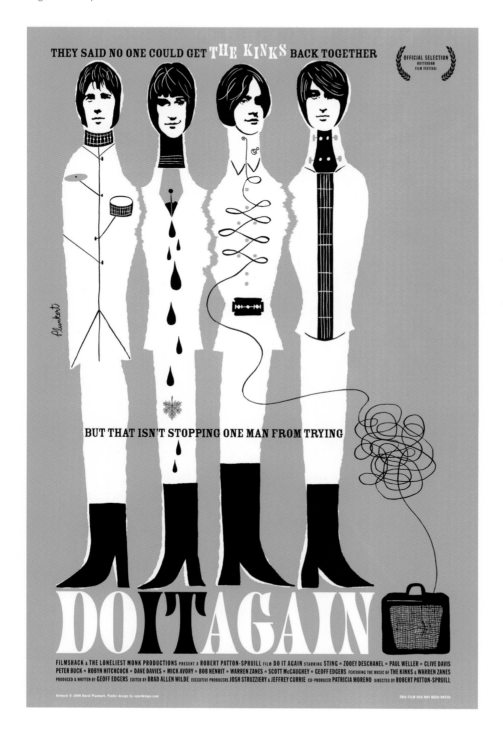

DAVID PLUNKERT
Unfinished Business
Illustration created for the David Plunkert poster retrospective at the *New York Times* Gallery 7. Each attendee received a poster that was completed with an original drawing at the opening.

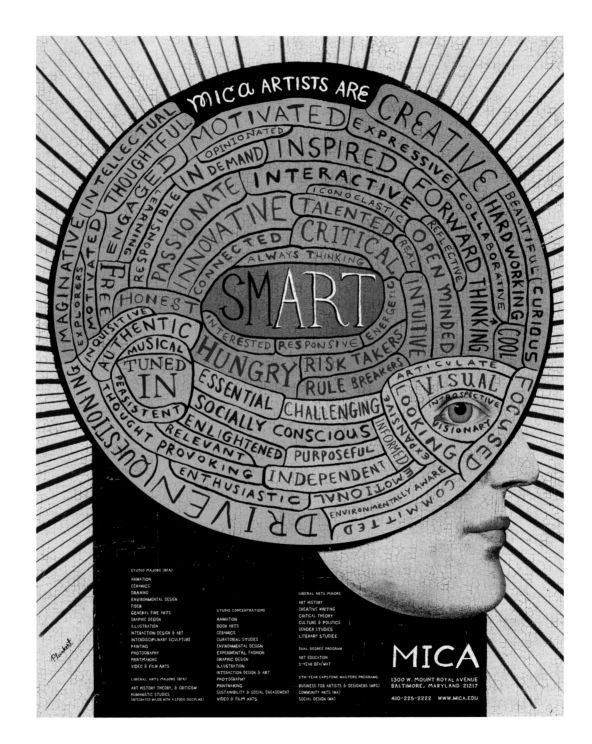

SATTU RODRIGUES

Colombo

EDEL RODRIGUEZ
Earth Hour
Poster for The World Wildlife Fund's Earth Hour energy-saving initiative,
encouraging people across the world to turn off their lights for one hour.

YUKO SHIMIZU
The Progressive Calendar

YUKO SHIMIZU
Amarillo Poster

YUKO SHIMIZU
Christian Louboutin

JOHN RUSH
Bronko Nagurski Poster
Bronko Nagurski was one of the Chicago Bears' great superstars. In my poster he is shown gaining yardage in the 1937 NFL championship game. He left football the next year to make more money as a professional wrestler.

STEVE SIMPSON
Inferno

I was approached directly by the client, bypassing the design agency altogether. As a start-up company, the guys in Mic's Chilli wanted an illustrative feel to their whole image. The "Day of the Dead" theme seemed the obvious direction to take. Using a scalpel, I cut the outline of the label and then traced it in Photoshop to help give a hand-made feel. All the artwork is done in pencil, then colored in Photoshop to give a grainy, retro feel, using a limited palette of four or five colors. The Inferno range has since expanded to four bottles with more to come.

MARK SMITH
Where Do You Stand?
This was commissioned by Antony Nelson at Abbott Mead Vickers and is part of a series that has used several different illustrators on a campaign for the *Economist*. The series poses the question, "Where do you stand?" and offers a variety of topics to the viewer. My brief was based on political attitudes towards Iran. These illustrations are split over two posters with the respective tag lines, "The West Should Not Use Force Against Iran's Nuclear Programme," and "The West Should Use Force Against Iran's Nuclear Programme."

OWEN SMITH

Silver Tassie
This poster art was used to publicize Druid Theatre's production of *The Silver Tassie* by Sean O'Casey. The epic play follows the lives of two football heroes from the tenements of Dublin to the battlefields of France, and their return home. Tony Award winner Garry Hynes directed this production that ran from August 2010 through October 2010. It played in venues in Ireland and throughout the UK, and at the 2011 Lincoln Center Festival in New York.

BRIAN STAUFFER
Oil Spill Poster

BRIAN STAUFFER
Music for the War

MARK STUTZMAN
T.I. Uncaged

T.I.'s album, *Uncaged*, was written while he was incarcerated for weapons possession. The album's release was to follow the end of his sentence. T.I.'s work on a film and another arrest delayed the album's release. Meanwhile, I worked on the concept: T.I., King of the South, and a lion, King of the Jungle, freely walking the streets at night, echoing T.I.'s new-found freedom. I worked with archive photos and a body double in a $1,500 leather jacket the art director and I chose online. Ka-ching! Then, I shipped the jacket off to New York for a photo shoot with the rapper. A photo from that shoot was selected for the CD cover, demoting my work to just the poster. And the album? It was retitled *No Mercy*, which I can completely relate to since everything that went into the original concept is no longer pertinent to the title.

POL TURGEON
Cirque 2

The Cirque du Soleil asked me to produce two different images that would be a kind of encounter between my world and theirs. I looked through a bunch of books and shows on DVD. I isolated different key characters or characters' costume details that struck me. From that point on I just let myself go free and came up with different, hopefully wild enough, propositions. This is one of the two they picked. Both were selected for a limited edition and are now part of the Cirque's Fine Art and Craft Collectibles.

STEVE WACKSMAN
Il Trovatore

BRUCE WALDMAN
The Knockout
This illustration was done for Christine Morrison of *Technical Analysis of Stocks and Commodities* magazine. The assignment was to capture the moment of impact when a fighter is knocked out. I tried to capture the frightening speed and explosive violence of the moment. This work is a monoprint.

SAM WEBER
Oryx

ANDREW WRIGHT

Top Shelf

Showing the product in a positive light was the only guideline for this assignment. After poring over numerous bad ideas, I went to the kitchen to clear my head. Opening the door to the fridge revealed the image we went to final with.

JAMES YANG

Underground

This advertising poster was for A/I Data, a company that does research and consulting for underground structures and engineering. They wanted an image to show a complex underground infrastructure that is invisible to the average person. The idea of winding pipes and electrical wires lent itself to creating an interesting, graphic visual pattern. The art director was Ken Karlic of Splice Design Group.

SCOTT BAKAL

Red Fish

This painting was created for the *Paint It Red* exhibition at the Society of Illustrators. I often think about the feeling of bliss and happiness, because really, isn't that what we all want? During the warmer months, I often find myself holding my face up to the sun to feel the wonderful sensation of having the warm sun and breeze caressing my face. I've also been thinking about fish a lot lately. Probably because of a recent sushi obsession I've acquired up in Boston because I just can't get the high-quality sushi I got when I lived in New York. Thinking about fish, I always love seeing schools of them glide through the water in tandem. It's beautiful. Almost like a soothing dance. Putting the images together to create this painting seemed natural.

RICK BERRY
Seraphs
Denizens of the KitKat Klub for the A.R.T.'s production of *Cabaret*, starring Amanda Palmer.

ANA BENAROYA

Beard Socks

The idea was to create a pair of socks that were not only fun and decorative, but also sculptural in concept. Once you step your foot into my Beard Sock, the sock transforms into the head of a man, and his expressions vary depending on how he's put on your leg and how your leg and foot move.

SERGE BLOCH
Mi Master

SERGE BLOCH

Stamps

THOMAS BLACKSHEAR II

Mother Teresa

In creating the stamp of Mother Teresa, the biggest challenge I faced was being haunted by the iconic painting of Mother Teresa done by Bob Peak. It was really a struggle to keep from painting something close to an image I considered to be almost perfect! I ended up doing three drawings and the postal committee selected the one of her smiling because they wanted to show her love of life and Christ. So they solved my problem for me! I painted the final illustration in watercolor and gouache.

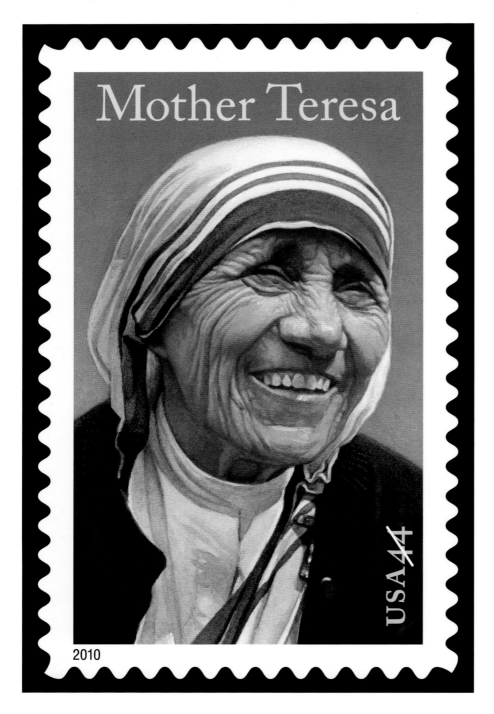

CALEF BROWN
The Exquisite Corpse Adventure, Episode Fifteen
This is one of many illustrations that I created for an online serialized story written as a collaborative effort by numerous authors. In the manner of the Exquisite Corpse, the celebrated Surrealist game, each writer added a chapter, then passed the story to the next participant. It was published on the website of the Library of Congress's Center for the Book–read.gov, and is due out in print form as well.

Nigel Buchanan
China

BILL CARMAN
Gondola Security
I was honored to contribute this piece to MicroVisions benefitting the Society of Illustrators student scholarship program. The painting is acrylic on copper.

BILL CARMAN

Narwhal Rain
I've been doing this illustration and painting thing for a lot of years. Why is it I still get giddy when the Society of Illustrators asks me to participate in something? This painting was for *Earth: Fragile Planet*, an exhibition with some incredible work included. Thanks again for asking.

RICHARD DOWNS
Save Them All
I was invited to create these Sea Turtle monotypes by Erica Heimberg, the director of the Sea Turtle Restoration Project. It was for an art exhibit and benefit to help restore habitat destroyed by the BP Deepwater Horizon oil spill. Erica had seen several personal pieces I'd posted after I'd read that BP was burning surface oil in which endangered Sea Turtles were trapped and burned alive. The Sea Turtle Restoration Project is a fabulous organization that continues remarkable worldwide conservation efforts for our sea creature friends through public support.

LEO ESPINOSA

Gitango
This piece was one of two limited-edition silkscreen series produced for Gitango, a solo show at Turbo Gallery in Buenos Aires, Argentina. It was also the image chosen for the promotional material of the exhibit.

LEO ESPINOSA
Shelter
One of a three-panel piece created for Gitango, a solo show at Turbo Gallery in Buenos Aires, Argentina.

Vivienne Flesher

Dowd and Friedman

Leanne Shapton was the art director of the *New York Times Op-Ed* for several years and we worked together many times; by the time she gave me this assignment she was very familiar with my work. It's the custom to display photographs of the *Op-Ed* columnists next to their articles on the *Times* website. Leanne thought it might look fresh to have their portraits illustrated, rather than photographed. Sadly, it wasn't an option with which the editors agreed.

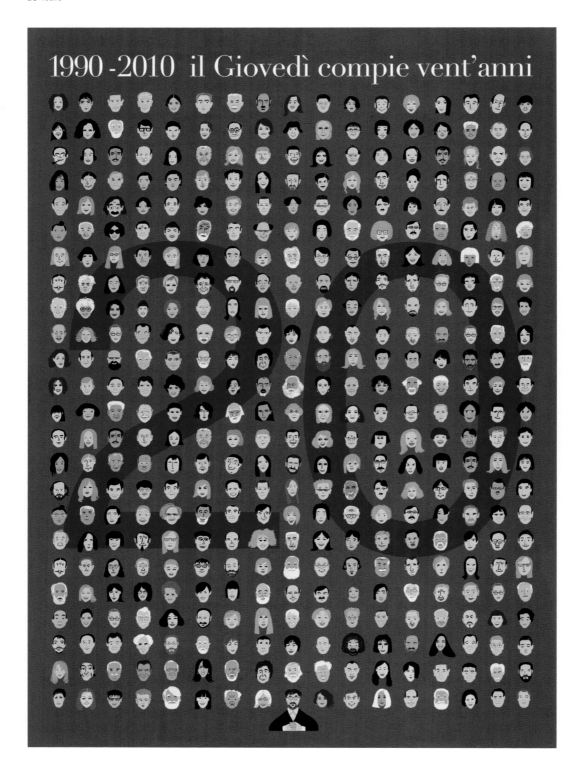

MICHAEL GIBBS
Time

ALESSANDRO GOTTARDO
Victoria Symphony Summer Season

DONNA GRETHEN

Best Foot Forward!

After hanging onto a mailer of mine for six years, Sung Hee Kim, the creative director of Sagetopia Design, found the perfect project for me. This poster was based on my mailer *Eight Ladies Dancing*, which pictured women's feet in a hurry shopping; a modern take on *The Twelve Days of Christmas*. I work in layers of gouache and collage, and I love working with pen and ink on Japanese paper. I love the blotchy uneven line. I do things several times, pick the parts I like, and collage them together. Because of this I can play with spatial layouts and perspective. I scanned my final work into Photoshop and sent it all digitally to Sung Hee. She and everyone at Sagetopia were fabulous to work with and the project was a blast!

CHERYL GRIESBACH AND STANLEY MARTUCCI

The Unexpected Guest

This painting, which was included in an exhibition at Private Gallery, was also used for the show's announcements. The gallery gave me unlimited use of my private paintings, which are somewhat disengaged from my commercial commissions. Initially the image didn't have the cat peering through the foliage; the change was at the suggestion of

Stanley Martucci, my husband and frequent collaborator. Is the mother bird positioning herself to protect her young? Will they be protected by the predator, who seems to pick up their scent? Can this image portray the precariousness of life?

GREG HARLIN
Loyalist Leaving
Surrounded, with surrender now shockingly inevitable, Loyalist troops attached to the British army of John Burgoyne splinter over the terrible decision now facing them: risk staying for the surrender (and face charges of treason), or use the darkness of a final night to attempt escape through the overwhelming American army. This illustration was part of a series of waysides for the newly opened Victory Woods section of the Saratoga National Historical Park. The intention is to bring to life an emotionally resonant moment at each wayside along the walking path.

Earth Day 2010

JODY HEWGILL
Earth Day 2010 Poster

JESSICA HISCHE
Beautiful Decay

I was asked by *Beautiful/Decay*, an art publication, to submit a t-shirt design for their fall line of shirts. They provided minimal art direction and let me run free, as long as the design appealed to both men and women.

JOEL ISKOWITZ
Inspiration of the Lincoln Cent

This project was born from the good fortune of having my reverse (tails) design selected for the minting of the 2009 Lincoln Bicentennial Cent. To know that my artwork and artist mark (JI) would appear on the reverse of Victor David Brenner's (VDB) storied 1909 Lincoln profile on the cent's obverse (heads) is still an overwhelming thought, considering that the profile is the most reproduced object of art in all human history. Picture the scene in the library study of President Theodore Roosevelt's summer White House, Sagamore Hill, in Oyster Bay, LI. Brenner is sketching TR. The two conspire to break precedent by placing the portrait of a person (Lincoln), rather than an allegorical figure, on United States circulating coins. It was significant that Mark Schlepphorst and I visited this room. If I achieved some sense of verisimilitude, it is because of my direct contact with the subject matter in the theater of action, even if it occurred a century ago.

BRENDAN LEACH
Hester Street

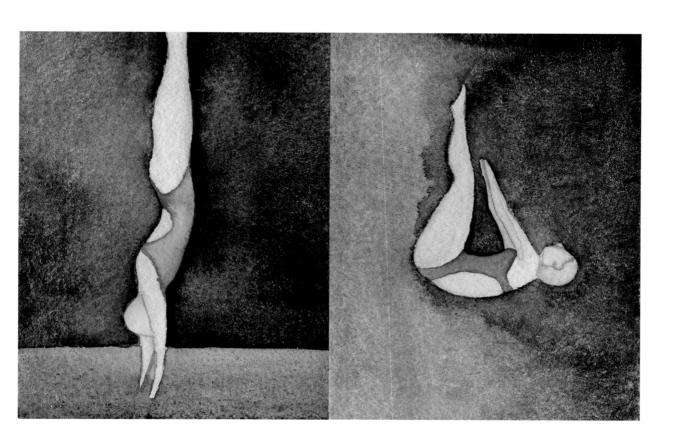

MARIA EUGENIA LONGO
Diving

KAM MAK

Year of the Tiger

The creation of the Narcissus painting began when I planted the Chinese Narcissus bulbs in a dish filled with pebbles and water. Growing up in Hong Kong, my grandma had taught me this Chinese tradition during the Lunar New Year, and it became an annual ritual for us. After several weeks, the Narcissus finally bloomed and I took numerous photos as references for my initial sketches. The Narcissus painting is based on the sketch that worked best and most harmoniously for the stamp size. If the Chinese Narcissus blooms exactly on the day of the New Year, the white flowers symbolize good luck and prosperity. It is believed to indicate good fortune for the ensuing twelve months.

GREG MANCHESS

Above the Timberline

This was produced for a video about my painting process, filmed by Massive Black. I love to paint snow. White subjects contain a wide range of color, which can help new oil painters understand the subtleties of mixing color. It demands that the painter use less for more dramatic affect. This is the first painting of a story about a young airship pilot, searching in uncharted ice lands for a mysterious mechanical city . . . and his lost father.

GREG MANCHESS
Edward Kennedy
Each year, the RAND Corporation puts out a calendar of interesting quotes from society's intellectuals, both contemporary and historical. This portrait sketch of Teddy Kennedy was created for the 2011 calendar.

BILL MAYER
Death of Frogs

CHRISTOPHER NIELSEN
Tug-O-War
The theme was "Untold Stories."

RAFAL OLBINSKI
Mona Lisa in Corrida

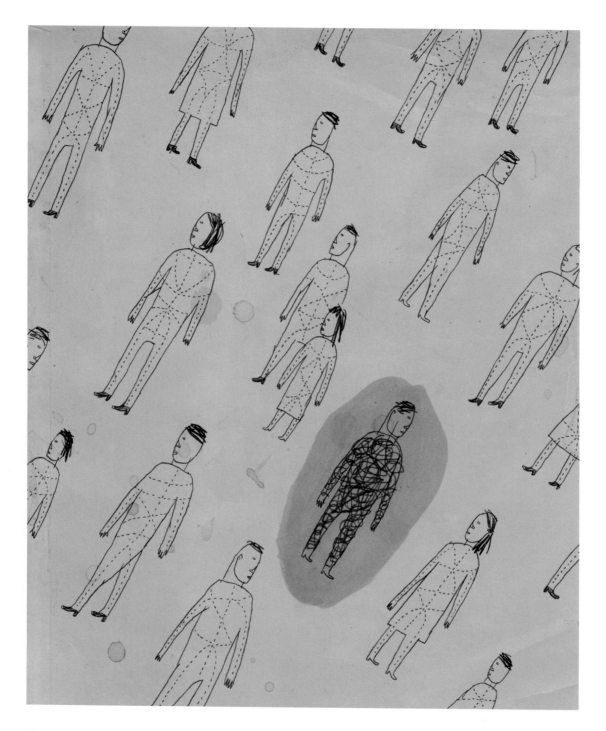

BRIAN REA

The Complexity of MS
Opener piece for a series on the challenges of understanding and evaluating the complexity of MS, a disease in which communication between the brain and parts of the body is disabled.

ROBERT RODRIGUEZ
Cowboys of the Silver Screen

Carl Herman, the art director, asked me to do Gene Autry in the style of the old cowboy movie posters, because he didn't have an existing poster that would work. We simplified it down to just the portrait, without stampedes, rustlers, and holdups in the background. Then the posters for the other cowboys in the series, which had all the background features, seemed too complicated for the small size of a postage stamp. So I wound up doing them all.

WHITNEY SHERMAN
Prometheus/Copernicus
Ethical behavior was the context for this illustration for the Templeton Foundation. The author compared two ways of thinking: Copernican (logical) and Promethian (emotional). The Greek vase styling gives a nod to the Titan Prometheus, while creating a crisp display of the tools of logic.

OWEN SMITH

Water

This is one of a series of three relief sculpture panels produced for Laguna Honda Hospital through the San Francisco Arts Commission. The purpose of this art is to add visual interest and character to the resident wings and serve as way-finding for the 740 residents. The water theme is a nod to the four classical elements that were represented in a set of WPA murals original to the hospital building. The sculptures are installed alongside a series of mosaic murals, also designed by the artist.

CARLO STANGA

Contemporary Gallery

In celebration of the 25th anniversary of the Arts for Transit program, I was honored to create an image that depicts the underground of a contemporary art gallery. I enjoyed working closely with the program's team to show, along with fellow artists, the multi-level stations and multicultural people as they rush below my interpretations of some of New York's most prominent buildings. The clients and Morgan Gaynin, my representatives, know that architecture is always present in my illustrations, and that this assignment fit my style like a hand to a glove. I hope to have successfully respected, as well as rediscovered, the characteristic New York atmosphere and state of mind.

GARY TAXALI
Row Box

GARY TAXALI
Any Thing Festive Goes

THE HEADS OF STATE
NPR
Cover for National Public Radio's 2011 Calendar.

THE HEADS OF STATE
Oil Drip
A call to action poster for green energy reform post-Gulf oil spill.

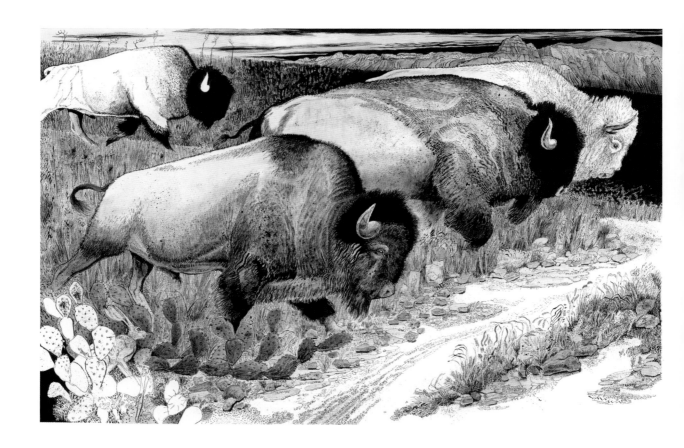

JACK UNRUH
Buffalo
A Texas Panhandle bank uses a buffalo as their brand. I was asked to draw a herd of buffalo to represent the corporate group. So I threw in the mythical white buffalo to enhance their stature.

ELLEN WEINSTEIN
Peter and the Wolf
The Nashville Symphony commissioned me to illustrate their program guide covers for the 2009/2010 season. *Peter and the Wolf* was one of this series. I felt great empathy for the wolf in this symphony. I wanted to capture him lost and alone in a forest of music.

SAM WEBER
The Fisherman's Wife

Sam Weber
Honey

KYLE WHITE

Good Game
This illustration is a commentary on Southern culture and the underlying racial tension that still exists. I often use metaphors and my own personal experiences to tell stories that can resonate with a much larger audience. The work was created using a variety of processes including, drawing, painting, and digital manipulation.

NATE WILLIAMS
Lions and Molecules

NOAH WOODS

Explore

It was a treat to create *Explore* for the St. Louis Central Library. The image was used as a huge outdoor banner to draw in not only children, but adults as well.

JAMES YANG

November

Artists were asked to illustrate a month of the calendar for the Society of Newspaper Designers. The only requirement was to incorporate newsprint into the final art. This was a chance to play with depth, pattern and character design. The art director for this piece was Deborah Withey of Cheese + Pickles Studio.

BOOK

CALEF BROWN
ILLUSTRATOR

Calef Brown's illustrations have appeared in *TIME*, *Rolling Stone*, *Newsweek*, the *New York Times*, *Entertainment Weekly*, the *New Yorker*, *Sports Illustrated*, and numerous other newspapers and magazines around the country and internationally. He has created CD and book covers, murals, and packaging for clients such as Target Stores, Coca-Cola, Adidas, Martha Stewart, E✳TRADE, Sony Music, and Nickelodeon. Calef has also written and illustrated many acclaimed children's books, including the #1 *New York Times* bestseller, *Flamingos on the Roof*, and most recently, *Hallowilloween: Nefarious Silliness*. He lives and works in Maine.

MARC BURCKHARDT
ILLUSTRATOR

Marc Burckhardt lives in Austin, Texas, but his work can be found in galleries and publications, and on book and album covers throughout the world. His work has received numerous awards, including Gold and Silver Medals from the Society of Illustrators, and has been profiled in *3x3* magazine, *Communication Arts*, *Illustration/Japan*, and *Juxtapoz*. In 2005, Marc was commissioned to produce a collector's portrait of Johnny Cash for SONY Records' "The Legend," which went on to win the 2006 Grammy® for Best Packaging of a Special Edition Box Set. He is past president of the Illustration Conference, chair of the Society of Illustrators 47th Annual Exhibition, and in 2010 he was named State Artist by the Texas Legislature and the Texas Commission on the Arts. His dog is named Gertie.

RODRIGO CORRAL
CREATIVE DIRECTOR, FSG

Graphic designer Rodrigo Corral is creative director at Farrar, Straus and Giroux, where he worked from 1996 to 2000 following his graduation from the School of Visual Arts. He also runs Rodrigo Corral Design, the nine-year-old studio behind such memorable book covers as those for James Frey's *A Million Little Pieces*, a shelf of Chuck Palahniuk novels, Debbie Millman's smashing *How to Think Like a Great Graphic Designer*, and Jay-Z's *Decoded*. Rodrigo's work has appeared in *New York* magazine, the *Atlantic*, and the *New York Times Book Review*.

ROBERT FESTINO
CREATIVE DIRECTOR, *MEN'S HEALTH*

Robert Festino is an award-winning art director and graphic designer, currently the creative director of *Men's Health*. Previously, he was the design director of *FORTUNE*, and held similar roles at several other publications. In 2005 *Photo District News* added him to their prestigious "Players" list, a rare honor for magazine art directors. That same year, *Adweek* awarded Robert the title of "Creative Team of the Year" for his work at re-positioning *Runner's World*. Infamous, among the Society of Illustrators, for his design of the *Illustrators 48* Call for Entries, he insists, "It was ahead of its time, or just plain bad."

KADIR NELSON
ILLUSTRATOR

Kadir Nelson is an award-winning artist and illustrator who has created paintings for *Sports Illustrated*, the Coca-Cola Company, the U.S. Postal Service, Major League Baseball, Dreamworks SKG, Sony Music, and the estate of Michael Jackson. Kadir's paintings are in the collections of notable institutions and public collections, including the International Olympic Committee, the U.S. House of Representatives, and the National Baseball Hall of Fame. He has also illustrated several best-selling picture books including *WE ARE THE SHIP: The Story of Negro League Baseball*, and *HEART AND SOUL: The Story of America and African Americans*, which he also authored.

ELIZABETH B. PARISI
CREATIVE DIRECTOR,
SCHOLASTIC

Elizabeth B. Parisi graduated from Rhode Island School of Design with a BFA in Illustration, which she immediately put to use as a book designer in children's publishing. As creative director in trade publishing at Scholastic, she oversees the creation of over 120 titles per year in various genres of children's books, though her heart is in the young adult market, where she has designed many award-winning titles. She is the art director and designer of The Hunger Games trilogy, soon to be a major motion picture. The winning solution for that series involved the amazing work of her husband, Tim O'Brien, who created all the front cover art. Elizabeth contends that she loves her job every day and never tires of the creative process involved in making imagery for fiction—in whatever form.

DUSTY SUMMERS
CREATIVE DIRECTOR,
THE HEADS OF STATE

Dusty Summers is co-founder and creative director of The Heads of State, a design and illustration studio formed in 2002 with Jason Kernevich. He is also an art director at Seattle's legendary Sub Pop Records and an adjunct professor of design and illustration at Tyler School of Art, where he received his BFA. He has won various awards and has done work for the likes of the *New York Times*, Starbucks, Wilco, Iron and Wine, and Penguin Books. He lives and works in Philadelphia with his wife, son, and cat. He has no major obsessions but is minorly afflicted by American football, globes, paperbacks, and westerns (revisionist or otherwise).

ANNE TWOMEY
VP CREATIVE DIRECTOR,
GRAND CENTRAL
PUBLISHING

Anne Twomey is a graphic designer specializing in book cover design. Currently VP creative director of Grand Central Publishing, she had been an art director for Pocketbooks and St. Martin's Press. As a creative director of a major New York book publisher, Anne has worked on covers for many esteemed and celebrity authors. More rewardingly, she has been able to collaborate with the most talented illustrators, photographers, graphic designers, and type designers in the business. Her work has been acknowledged for excellence in design and art direction by AIGA, the Art Directors Club, *Communication Arts*, *Photo District News*, *Print*, the Society of Illustrators, and the Type Directors Club. She lives in New York City.

HELEN YENTUS
ART DIRECTOR,
RIVERHEAD BOOKS

Helen Yentus has been designing book covers for nine years, first as a designer for Paul Buckley at Penguin, and then for John Gall at Vintage, before returning to Penguin as art director of Riverhead Books. She also designs with her husband and partner as Yentus & Booher. Their clients include the *New York Times*, *Metropolis*, *Wired*, Gibney Dance, as well as numerous publishing houses. Her work has been featured by the AIGA, *Print*, *Graphis*, *Communication Arts*, the Design Museum in London, and various design books and blogs. She lives in Brooklyn with her husband and daughter.

GOLD MEDAL WINNER
Anna and Elena Balbusso

Northanger Abbey
Cover illustration for the novel *Northanger Abbey* by Jane Austen, published in 2010. We wanted to represent the emotion and thoughts of the female protagonist by showing her reading. The seventeen-year-old Catherine is obsessed with Gothic novels; she confuses what goes on in the books with real life, imagining that her friend's house is a crime scene. Created in acrylic and digital, the original art in the exhibition was a limited edition fine art print on 100% cotton, acid-free Velvet paper.

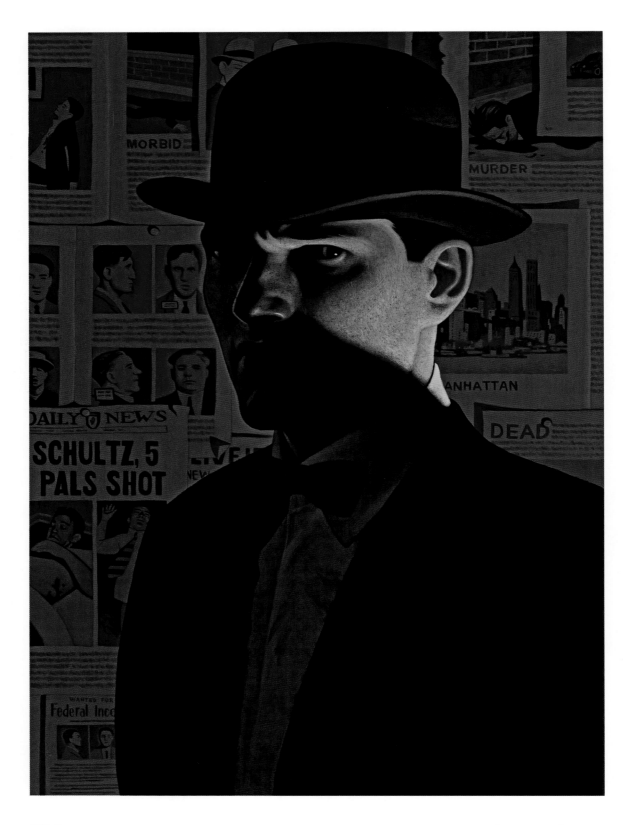

GOLD MEDAL WINNER
THOMAS EHRETSMANN

Murder Inc.
This is one of the covers I did for a series of French comic books called MafiaStory. The question was how to create a strong and personal piece from true historical events, which happened almost a century ago on another continent and were reported in a rather neutral way by the authors. The previous illustrations in the series suffered because I wanted to include too much documentation and reference in the work. This time, I just closed my eyes and put myself in the main character's place. The bad mood I was in on that particular day was also a great help in creating the atmosphere of the picture. I want to thank the publisher, Guy Delcourt, and the authors, David Chauvel and Erwan LeSaec, for trusting me.

Now Billy Can Concentrate
From my book, *In and Out with Dick and Jane: A Loving Parody*, written with James Victore, published in 2011 by Abrams Image. It's a simple book that tells a timeless tale of children and their world. A beautiful, sunny, joyful world filled with foreclosures, gun culture, school shootings, abuse by priests, serial killer clowns, meth labs, racism, the Times Square bomber, latch key kids, Viagra, obesity, litter, pollution, big box stores, credit card debt, sex education, ADHD drugs, bad school lunches, soccer dads, bestiality—in other words, a world much like our own.

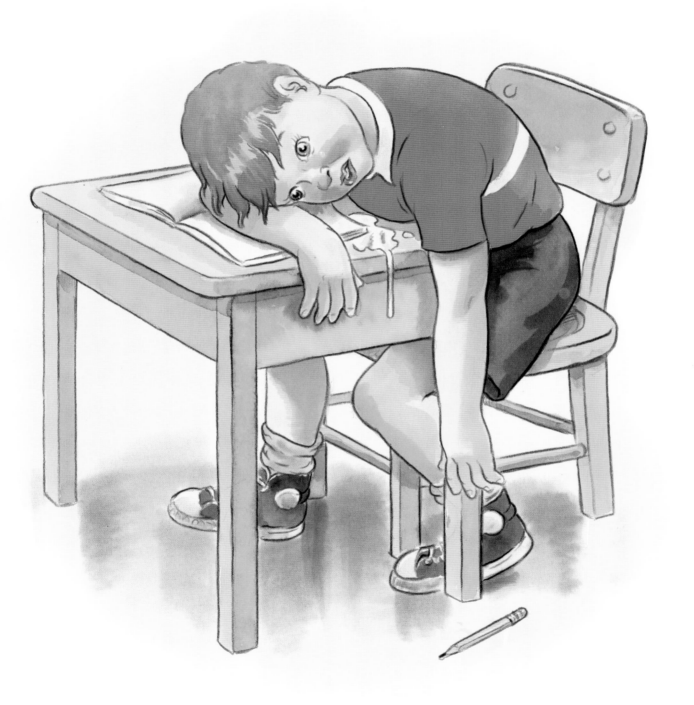

SILVER MEDAL WINNER
Josh Cochran

Zombies vs. Unicorns

I referenced Hieronymus Bosch's *Garden of Earthly Delights*, and used it as a starting point. I even included a Bosch character in my drawing. Since this was a Young Adult cover I wasn't too sure how far I could take the imagery. The art director, Lauren Rille, wanted me to do a sample of what it could look like so she could sell it to the editor and her creative director.

After seeing this, they basically let me go wild with it; I just couldn't show any nudity or sex. This project was a total dream assignment for me because of my love for both unicorns and zombies. The art directors, Lauren Rille and Sonia Chaghatzbanian, gave me a lot of freedom and pushed me creatively. Luckily we were all super happy with the results.

The Perfect Joke
It's a book cover image for a novel about the relations between a dad and his son. The dad is an old school comedian for a '60s TV program. His son is a comedian of the present day, where the TV culture, and everything else, is much more vulgar, silly, and without any values. The technique is a mix: digital, drawing on paper, and textures.

Yiddishkeit: Coney Island
This was created for a book illustrating Yiddish art and culture. It is a little ironic that I find myself doing more and more art related to Judaism, given that I was brought up by two atheists. I certainly feel Jew-*ish* but ultimately I'm a *Manhattanite* and try to sketch the city religiously.

LINCOLN AGNEW
Cookiebot Centerfold

LINCOLN AGNEW
Cookiebot Storm

ANNA AND ELENA BALBUSSO

Prisoner

The illustration is part of a series of 28 images of the illustrated book, *Le Horla*, published in 2010. "Le Horla" is a famous short horror story written by French writer Guy de Maupassant in 1887. The story is written in the first person in the form of a diary. The narrator, a solitary bourgeois man, reported his troubled thoughts and feelings of anguish. All around him, he senses the presence of a being without form and consistency.

He calls it the "Horla," a strange invisible creature, a threatening presence that has come to make him his slave. The narrator feels imprisoned, lost, and possessed to the point that he is ready to kill either the Horla, or himself. Created in acrylic and digital, the original art in the exhibition was a limited edition fine art print on 100% cotton, acid-free Velvet paper.

LOU BEACH
Elephant Milk

DIVERSITY

VINCENT BOURGEAU
Un Ogre

CALEF BROWN

The Poltergeyser

This painting accompanies "The Poltergeyser," a poem in my book *Hallowilloween—Nefarious Silliness*. The poem concerns a ghostly fountain at the base of a haunted mountain. A strange waterspout visible only to those who keep an eye out on nights that are especially dark in a certain National Park.

DANIEL BUENO

A Janela do Meu Primo

Illustration for *A Janela de esquina do meu primo (My Cousin's Corner Window)*, written by E.T.A. Hoffmann in 1822. An image of 47.2" x 35.4" was created to appear in fragments and in its entirety in the book. It explores the movements of the cousins' eyes as they observe—closer in and far-ther away—the market in Gendarmenmarkt, a square in Berlin, from a corner window. Research of historical clothing, architecture, costumes, and other elements, was used to appropriately illustrate the observations made by the characters in this example of Hoffmann's late, realistic style.

MARC BURCKHARDT
Nashville Chrome

This group portrait of the Browns, a real-life country trio of the 1950s–'60s, was for the cover of the fictional novel titled *Nashville Chrome*, which was based loosely on their lives. Using the bright palette and snug grouping typical of the time, I tried to capture the era and the group's sunny, wholesome sound, and their humble roots.

CHRIS BUZELLI
Door in the Forest
This painting was for a wraparound book cover for *The Door in the Forest*.

RAÚL COLÓN
Once Upon a Time
Having spent time in the country visiting my cousins, I was familiar with
chickens, roosters, and farm animals in general, which helped in developing this character. However, the feathers in this particular rooster were
inspired by a wooden folk sculpture I once saw in a magazine.

ANDRÉ DA LOBA
The Forest

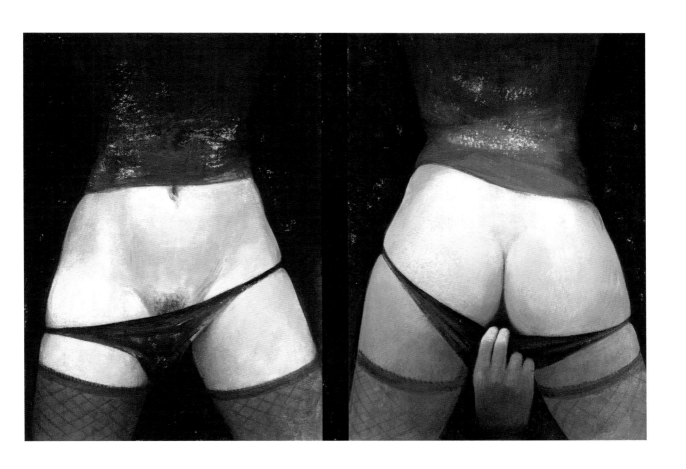

GÉRARD DuBOIS
Les Adventures de Minette

LEO ESPINOSA
Lullaby
This was my contribution to *I Heart Haiti*, a limited edition book featuring the work of 31 Colombian illustrators, designers, and photographers, created to collect funds for the reconstruction of Haiti through Architecture for Humanity.

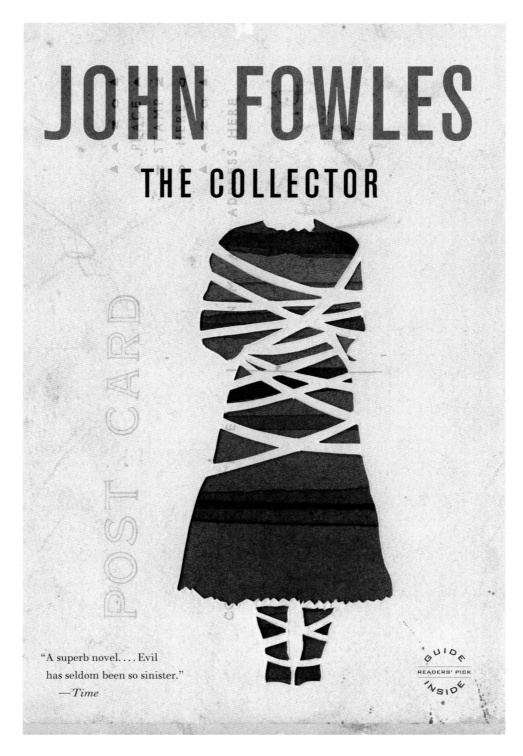

SHANNON FRESHWATER
The Collector

CHRIS GALL
White Lady
One of several hundred illustrations I created for the *The PDT Cocktail Book: A Modern Bartender's Manual*. The object was to use illustration to capture the modern cocktail culture with artwork that suggests intriguing narratives while avoiding traditional glassware depictions. This particular illustration accompanies the recipe for a White Lady.

CHRIS GALL
Bull
This illustration accompanied the recipe for Cranberry Cobbler.

ALESSANDRO GOTTARDO
Landscape of Fire

JESSIE HARTLAND

Sphinx

A spread, from my children's book, *How the Sphinx Got to the Museum*, is of museum conservators busily at work assembling a broken sphinx. I also wrote the book. It's the story behind how the Sphinx of Hatshepsut actually found its way to New York's Metropolitan Museum of Art.

NURSE, SOLDIER,
MARISSA MOSS
SPY
JOHN HENDRIX
THE · STORY · OF ·
SARAH EDMONDS
A CIVIL WAR HERO!

John Hendrix

Sarah Edmonds Cover

Cover art for the true story of Sarah Edmonds, a passionate woman who wanted to fight for the Union in the Civil War. In order to enlist she dressed up as a man and called herself Frank Thompson. In this book, we tell the tale of her enlistment, her exceptional abilities in the battlefield, and her adventures as a spy behind the Confederate lines. Because of her bravery she was sent on many clandestine missions, dressed up as woman, a runaway slave, or traveling peddler. She was a woman dressed as a man dressed as a spy—wearing two disguises at at the same time!

John Hendrix

Our Little Woman
Interior art for *Nurse, Soldier, Spy*. The soldiers in Sarah Edmonds's company had no idea of her deception and merely saw her as a girlish young boy. They often teased "Frank," affectionately calling her "Our Little Woman." But, her exceptional bravery on the battlefield won her the loyalty and praise of her fellow soldiers.

JEREMY HOLMES

Sensing Jesus: Pastoral Musings for Ministry
While gathering research, I came across many images of Jesus's face that people had found in everything from smoke stains to plant life. My gut told me this was the solution, but I wasn't exactly sure how to apply this to the assignment—until I sketched a fingerprint.

Rod Hunt
Paddy Clarke HA HA HA
I was asked to create the cover for the Vintage reissue of Roddy Doyle's 1993 Booker prize-winning book *Paddy Clarke Ha Ha Ha*. I had to visualize Barrytown, the 1960s hometown of the ten-year-old Irish protagonist, and the key events from the text. To emphasize the historical time setting, we decided to use an almost monochrome, limited-color palette, punctuated by a strong red spot color.

HIROMICHI ITO

Place of Winter

I needed to draw a traditional Japanese house this time. This kind of
house rarely exists now, so it was difficult to find and gather the research
material. But I was lucky because the authors of the book helped to collect
the information for me, so I could make a fantastic, traditional Japanese
atmosphere in my illustration. If you feel coolness and silence in my illustrations, I will be so happy!

PAT KINSELLA
Houdini

TATSURO KIUCHI

The Memories of Festivals
The novel deals with recollections of various festivals throughout Japan. It was difficult to show a particular festival as a cover image because it wouldn't represent the novel as a whole. So I chose to depict a night stall, which is typical to any festival in Japan.

PATRICK LEGER
The Midwich Cuckoos

PATRICK LEGER
The Chrysalids

ROSS MacDONALD

Some Kids Have Hobbies

The following three illustrations are from my book, *In and Out with Dick and Jane: A Loving Parody*, written with James Victore, published in 2011 by Abrams Image.

The book was over 15 years in the making. This illustration was sketched for the *New York Times Magazine* around the time of the school shootings in the mid-1990s, but before Columbine. James Victore and I had written a few humor pieces together for magazines and were casting about for a more ambitious (lucrative) project. I don't remember exactly, but I'm guessing we looked at the killed sketches hanging on my wall and little light bulbs appeared over our heads.

ROSS MACDONALD

Billy Liked Dressup
This illustration from my book, *In and Out with Dick and Jane: A Loving Parody*, was originally sketched for the *Los Angeles Times Magazine* around 1994. The sketch was killed.

JOSÉE MASSE

Bears in the News

The challenge was to create illustrations divided into two parts. They were to accompany poems that could be read both forward and backward, with a different outcome either way.

"Asleep in Cub's Bed, Blonde Startled by Bears," the headline read. Next day Goldilocks claimed, "They shouldn't have left the door unlocked." She ate the porridge. She broke a chair. "Big deal? No! They weren't there."

They weren't there. No big deal?! A chair broke. She ate the porridge. She unlocked the door. "They shouldn't have left," Goldilocks claimed. Next day the headline read: "Bears Startled by Blonde Asleep in Cub's Bed."

JOSÉE MASSE

The Sleeping Beauty and the Wide-Awake Prince
Typical. Hacking through briars, looking for love—the prince at work. But I have to be sleeping, never partying, never out in the world. It's no fun being in a fairy tale.

In a fairy tale. It's no fun being out in the world, never partying, never sleeping. But I have to be the prince at work, looking for love, hacking through briars. Typical.

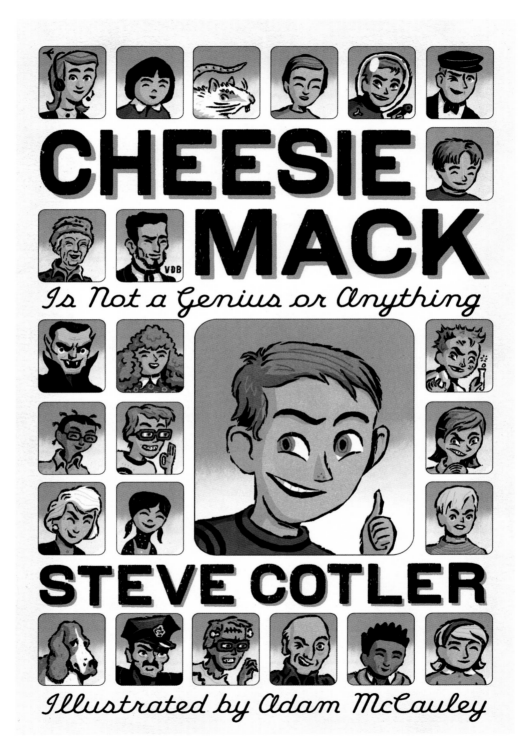

GRADY McFERRIN

Where Things Come Back

This book takes place in a small Arkansas town, where a woodpecker, which was long-thought extinct, was spotted. The main character in the story is not the woodpecker, but a young man whose brother had recently disappeared mysteriously. The bird, however, steals all media attention and captures the hearts of the nation, whose eyes are glued on this town where things come back from the dead. The narrator hopes, waits, and prays that his brother will come back as well. The art director, Michael McCartney, knew the importance of having the symbolic bird at the center of the cover. I'm very pleased that he insisted we try several different variations on that theme. I also really like the way the blue oval in the center feels like a break in the fabric, or a peak through the wood, beyond the void that reveals the bird shining and happy.

SCOTT MCKOWEN

Dracula

Dracula begins with Jonathan Harker's visit to Castle Dracula, to complete formalities for the Count's purchase of a property in England: Carfax Abbey. Carfax is fictional, but it was inspired by a visit Bram Stoker made to Whitby Abbey in North Yorkshire. Stoker sets several chapters of the novel in Whitby, so Scott McKowen based his version of Carfax Abbey on Whitby Abbey. The Count stands atop the Abbey walls, half Batman, half Wim Wenders' *Wings of Desire* angel.

CHRIS SILAS NEAL
A Room with a View

KADIR NELSON
Mama Miti/Crowd
I began working on the book *Mama Miti* with the intention of creating the artwork with natural materials like sand, dried plants, rocks, and so forth, but I quickly realized the limitations of important things like color and variety. Instead, I chose to use patterned cloth, and found intricate images like this one to be quite a challenge, but I like the end result.

KADIR NELSON

Mama Miti/Madonna

I thought it would be interesting to turn an ordinary situation like this one, a woman asking for help, into an image of hope, with both spiritual and religious connotations. It was merely an experiment inspired by a painter by the name of Barkley Hendricks.

KADIR NELSON

Mama Miti/Grid

Creating the artwork for *Mama Miti* was the first time I'd ever worked with fabric. I found that I needed to use very little paint for this series of paintings, and it gave me an opportunity to find depth through patterns and color versus light and shadow. The challenge was finding the right patterns and colors to help tell the story while keeping the emotional integrity of each image.

TAO NYEU

Please Don't Pick in Public
I was originally going to paint this scene, but after doing a color sketch it looked like an embroidery piece to me, so I had no choice but to make it so. I was pregnant at the time so it was also a perfect non-toxic medium and my belly provided a perfect table on which to work.

TIM O'BRIEN

Elkhorn Tavern

For a cover for Anthony Ramondo at Penguin, I was asked to paint Elkhorn Tavern, a two-story, wood-frame structure that served as a physical epicenter for the battle of Elkhorn Tavern, which was fought in northeastern Arkansas on March 7th and 8th 1862. I had the most fun painting the sky.

RYAN PANCOAST
At the Queen's Command

HyeJeong Park

The Headless Lady

I had to draw the cover for a horror/crime novel, *The Headless Lady*, in which the victims' bodies are headless. Instead of gore, the client wanted mystery and a beautiful woman's face (looking alive). I read the book, so I knew I wanted a female figure that ended at the neck to make it ambiguous: the viewer wouldn't know if it was a victim, the killer, or someone else. The book design team used a folding cover, which showed only the face being touched, but when the cover is unfolded, we see that the head is held in the headless figure's hands, creating an ingenious illustration with a twist ending.

C.F. Payne
Late for School

CRAIG PHILLIPS

Red Riding Hood
The art director had a very specific image in mind for this particular jacket and provided me with a solid comp to work from. The goal was to keep the composition and color as minimal as possible, and to work with positive and negative shapes to achieve a simple graphic statement. The snowy landscape and starkness of Red Riding Hood's classic crimson cloak served that goal well.

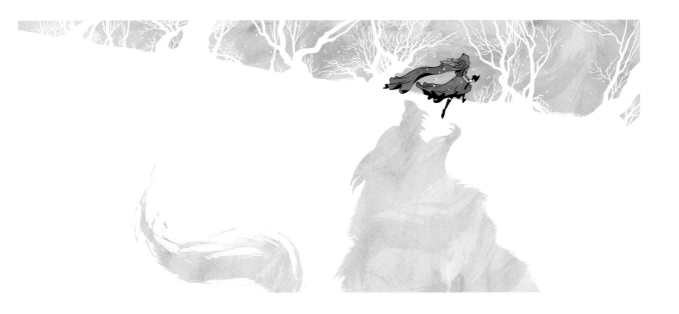

JEFFREY PIKE
Charlie Chaplin
A chance meeting with poet Ryan Fox led to a collaboration that became
After Love, published by the Virginia Arts of the Book Center. Mr. Fox's
poem, "Charlie Chaplin," is based, in part, on a specific scene from a
Chaplin movie. So, it was important that the Little Tramp character be
present, but hopefully not as a primary read.

ANTOINE REVOY AND KELLY MURPHY

The Lodge

This was created to illustrate one of the 10 chilling tales of *Haunted Houses*, the first volume of the Are You Scared Yet? series written by Robert D. San Souci. Kelly Murphy and Antoine Revoy decided to work on this book collaboratively in hopes of developing an unexpected hybrid style that would conjure eerie impressions. "The Lodge" is the story of the ghost of a mother looking for her lost child in the woods. The artists chose to limn the apparition's horrific drama with understated theatrical means, revealing the mother's phantasmal nature solely by the absence of her reflection in a pond. Antoine's crow quill drawing was combined with Kelly's ink wash painting, inviting traditional craftsmanship to produce a spectral atmosphere.

JUNGYEON ROH
American Boys—Broadway

GUIDO SCARABOTTOLO

Hypothermia

Arnaldur Indridason is an Icelandic writer of crime fiction. I have to make about one cover per year for the Italian edition of his novels. It is a kind of serial work, so I decided to suggest the really dark and scary atmosphere of his stories by always using a nervous and messed up pencil mark and only one or two colors. The English title required a cold color, but I had used a blue-gray for the previous cover, so I preferred black and brown for this one; luckily the Italian title does not refer to the cold.

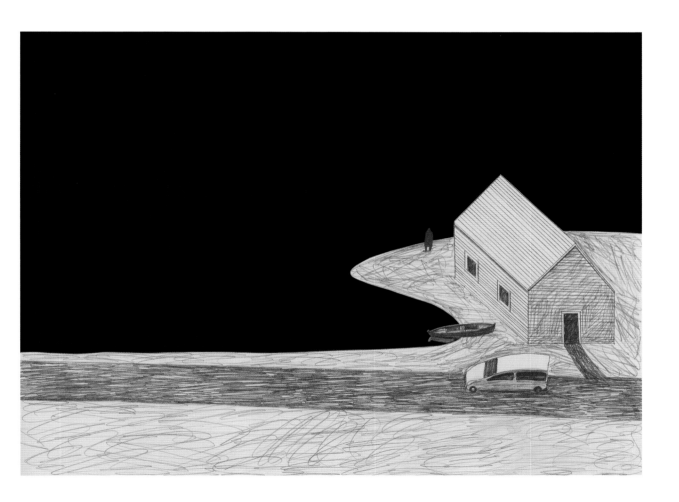

YUKO SHIMIZU
Unwritten 19 cover

YUKO SHIMIZU
Unwritten 16 cover

LAURA SMITH

Pricing and Ethical Guidelines Cover
Since I was already familiar with the *Graphic Artists Guild's Pricing and Ethical Guidelines*, and with the Guild itself and what it stands for, it was relatively easy for me to come up with concepts that would tell the story for this project. Once they were approved, it took a bit more time to work out the details, which included my creating copy as well as the configuration of the type design. Sara and Simms were supportive and really great to work with. All in all a fun project!

OWEN SMITH
Stands

STEVEN TABBUTT

Dogwood
This painting is part of a series featured in an art-themed, children's ABC book. I was asked to create a group of paintings inspired by famous movements and artists. This particular piece stands for the letter A for Art, and was inspired by the work of Italian Renaissance painter Giuseppe Arcimboldo. Like him, I created my subject out of natural elements.

THE HEADS OF STATE
Solo
A cover for a sprawling tale that views the events of the 20th century through the life of a 100-year-old blind man on his deathbed.

SAM WEBER
Enchanted Ivy

UNCOMMISSIONED

CATHIE BLECK
ILLUSTRATOR

Cathie Bleck has exhibited at over 50 galleries around the world and is a Gold medalist from The Society of Illustrators in New York. She has been commissioned by the *New York Times*, *Esquire*, *TIME*, and *Martha Stewart Living*, as well as the U.S. Postal Service, Sony Records, and Random House. Recent projects include the U.S. State Department Earth Day image, and covers for *Dante's The Divine Comedy* and *One Hundred Years of Solitude*. With the publishing of her monograph, *Open Spaces*, in 2006, Cathie went from respected illustrator to exhibiting gallery artist. In 2008 she had solo retrospectives at The Butler Institute of American Art and The New Britain Museum of American Art. Her work is also a part of many private and corporate collections. Cathie has also served as president of ICON 3, lectured internationally, conducted workshops, written for art magazines, and been featured in many art and design magazines.

DOUGLAS FRASER
ILLUSTRATOR

Born in Lethbridge, Alberta, Douglas Fraser attended the Alberta College of Art and Design in Calgary, Canada, where he studied graphic design and illustration for four years. He then received an MFA from the School of Visual Arts in New York. The focus of his graduate study was illustration for the publishing industry. An award-winning illustrator for 26 years, he has worked for an array of international clients, which include the *New York Times*, the *Washington Post*, *TIME*, *Newsweek*, *BusinessWeek*, *Wirtschafts Woche*, *Rolling Stone*, *Mother Jones*, *Motor Trend*, NHL, IBM, and Levis. He works in both traditional and digital media. A member of the Society of Illustrators in New York since 1993, he has exhibited in the United States, Canada, Europe, and Japan.

TIM J. LUDDY
CREATIVE DIRECTOR,
MOTHER JONES

Tim J. Luddy is the creative director for *Mother Jones* magazine and motherjones.com. He has worked as a designer and art director in New York and San Francisco for publications including *BusinessWeek*, *eCompany Now!* (also known as *Business 2.0*), *PC World*, and *Diablo*. He has lectured on publication design at the California College of Art, San Francisco State University, UC Berkeley Extension, and the University of San Francisco. *Mother Jones* has received the National Magazine Award for General Excellence twice during his tenure there. His work has been recognized by the Society of Publication Designers and *Print*, and he has commissioned illustrations that have appeared in *American Illustration*, *Communication Arts*, and the Society of Illustrators annual exhibitions and books.

GREGORY MANCHESS
ILLUSTRATOR

Gregory Manchess exhibits frequently at the Society of Illustrators in New York, where he has won a Gold and four Silver Medals. His peers there honored him with the Hamilton King Award in 1999 for the best illustration of the year by a member. The following year they awarded him the prestigious Stevan Dohanos Award, based on an artist's career accomplishments. He received two Silver Medals and a Best in Show Award from the Society of Illustrators in Los Angeles, and *Artist's Magazine* gave him First Prize in their 1990 Wildlife Art Competition. He was featured in *Communication Arts* in 1995, and featured in 1996, 1998, and 2000 in *Step-By-Step Graphics*. He has since appeared in many issues of the *Communication Arts*, *Step-By-Step*, and *Spectrum* juried annuals. Gregory is included in Walt Reed's *The Illustrator in America, 1860–2000*.

ROBERT NEWMAN
EDITORIAL AND DESIGN
CONSULTANT

Robert Newman has been the design director of the *Village Voice*, *Guitar World*, *Entertainment Weekly*, *New York*, *Details*, *Vibe*, *FORTUNE*, and *Real Simple*. He's currently consulting for print and digital publications of all kinds. Recent clients include AARP, *TV Guide*, and *Reader's Digest*. His most important projects are his two daughters, Ivy and Lillian. You can follow his Twitter feed, @newmanology, or his Facebook page, www.facebook.com/newmanology for all kinds of news, updates, and inspiration from the world of publication design and illustration.

JEFF SOTO
ILLUSTRATOR
Jeff Soto is an artist, illustrator, and muralist who has exhibited in galleries and museums around the world. The artist's distinct color palette, subject matter, and technique resonate with a growing audience and bridge the gap between Pop Surrealism and graffiti. In 2002, Jeff graduated with distinction from Art Center College of Design in Pasadena, California. In 2008, his work was the subject of an exhibition at Riverside Art Museum. Jeff was born and raised in Southern California, where he currently resides with his wife and two daughters.

ADOLFO VALLE
COVER ART DIRECTOR, *NEWSWEEK INTERNATIONAL*
Being on this jury is the culmination of years doing what I love best: judging *other* people's creativity! I've done that for close to 15 years as designer and art director at *Newsweek* magazine, where I've worked since I graduated with a BA in 1997 from the School of Visual Arts in New York City. Before that I attended that hidden jewel of Brooklyn, Kingsborough Community College, cutting my teeth in the graphic arts while yearning to become an illustrator and hanging out by Sheepshead Bay. I even took a turn as an instructor of editorial design there, earlier in the century. At *Newsweek International*, where I've been the cover director since 2002, I have designed over 400 covers.

DENA VERDESCA
ASSOCIATE ART DIRECTOR, *MEN'S HEALTH*
Dena Verdesca is a designer living in Brooklyn, NY. She has worked at *Glamour, ym, Best Life*, and is currently the associate art director at *Men's Health*. Her work in design and art direction has appeared in *American Illustration* and *American Photography* and has received Gold and Silver Medals from the Society of Publication Designers. Dena was part of the team whose redesign of *Men's Health* helped win the National Magazine Award for General Excellence. She has been a juror for illustration student scholarship competitions, and has had the privilege of collaborating with many amazing illustrators. Outside of magazines, she makes things out of silk dupioni and designs textile prints.

AUTUMN WHITEHURST
ILLUSTRATOR
Autumn Whitehurst is originally from New Orleans, LA. She received her BFA in general fine arts from the Maryland Institute College of Art and is now living in Brooklyn, NY, as a full-time freelance illustrator. Her work is recognized by its clean digital realism, and her creative focus is primarily beauty and fashion, although she's been commissioned by a broad spectrum of publishing, editorial, and advertising clients, notably Coke, Sapporo, Lillet, Target, Ray-Ban, Nieman Marcus, and the Principality of Monaco. She has also been published in several books including *100 Years of Fashion Illustration* (Cally Beackman), *Wonderland*, and *The Beautiful* (Gestaltan). All work and no play makes Autumn a dull girl. She finds great satisfaction and pleasure in traveling, partying with close friends, and watching really sad movies.

GOLD MEDAL WINNER
Marc Burckhardt

Himmelblick
This piece was created for the exhibition *Images of the Afterlife*, curated by Monte Beauchamp of *BLAB!* fame. Artists were invited to present their view of what follows death—a question as old as mankind, and one each individual has a unique vision of. I'm personally doubtful of pearly gates and choirs of angels—or fiery pits of sulfur—but think the residue of one life is the building block of another. Utilizing the classic tradition of *momento mori* allegory as my framework, I created this image of the life (and death) cycle.

GOLD MEDAL WINNER
KOREN SHADMI

Ebb & Flow
I came up with this concept while visiting the Puget Sound shore in Washington State. During my stay I got interested in the abundance of life that kept washing up on the shore: mussels, oysters and barnacles, small crabs lying under rocks, and so on. My initial thought was to draw two embracing figures coming out of the waters covered with various sea life, to the point where they are unrecognizable. I held off though, feeling that something was missing from the rough sketch I'd made. Other projects kept coming in and I had to put this idea in my mental drawer. A few months later, I came up with the solution, only one of the figures will be obscured by sea remnants, the other will be bare—as contrast to the first. I also changed the angle, putting the girl high above and the other figure coming from below, to add more tension to the composition. The drawing, and even more so the colors, were inspired by the Japanese woodblock print artist Kawase Hasui. In his prints there is often an impression of nature and man's mark in it, at a certain time of a day or season of the year.

Paper Tiger
"Paper tiger" is an old expression my mother brought to America and told me about when I was younger. It's meant to describe anything that tries to give off an aura of shock and awe, but in reality is harmless. My assignment was to describe a story in "Missed Connections" on Craigslist. I found an entry of a guy who pretends to be confident and impressive but buckles when it gets to the nitty gritty of asking a woman out. Remembering the metaphor, I wrapped it around the story and created this paper cat with painted stripes who thinks he's a tiger.

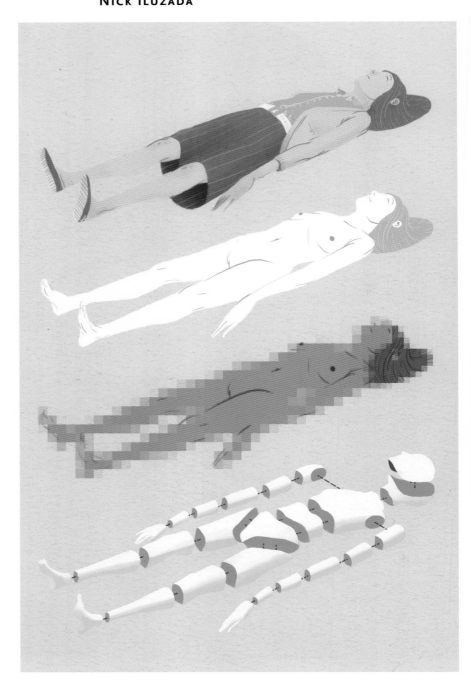

After Life

For the first semester of my senior thesis project at MICA I focused on illustrating episodes from WNYC's program *Radiolab*. This podcast explores exactly what happens at the moment when we slip from life, and what it means to be gone in a variety of different contexts. The episode is a series of meditations, and I wanted the concept and composition to mirror that idea. The underdrawing was done in pencil, then elements of the drawing were created using a variety of media on denril. The separate sheets were then scanned and compiled in Photoshop. Additional digital coloring was done on top of the other layers.

&

This piece is part of a personal series I had been working on in order to combine different aesthetic qualities that I'd been exploring in my sketchbooks. A fair amount of my uncommissioned work focuses on nostalgia and the particular emotions that are experienced when one revisits the memories of things past and lost. In this case, inspired by post-mortem photography and without saying too much, I was interested to see what kind of story could be told about the life and death of this man & his wife, who can be found on page 492.

Saints Preserve Us
This painting was created for Pulse Art Fair New York in 2009, which ran in conjunction with the city's annual Armory Show, and was exhibited by Copro Gallery of Santa Monica, California. The painting explores the idea of humanity's focus on artificial self-preservation in a time when our excesses seem to be leading the natural world into a state of confusion and change. The abandoned fridges in this piece allude to our artificial solutions to forecasted issues, but in their tombstone-like presentation also suggest the theme of death. These relics, standing in for the polar bear's missing ice floes—and the butterflies that she's chasing—hint at a perversion of the natural state. Collection of Michael LaFetra.

NISHAN AKGULIAN

Subway Riders, New York City
This piece is based on a sketch I did while riding the New York City subway.
I enjoy sketching subway riders, who are like a cast of actors on a stage that
changes with every station stop. In my studio I interpret my pencil sketches
into drawings that, through mixed media, celebrate the individuality of each
rider, while creating a rhythm that unifies the composition.

SCOTT BAKAL
Tea Party
This drawing is a result of my views of the Tea Party Movement in 2010 and
how unabashedly racist and shortsighted some of the representatives are.

JOHN-PAUL BALMET
Pursuit
This piece was created as an homage to the dystopian totalitarian futures in books like *1984* and films like *THX 1138*. I was also inspired by night photography of North and South Korea. I imagine someone running from these police, wondering if these are men or machines.

CATHIE BLECK
Riding on the Hope Horse

SAM BOSMA
Sub Rosa
This piece was created for a gallery show held by Rotopol Press in Kassel, Germany. The prompt was open, save that the pieces had to relate to the show's title, *Secret Service*. Throughout history, a rose placed, drawn, or carved over the door to a house or room meant that whatever occurred within was to remain secret, and anyone who passed beneath the rose was held to that pledge. The term *sub rosa*, literally means, "beneath the rose."

MARC BURCKHARDT
Flight
I was invited to create a piece on the theme of "Air" for the exhibition *Earth: Fragile Planet* held at the Society of Illustrators. Animals have long been used as a first-alert measure of the quality of our environment, and none more traditionally than the "canary in a coal mine." Starting with this simple concept, and adding the physicality we associate with birds felled in hunting, I hoped to give a sense of immediacy to this issue. The circular shape alludes to the broader theme of the exhibit.

CHRIS BUZELLI

M-44

M-44s are devices used by Wildlife Services, an agency housed within the U.S. Department of Agriculture, to protect livestock against predators. When the animal triggers the pipe-like device sticking out of the ground, the device shoots sodium cyanide—one of the most toxic chemicals approved by the EPA—into an animal's mouth, killing it within minutes. M-44s are set by Wildlife Services agents targeting coyotes and foxes, but the poison also kills wolves, bears, bobcats, eagles, and dogs. The devices are indiscriminate killers; any animal will likely be killed if it tugs on the meat-scented lure. Unbeknownst to most Americans, M-44s are strewn across our public lands. Today, the agency spends over $100 million annually to kill millions of animals each year.

HARRY CAMPBELL
Myth Urn
This started as one of several roughs for a cover assignment entitled
Myth. Another of my ideas was chosen for the final but I was excited
about all the roughs, so I finished this one.

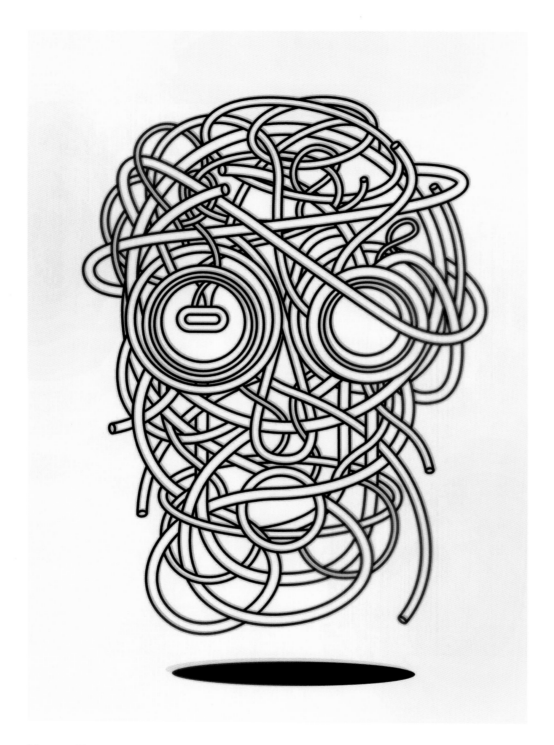

HARRY CAMPBELL
Wire Head
This was done as part of a group show, *One Hundred Heads for Haiti*, a benefit to aid the disaster relief in Haiti.

BILL CARMAN

Oh Crap, Sorry

To soften a rigorous painting schedule I do drawings, which are simply breakings of cerebral wind. This is ink and acrylic on watercolor paper. Wonderful surface.

Q. Cassetti
Holiday Nutcrackers

This is one of 32 illustrations I created and posted online daily from December 1- 25 as an Advent Calendar, and as a personal challenge and delight. These illustrations were a way for me to talk to myself (and inevitably my online friends) about my vision (albeit not the most happy) of the holidays. Additionally, by creating an online expectation for a new illustration a day during this time, drove more traffic and interest in my work. These nutcrackers were inspired by my collection of nutcrackers that my son and I have assembled as part of our holiday traditions. I particularly love how frightening these figures are with their odd calligraphic mustaches and eyebrows, their fearsome eyes and their chomping, scary mouths.

EFI CHALIKOPOULOU

Yellow Fat Hate Eating My Lilies
This is one of the nine drawings in a continuing series of works titled All About Love. This series was inspired by the end of a relationship and the beginning of a new period in my personal life. The fat, greedy figure of a man-drone mentally devouring the fresh lily of female romance, represents the sharpness of the pain that a loss can cause. Sometimes love pretends its existence and hate is painted yellow.

ANGY CHE

Sipping Water

The objective of the assignment was to create an indirect portrait, in this case, of my friend Grace. Instead of having the main focus being on the face, the portrait is hinged on body language, posture, and attitude. Her gesture was constructed with simple shapes and value design. I included details selectively to accentuate Grace's unique features. I enjoy using acrylics because, besides the fact that they dry fast, they work well for both flat color and rendering. Working with acrylics on a wood panel allows me the freedom of experimenting with different textures. The unpredictable behavior of the paint is sometimes the most fun part.

PHILIP CHEANEY
The Leviathan
Part of a Biblical bestiary, featuring the fantastic beasts and beings found in both the Old and New Testaments.

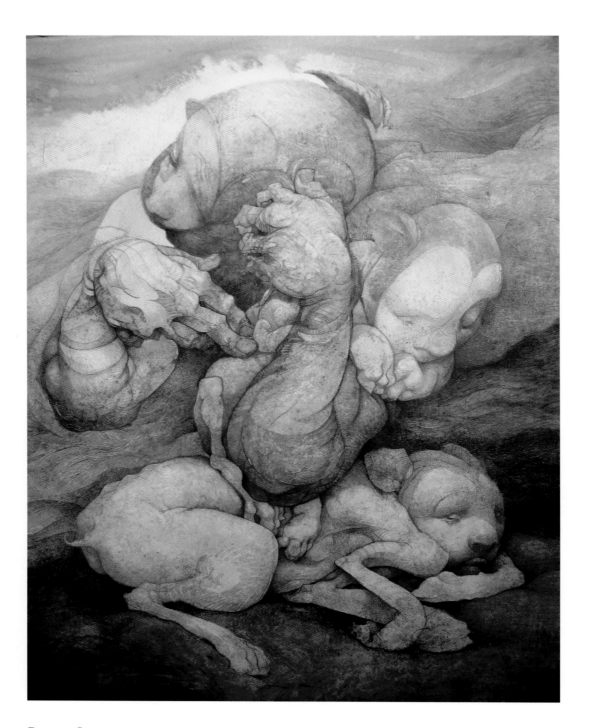

DAVID CHRISTIANA
Five and Dime

As a writer I've relished the use of the personal narrator to tell a story. Recently I've employed that approach to my visual work by imagining I'm someone else making the picture—someone with a different history and a different point of view. I begin by channeling this fictional character with a pencil and a panel. Something like channeling letters on a Ouija board, but rather than letters I get lines, then egg tempera (powdered pigment, egg yoke and water). This picture illustrates a fatally stubborn man and his relationship with two loved ones.

TIMOTHY COOK

Raven Girl
I created this drawing for my daughter and then used it for a self-promotion piece. I traced a guitar pick to create some of the shapes.

ALL GOOD

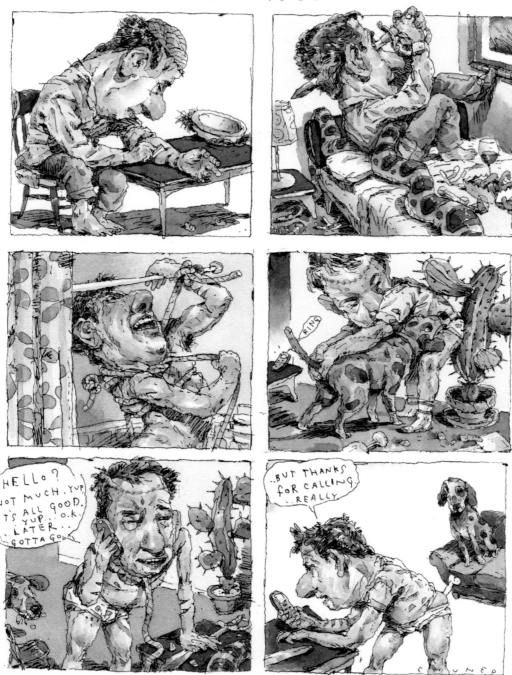

JOHN CUNEO

All Good

A personal piece. One from an ongoing series of drawings about shame, self-esteem, cutlery, and catharsis.

PETER DIAMOND
A Dream of a Killing

In 2010 I made a number of portfolio pieces to strengthen my body of work using images drawn from personal experience and knowledge. This illustration was drawn from a powerful nightmare I had some years ago. I woke from it in a kind of shock, and the idea was to freeze that moment when one sees the last fragments of a dream with waking eyes and feels halfway between dreaming and waking.

JOHNNY DOMBROWSKI
Homo Ferus

JOHNNY DOMBROWSKI
Passerby

BIL DONOVAN
Crossroads of the World

This piece was initiated and completed during two three-hour drawing sessions in Times Square. I teach a documentary class at the Fashion Institute of Technology and take the students out to different locations to draw on site. Drawing outside of the safe confines of a studio setting is challenging and invigorating. You have to make allowances for the un-expected and allow the energy and the moment to intuitively filter into the work. Times Square is a rich reserve of lights, action, and energy; my intent was to capture this energy with an overlapping of line shape and color. My intent was to allow this energy to direct the work through line, repetition, color, and chance.

BIL DONOVAN

Opera Queen

I wanted the image to capture the allure and attitude of Maria Callas and the glamour and stature of Ava Gardner. *Opera Queen* evolved through an editing process, which allowed the essence of the image to emerge. Selectivity is the guiding force, and what is absent is as essential to what is present in the drawing. A brush stroke can become a shoulder, wing, or exclamation mark for the figure, leaving the viewer to create the narrative. Initially uncommissioned, *Opera Queen* was used for promotion by *Elle* magazine.

SAMUEL FARINATO
The Last Leaf of Winter
This work is the first image seen in my book, *The Angry Winter*. This story of journey and perseverance is told entirely through the illustrations, leaving out any text in favor of letting readers wander on their own, interpreting the story for themselves. From conception to completion, all of the work was created digitally as flat shapes in Photoshop, then layered with scanned mulberry and rice paper textures to give a more organic feel to the work.

PETER FIORE

Killing Field

Over time subjects emerge, commanding their importance. Walking on a path that parallels the Delaware River, the white pine trees along the way have become my latest motif. Trees have always been an important subject for me, and I believe on many levels that they are metaphors for life. They have long histories and many stories to tell. I'm often struck by how some trees are more than just trees—they are very much a presence. I have made many paintings of these pine trees. Visiting often throughout the seasons, I have come to visually own these trees.

CARLO GIAMBARRESI
Nazi Censorship
This work is a self-promotion piece inspired by an article about censorship against books, newspapers, and writers during the Nazi dictatorship. I wanted to represent the violence with which this prohibition was applied. I had fun playing with India ink and Photoshop, and I am very happy with the final result.

CHAD GROHMAN

Duet

This was done for self-promotion purposes. It's part of a group of digital paintings made to help change over my portfolio. I spent a lot of years doing vector illustration and have recently headed back to painting, both digitally and traditionally. Here, I included the lion and the deer to reflect the violin and the piano. The animals are also meant to relate the musical story the duet might be telling with their instruments.

REBECCA GUAY

Pandora

DAVID HENDERSON
The Rose Farm, Gettysburg

This work illustrates my approach to landscape painting. My strongest passions have always been American history, landscape, and architecture. I was academically trained and continue to work in a traditional way. It's important to me that every work begins with a drawing. Viewpoint, space, perspective, and the strong sense of light I have become known for are all worked out during this stage. My favorite medium has always been oil because of its permanence, depth of color, and workability. Every American should walk the fields of Gettysburg at least once in their lifetime; you cannot do so and not be deeply moved. I've painted these places as I felt them. They hold their history with beauty and a quiet dignity—powerful and at peace.

JODY HEWGILL
Speechless

484 Uncommissioned

NICK ILUZADA
Animal Minds
For the first semester of my senior thesis project at MICA I focused on illustrating episodes from WNYC's program Radiolab. This particular one was about how and/or if we as humans can ever truly understand what other organisms on this planet think and feel. The underdrawing was done in pencil and then elements of the drawing were created using a variety of media on duralar and denril. The separate sheets were then scanned and collaged together in Photoshop. Additional digital coloring was done on top of the other layers.

TARA JACOBY

Anti-Fur Poster

This piece was done to express the cruelty hidden behind the fur industry. Each year tens of millions of rabbits are raised in cramped conditions and then brutally killed so their fur can be used to trim coats, jackets, boots, gloves, and scarves. Their fur is also used to produce toys, stuffed animals, ornaments, pet toys, blankets, and other fashion and household textiles. Rabbits are not the only animals subject to the murderous hand of fashion. Over 75 million factory-farmed animals die every year for their fur, as well as millions of wild animals that are hunted and clubbed to death or suffer and die in traps, solely to indulge the whims of fashion. My goal with this piece was to make the viewer aware of the savagery that lies beneath this very unnecessary fashion faux pas.

LEW KEILAR

The Bridge

Whether a scene in real life or from a movie, my sketchbook is ever ready to capture it. My starting point for this uncommissioned piece was the briefest of scenes from *The Painted Veil* with Edward Norton and Australian actor Naomi Watts. The bridge was a tiny detail in a transition shot from one key scene to another, but I loved it and drew it. Once started, I then improvised the rest of the scene, finishing with the lone character who seems to be challenging the temple with his presence. My color and texture choices then heightened this drama, amplifying the mood of the drawing.

ANITA KUNZ
Stork

I've been working on a series of personal work that has to do with our collective narratives and storytelling. We have all heard stories that have persisted through the ages. Here I'm tackling the story of the stork bringing babies to hopeful parents. I've retold it in my own way, sort of a "stork redux." The painting is acrylic on paper.

ROBBIE LAWRENCE

Portrait of a Lady

This portrait of Gaga was an experiment with color for the most part. I enjoy her offending fashion; it gives a lot of room to play. I wanted to capture her colorful, bizarre nature and her classy, polite demeanor in one piece, combining her shocking appearance with something dainty and lady-like. Tea seemed perfect. I drew her while watching an interview, changing her makeup and clothes. After scanning the drawing into Photoshop I experimented with color, trying to make her skin just as loud as her clothes. I think if she could change her skin at will, she would.

FRANK LIN
Thao

I wanted to experiment with a square composition. I started by playing with negative shapes. Next, I added a multiple layer for some color, then burn-tooled the painted layer to add value in certain areas. Made selections to curve for more value variety, then added textures and gradients on top.

NIMIT MALAVIA
&&

This piece is part of a personal series I had been working on in order to combine different aesthetic qualities that I'd been exploring in my sketchbooks. A fair amount of my uncommissioned work focuses on nostalgia and the particular emotions that are experienced when one revisits the memories of things past and lost. In this case, inspired by post-mortem photography and without saying too much, I was interested to see what kind of story could be told about the life and death of this woman & her husband, who can be seen on page 451.

MARION McCALLY
Cookie
Driving in San Pedro, California, one day, I saw this woman waiting for the bus. I was struck by her soulful face and the graphic quality of her red coat. I pulled over and asked her if she would pose for me. Her bus was coming, so the encounter was brief. I experimented with the composition but kept the background and surroundings true to the location. Next, I drew the background and figure directly onto the canvas (not using photo projection), then I painted in oil.

NICHOLAS McNALLY
Shirayuki
Here's an acrylic painting from my yet-to-be-published picture book entitled *Shirayuki*. "Shirayuki" is how you say "Snow White" in Japan—16th
century Japan, that is. Why settle for deciduous forests, dresses, and
dwarves, when you can have cherry blossoms, kimonos, and Kurosawa's
seven samurai?

TONY MONTAÑO
Cheryl

496 UNCOMMISSIONED

CHRIS B. MURRAY
Radio Dead
The piece is the second version of a painting I did in 2008 titled *Radio Head*. It's my take on how commercial music is perceived in today's society and its lack of longevity, with its listeners leaving it disposed of—or "Dead."

TIM O'BRIEN
Giraffe Alley

TIM O'BRIEN
Fire Frog

GEORGE PRATT
Unknown Solider

ANDY RASH

President Iotacons

I call these pixel mosaics "iotacons" because they are icons created with an extremely small amount, or iota, of information. If the 44 presidents of the United States were not real historical figures but rather sprites from an early '80s video game, they might look like this.

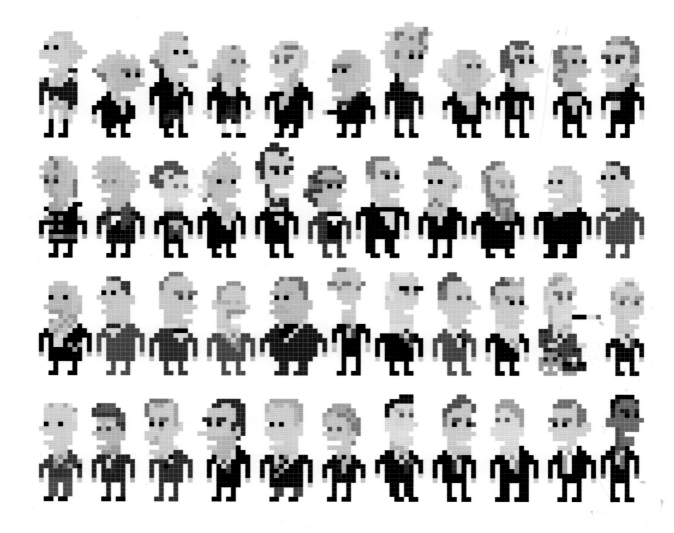

OMAR RAYYAN

Full Gallop

This is but one of a series of paintings documenting the "Great Turtle Race," a mouse-riding-tortoise steeplechase. In this instance, the need to convey the speed and excitement of the "and they're off!" moment was paramount. So, I took a ground-level vantage point to put the view-er in the action, and to offer easy comparisons of color and texture of the various racing reptiles bumping and pushing from the crowded left, leaping into the open "race track" at full gallop!

EDEL RODRIGUEZ
Luz
One of a series of paintings done for a solo gallery exhibition.

EDEL RODRIGUEZ
Guardian
One of a series of coffee drawings done for a solo gallery exhibition.

KIM ROSEN

Jhumpa Lahiri

Every book I have read from author Jhumpa Lahiri has been a truly inspiring experience. Lahiri's work evokes emotions of being torn between two worlds. The old world of childhood memories and traditions seems to be in constant battle with the modern world of western culture. We can all relate to changes in our lives that lead to familial guilt that forces us to reflect on our choices. My goal was to capture the strength of the author while also showing the dependence and importance of her past.

PHYLLIS SAROFF
Chanticleer and the Fox

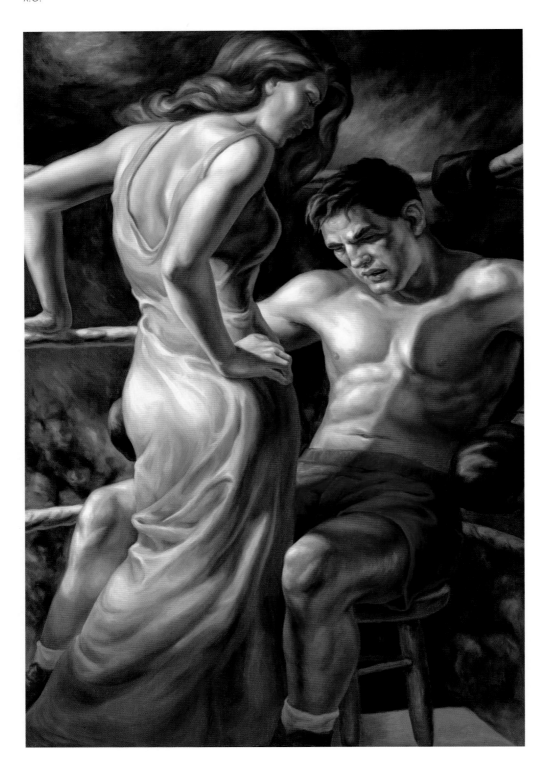

JAMES STEINBERG
Sideshow #3

GARY TAXALI
Toy–Car

SACHIN TENG
Contact

JOHN THOMPSON

One Cow

Early one morning, while walking along a street in Nawalgarh, India, I met up with this cow, who seemed to be out for a leisurely stroll. *One Cow* became the first in a series of animal paintings I'm working on for a yet-to-be published book proposal titled *Animals of India: A Counting Book*.

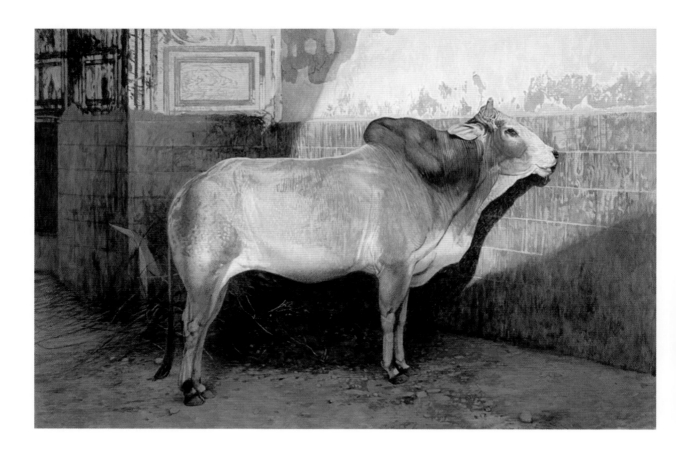

DAISUKE TSUTSUMI

My Piano Teacher Mrs. Asaoka

Created for a gallery show, *Cuter Than Stranger*, at Gallery 1988 in San Francisco, May 2010. This is based on Tsutsumi's childhood experience of taking piano lessons from a lady named Mrs. Asaoka. The artist's only memories of the lessons were Mrs. Asaoka slapping his hands, her garish dresses, and the marble angel statues by the gate of her house that scared him. Tsutsumi believes he would have been playing in Carnegie Hall instead of drawing cartoons today if his music talent hadn't been destroyed by this experience.

CARL WIENS

Inspiration
This piece is the result of visual experimentation—a digital assemblage.
It is a combination of natural and man-made elements that took flight in
my studio late one night.

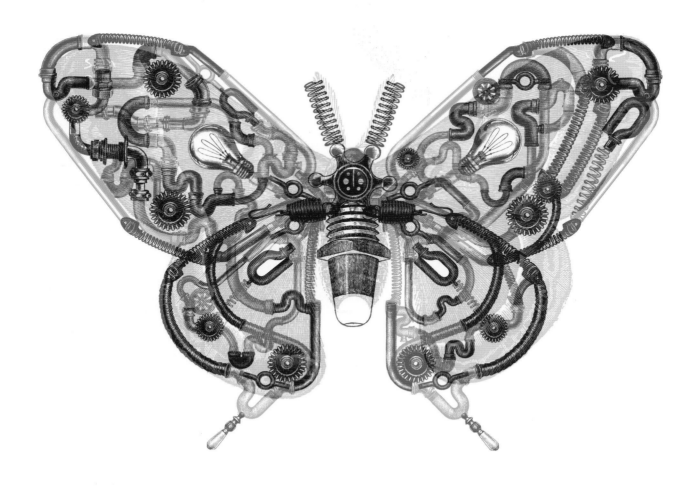

NATE WILLIAMS
Summer Camp

SEQUENTIAL

MONIKA AICHELE
ILLUSTRATOR, DESIGNER

Monika Aichele was educated at the Stuttgart Academie of Fine Arts, Germany. Her work has been recognized by the Society of Illustrators, *American Illustration*, the Society of Publication Designers, the Art Directors Club Germany, and many more. Her inflatable monkey sculptures, which she created for Stefan Sagmeister and the Six Cities Design Festival in Scotland, was selected as Best of Show by *3x3* magazine in 2008. Exhibitions of her work have been held in New York, London, Barcelona, Rome, Hamburg, Venice, Toronto, Naples, Milano, Paris, and Shanghai. Monika is based in Munich and Berlin. She teaches illustration at the University of Applied Sciences in Mainz, Germany. Find more about her on monikaaichele.com.

NICHOLAS BLECHMAN
ART DIRECTOR,
THE NEW YORK TIMES BOOK REVIEW

Nicholas Blechman, an internationally recognized illustrator, art director, and designer, is the art director of the *New York Times Book Review*. He previously art directed the *Op-Ed* page of the *Times*, where he initiated the *Op-Art* section. Since 1990, Nicholas has published, edited, and designed the award-winning political underground magazine *Nozone*, featured in the Smithsonian Institution's Design Triennial. His illustrations have appeared in *GQ*, *Travel + Leisure*, *Wired*, and the *New Yorker*. He co-authors a series of limited edition illustration books, One Hundred Percent, with Christoph Niemann, and is the author of *Fresh Dialogue One: New Voices in Graphic Design*, 100% EVIL, *Nozone IX: Empire*, and *Nozone X: Forecast*. Nicholas is a member of Alliance Graphique International (AGI), and lives in Brooklyn with his wife and son.

LEO ESPINOSA
ILLUSTRATOR

Leo Espinosa is an award-winning illustrator and designer from Bogotá, Colombia, whose work has been featured in a variety of publications, products, animated series, and gallery shows worldwide. His short list includes the *New York Times*, *Wired*, *Esquire*, the *Wall Street Journal*, *FORTUNE*, Nickelodeon, Swatch, Hasbro, American Greetings, and Coca-Cola. Leo's illustrations have been recognized by *American Illustration*, *Communication Arts*, *How*, Pictoplasma, and he was awarded two consecutive Silver Medals from the Society of Illustrators in 2009 and 2010. After living in New York, Barcelona, and Boston, he moved to Providence and became an adjunct professor at the Rhode Island School of Design.

TOMER HANUKA
ILLUSTRATOR, CARTOONIST

Tomer Hanuka is an illustrator and a cartoonist based in New York City. He works on a range of projects for magazines, book publishers, ad agencies, and film studios. His clients include the *New Yorker*, D.C comics, Nike, and Microsoft. He has won multiple Gold Medals from the Society of Illustrators and the Society of Publication Designers, and was showcased in *Print* magazine and *American Illustration*. In 2008, a book cover he created won the British Design Museum award as part of the Penguin Classics Deluxe Editions. *Waltz With Bashir*, an animated documentary for which Tomer contributed art, was nominated for an Oscar in 2009, and won the Golden Globe that same year. Currently he teaches at the School of Visual Arts and is working on a graphic novel with his twin brother, Asaf, and writer Boaz Lavie.

AVIVA MICHAELOV
ART DIRECTOR,
THE NEW YORK TIMES OP-ED

Aviva Michaelov is the art director of the *Op-Ed* section at the *New York Times*. Previous assignments include art direction of the newspaper's *Week in Review* section, the design of "2007: The Year in Pictures," and, with Nicholas Blechman, the redesign of the *Book Review* section. While at Parsons School of Design, Aviva worked as a print and web designer at pixelpress.org, a multidisciplinary studio. She also received a Type Directors Club Scholarship Award given to promising students of typography. After graduation, she freelanced for RG/A, working in web design. In 2004, she began working at the *New York Times* as a designer and later on as art director. Her work at the *Times* has been recognized by the Society of Newspaper Design.

FRANÇOISE MOULY

ART DIRECTOR OF COVERS, *THE NEW YORKER*

In 1980 Françoise Mouly was the founder, publisher, designer, and co-editor, with her husband Art Spiegelman, of *RAW*, which launched artists such as Charles Burns, Sue Coe, Chris Ware, Xavier Mariscal, and others. In 2000 she founded a RAW Junior division, publishing the Little Lit collection of comics by the likes of Maurice Sendak, Paul Auster, Ian Falconer, David Sedaris, Jules Feiffer, Gahan Wilson, and Neil Gaiman. In 2008, she launched TOON Books, her own imprint of hardcover comics for emerging readers. She joined the *New Yorker* in 1993 and has been responsible for over 900 covers, many of which were awarded "best cover of the year" by the American Society of Magazine Editors. Born in Paris, Françoise studied architecture at the Beaux Arts, and moved to New York in 1974. In 2001 she was named chevalier in the order of Arts and Letters by the French Ministry of Culture and Communication.

GEORGE PRATT

ILLUSTRATOR, GRAPHIC NOVELIST

George Pratt's work is in private collections internationally and has been exhibited in the Houston Museum of Fine Art. His one-man show in Belgium and Paris featured his First World War drawings and paintings. His numerous awards include the coveted Eisner Award for Best Painter and Best Feature Documentary at the New York International Independent Film Festival. He is working on a new documentary film on the artists at the front during World War One, and on a new graphic novel. George is a full-time faculty member at Ringling College of Art and Design, and he teaches at the Illustration Academy and TAD (The Art Department).

GRAHAM ROUMIEU

ILLUSTRATOR

Graham Roumieu is the creator of the faux Bigfoot autobiography books *In Me Own Words*, *Me Write Book* , and *I Not Dead*; as well as some non-Bigfoot-related books such as *Cat & Gnome* and *101 Ways To Kill Your Boss*. Since starting work in 2001, his illustrations have appeared in publications such as the *New York Times*, the *Atlantic*, the *Guardian*, *Men's Health*, and in other advertising, editorial, character design, and book venues. His work has garnered awards from *American Illustration*, D&AD, *Communication Arts*, the Society of Publication Designer, and the Society of Illustrators. Graham is a member of the Advertising and Design Club of Canada, and instructor at the Ontario College of Art and Design.

MARK ALAN STAMATY

ILLUSTRATOR, CARTOONIST

Mark Alan Stamaty has worked in a variety of disciplines over the past four decades: children's books, editorial illustration, advertising, graphic novels, printmaking, cartooning, cartoon reporting, and teaching. He is the author/illustrator of the cult classic children's book *Who Needs Donuts?*, among others, and the creator of numerous comic strips, including "MacDoodle St.," "CARRRTTOOOONNN," "WASHINGTOON," and "BOOX." His work has appeared in many publications, including the *New Yorker*, *GQ*, *TIME*, *Newsweek*, the *New York Times*, *Esquire*, *Harper's*, and others. For 12 years he did a syndicated political comic strip that was a fixture on the op-ed page of the *Washington Post*, and in the *Village Voice*, as well as newspapers nationwide. Among his awards are two Gold Medals and a Silver from the Society of Illustrators.

GOLD MEDAL WINNER
ASAF HANUKA

The Realist Comics
The Realist started as a weekly autobiographic comic about my life as a 30-something family man taking on the challenge of mortgage payments. As the weeks passed, the strip changed its focus when I started writing more about family interaction rather than about billing and payments. I thought becoming a homeowner was the biggest challenge I had ever faced, but was I wrong. My kid just turned two and started to talk. He asked me questions and called me Dad. My wife and I faced the dilemma of trying to make the right choices in raising our son. I had to find a way to explain to him in simple terms how the world works, while I asked myself if I understood it. That was a bigger challenge than any debt to the bank. And I'm still not sure I got it right.

ILLUSTRATION CLASS

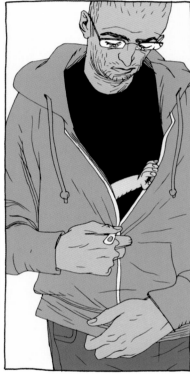

Kamikaze
This piece is one of a series of biographical comics I created based on the real lives of people who have experienced war, but who are unknown to the general public. *Kamikaze* is a 10-page narrative that tells the story of a WWII Kamikaze pilot who survived his mission because of an unexpected plane engine problem. When his plane crashed on the open sea, he was able to save himself by swimming to an isolated island. Due to the island's location he was forced to remain there until just before the war ended. The story was created for *SPRING*, a German comics anthology, featuring stories around the theme of "Happy Ending."

Ein junger und sehr begabter Pilot namens Seki wurde gefragt, ob er den ersten Spezialeinsatz übernehmen und als Kriegsheld sterben wolle.

Bitte akzeptieren sie meine Zusage.

Seki hatte vor kurzem geheiratet.

Ihr seid schon jetzt Götter. Und als Götter habt ihr kein Verlangen mehr. Ihr werdet lange schlafen.

Er wollte keinen Selbstmord begehen.

Vor seinem Abflug überreichte er einem Offizier eine Haarsträhne,

die kurz nach seinem Tod seiner Mutter übergeben wurde.

Ab sofort wurden junge Soldaten gefragt, ob sie freiwillig in die Spezialeinsatztruppe eintreten würden. Die meisten waren zwischen 17–26 Jahre alt.

Freiwillige sollten ihren Namen auf ein Blatt Papier schreiben— alle anderen das Papier unbeschrieben lassen.

Fast alle Piloten meldeten sich. Kein Pilot wollte seine Freunde sterben sehen und selbst am Leben bleiben.

Weigerte man sich, so wurde man trotzdem aufgelistet.

Einige Wochen vergingen,

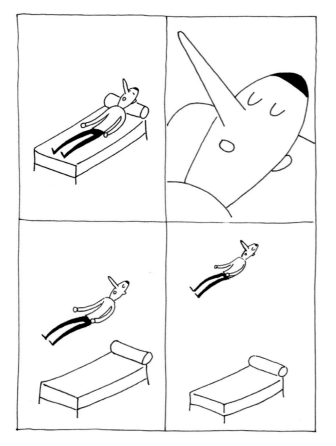

The Arms of Morpheus
This story is about dreams where things can turn magically into their opposites. Here, an attractive girl will be replaced by a repulsive pig, and death itself (a huge black cloud) will transform into life again.

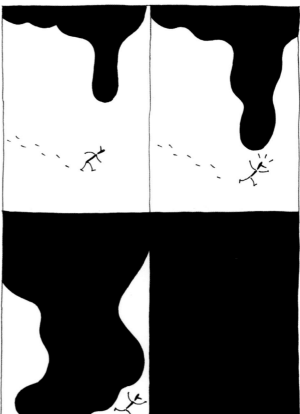

Modern Love

The pictures for the Modern Love series have roots in drawings I produced for my partner during the time she and I lived apart. Those drawings (one each day) helped simplify my drawings and added an emotional level to my work. The essays written each week for the column are accounts of different writers' experiences with relationships and love. They are at times heartbreaking, humorous, witty, painful, sometimes nostalgic, and more often than not—familiar. I don't try to illustrate the essays. Instead I try to create a drawing that runs parallel to the story, one that pulls from my own experiences and emotions, and provides a familiar tone to that of the writer's experience.

The Silent Truth

The Silent Truth is a documentary that tells the story of LaVena Johnson, an American soldier serving in Iraq. LaVena enlisted directly after high school. She made it through boot camp, and was sent to Kuwait City. While waiting there to be deployed into Iraq, she died under circumstances the U.S. military called a suicide. Her family, once seeing the body of their daughter, felt they had reason to have the body examined. During the examination they found that the evidence they received from the coroner did not match that of the official military report. LaVena's nose had been broken, her body set on fire; the bullet wound was not inflicted by the gun the military claimed. The M16 the military said she used in her suicide would have been too long for LaVina to self inflict such a wound. Her family came to the conclusion that their daughter had been raped and murdered. These illustrations were used as still frames, and in animations (animated in After Effects) to tell LaVena's story of her time in boot camp, and in Kuwait City leading up to her death. The narration for these events was taken from letters she wrote to her parents during this time.

A. RICHARD ALLEN
Brat Farrar (book cover and interior plates)

CHI BIRMINGHAM

Life in These Old Bones Yet

This work was inspired by the history and natural beauty of my hometown, Big Sur, California. The story began with a few sketches of an aging prospector and his mule, and a plan to create a wordless comic book. As I researched written accounts of the 1800s, I began a storyboard where I tested my characters with increasingly arduous physical challenges. The thumbnails sprawled out shapelessly for a while, but when I was ready to begin making the final art, I decided to cut my original 150 panels into 20 images which would stand alone as full spreads. In the editing process I found myself drawn to the little moments of rest where I felt the characters best expressed themselves.

MATT DORFMAN

The Terrorist Mind: An Update

Kelly Doe at the *New York Times* called me late on a Thursday with an assignment requesting six illustrations in less than 24 hours. They were to accompany a piece for the *Week in Review* which examined the nascent science of studying terrorism via direct interviews conducted with ex-radicals who have abandoned their causes. Wrestling a brutal cold at the time, I turned the assignment down. When Kelly persisted and I accepted it, I pitched concepts that would require using only one illustration. Kelly again persisted and strongly encouraged me to work with multiples. I made strong tea that evening and gave those pictures all the energy that I had. Kelly's good.

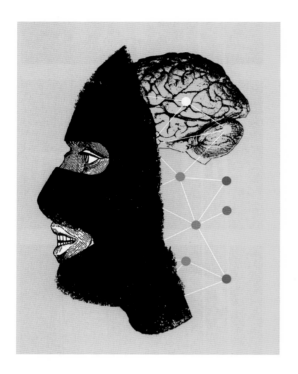
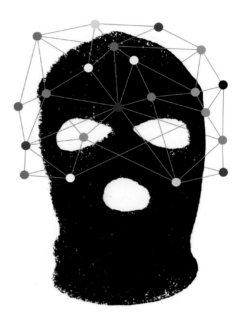

THOMAS FUCHS
Tausche Bag Artists Flaps

ALESSANDRO GOTTARDO

The Lady and the Dragon

STEVEN GUARNACCIA

Lament on the Death of Willie

I researched nonsense poems of the late 1800s and early 1900s, looking for poems that would lend themselves to being illustrated in a comic strip format. Many of the poems had an ironic, dark humor that made them seem very contemporary. This story was so vivid that it produced the sequential images I used in the strip almost spontaneously.

ERIK T JOHNSON
The Outliers
This is a work-in-progress comic book/adventure story. It is the coming-of-age story of a boy who is misunderstood by his peers, but able to see and communicate with a world beyond their perception.

KAKO

Itadakimasu!

Short story created for the anthology *MSP+50*, celebrating the 50th anniversary of Brazilian comic book artist Mauricio de Sousa's career. Each of the 50 invited artists was asked to choose one of the comic book characters and make a new and free interpretation of it. Even though Mauricio's stories take place in Brazil, I chose to place Magali and her cat, Mingau, in a small town in Japan as a reminder that his stories can be read and understood by any child in any part of the world.

NORA KRUG
Red Riding Hood Redux

PETER KUPER
The Road

This piece was inspired by many book tours and lectures that went.... imperfectly. Playing off of Cormac McCarthy's book title, this post-apocalyptic world is the one we live in now, as print media goes the way of all things digital. Of course I used a computer to digitally color the scratchboard drawing, so I can't gripe about the computer world too much. Then again....

THE ROAD

An author struggling to survive the post-print apocalypse

ADAM MCCAULEY
Greece is Broke

LEIF PARSONS

It's a Wrap

I, along with the good people at The Pencil Factory, decided to put together a fun promotion for the season. We wanted to print on newsprint, and in the spirit of a somewhat disposable medium, thought it would be nice if it could be recycled for wrapping paper after it was viewed. This became our theme, and I used it as a starting point for a playful narrative piece.

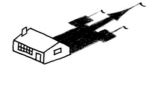

Eight little zombies

chasing after Kevin

Kevin shot his shotgun

Now there are seven

ANDY RASH

Ten Little Zombies: A Love Story
This project started as a Halloween story published in installments on my blog and on Facebook. I tagged the zombies with the names of my friends, who started rooting for their zombie to be the last one standing. When the story was done, I showed it to Chronicle Books. They published it pretty much as is, but added the subtitle A Love Story, which I thought was very funny.

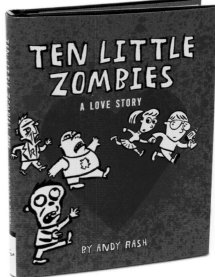

Edel Rodriguez

Chike and the River

This is a series of images used on the cover and interior of a book titled *Chike and the River* by Chinua Achebe. The story is about a boy's adventures while attempting to cross a river in Nigeria. The art director was John Gall of Random House.

EDEL RODRIGUEZ

China Takes Over

A series of images for *Newsweek* magazine for an article about China's world dominance in many fields, from technology to the economy and space exploration.

Your Assignment - 26 - W4M

In 4-6 sentences describe what you would do to me to make my toes curl. Please refrain from using run-on sentences.

Guitar Hero
I'm a Guitar Hero Groupie - 19 - W4M

I want to invite 3 guys over and have a competition. The one with the highest score wins me.

Punch You In the Face - 22 - W4M

I just want to punch you in the face, but am open to other ideas if you have any. I would bring my best friend along just to be safe.

Furry Sex - 32 - W4M

What I would like to do is have each of us dress up in bear costumes. I'll fix up my bedroom with forest decorations to give the whole scene some more authenticity.

Single Mother Needs Some Lovin - 26 - W4M

Im lookin for someone that can come over to my place for something fun but quick. I can't drive because my son is here sleeping.

GRAHAM ROUMIEAU
Bogus Booty Calls

YUKO SHIMIZU

The Beautiful and the Grotesque Book Illustration

MICHAEL SLOAN

My Hong Kong Sketchbook

I made these sketches during a two-week trip to Hong Kong with my family in July 2010. Torrential rain during the first week forced me to work quickly in black and white instead of using my usual watercolors. My sketches were transformed when I began using a brush marker, a tool that was new to me and very liberating. Suddenly I was able to draw with a brush from different and exciting vantage points (such as standing on a busy street corner), where it would have been difficult to sit and paint for any length of time.

JEFFREY SMITH
Shadow Knights

I got a call from David Talbot, founder and former editor-in-chief of *Salon.com*, who asked me if I'd be interested in a book project titled *Shadow Knights*, to tell the story of Winston Churchill's SOE (Special Operations Executive) and the courageous men and women who fought a secret war against the Nazis and Adolf Hitler. People like Noor Inayat Khan, Harry Ree, Claus Helberg, Winston Churchill, Hugh Dalton, Brigadier Colin Gubbins, Selwyn Jepson, Jens Poulsson, Knut Haugland, and many more. I felt the project important enough to make a trip abroad. In Paris I wanted to see some of the places where Noor Inayat Khan lived, fought, and died for freedom. The book's author, Gary Ka-

miya, gave me addresses—places like 40 rue Erlanger in Auteuil, where Noor first arrived; No. 3 Boulevard Richard Wallace, mostly occupied by SS officers; 98 Rue de la Faisanderie, where Noor was arrested; Avenue Foch, 82 and 84, the Gestapo headquarters; and finally, Fazal Manzil, the house in Suresnes where Noor grew up. It was a strenuous trip, but I'm glad I went. It gave me the grit to stay focused on a project that would take over seven months, to research thousands of photographs, to shoot 567 photographs of models and myself, produce 22 photographic comps, many more sketches, 22 full-page paintings, and 2 covers for this wonderfully exhausting project.

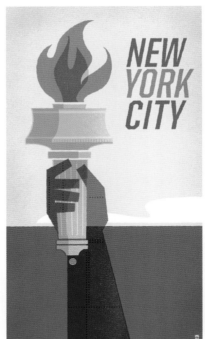

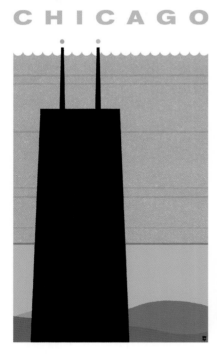

THE HEADS OF STATE
Travel Posters
Vintage Posters

MARK TODD
Portraits of Writers

These pieces were created with brush and ink, and colored digitally. I wanted to keep the colors soft and diffused, using a restrained palette. The overall mood of the piece is melancholy.

Miranda July

Junot Diaz.

George Saunders.

Anthony Doerr.

STEVE WACKSMAN
The Millner's Campaign

OLIVER WEISS

The Well-Tempered Year Calendar

I created these illustrations for my self-promotional calendar, which was professionally printed on heavy-coated paper, and mailed out to clients. The calendar is titled "The Well-Tempered Year" and contains 13 full-sized whimsical illustrations for every month. The titles mock famous novels (*Of Mice and ZEN, The BOLD MEN and the Sea, Brave BLUE World, Howard's FRIEND, Finnegan's LAKE*, etc.). The artwork makes abundant use of black-and-white contrasts, and uses only two colors: a dark brown and one spot color for each month. All images were created digitally and incorporate textured paper with a slightly warm tone.

STUDENT SCHOLARSHIP
AND
DISTINGUISHED EDUCATORS IN THE ARTS

The Society of Illustrators fulfills its education mission through its museum exhibitions, library, archives, permanent collection, and, most proudly, through the Student Scholarship Competition.

The following pages present a sampling of the 205 works selected from 7,002 entries submitted by college-level students nationwide. The selections were made by a prestigious jury of professional illustrators and art directors.

Scott Bakal chairs this program and major financial support is given by the Society of Illustrators as well as various other generous private and corporate donors, including Blick Art Materials, The Art Department, the Master Class Program, the late Arthur Zankel, and the late Joyce Rogers Kitchell, and other bequests established in memory of family and colleagues.

An endowment from bequests and corporate support makes possible over $50,000 in awards to the students.

Distinguished Educators in the Arts is an annual award selected by a distinguished group of illustrator/educators from a large pool of candidates.

IN MEMORIUM
JOYCE ROGERS KITCHELL
[1945 – 2008]

The Society of Illustrators is dedicated to preserving the memory of Joyce Rogers Kitchell, a nationally reknowned watercolorist whose illustrations were sought for both private collections and commercial advertising.

We are committed to honoring her legacy and fostering her spirit of kindness and generosity.

Illustration by Joyce Rogers Kitchell, 1989

PAIGE VICKERS

MARYLAND INSTITUTE COLLEGE OF ART

Campede
Graphite and ink, digitally colored
Maryland Institute College of Art
Zankel Scholarship

Zankel nominees: Paige Vickers (Maryland Institute College of Art), Alyssa Winans (Rhode Island School of Design), Craig Bowers (Maryland Institute College of Art) and Neiko Ng (Academy of Art University)

The Society of Illustrators proudly presents the Zankel Scholar named in memory of Arthur Zankel, whose generous bequest has made this scholarship possible. Mr. Zankel was a firm advocate for higher education. This is the fifth year the Society has been honored to seek, in his name, the best of the junior class and to financially support his or her senior year of college.

2011 Zankel winner Paige Vickers with Judy Francis Zankel.

JOHN LA GATTA

[1894–1977]

Glamour, grace and beauty epitomized John La Gatta's work and life. One of the most famous illustrators of the early decades of the 20th century, La Gatta depicted the well-heeled in the pages of nearly all the mainstream magazines such as the *Saturday Evening Post, Ladies' Home Journal,* and *Cosmopolitan*, as well as for swank advertising campaigns. His success afforded him a lavish lifestyle, befitting his own celebrity status. The changing tastes of the public and the advent of photography, found the artist, now in California and in faltering health, struggling to rejuvenate his career. Then, in 1956, came the call from Edward A. "Tink" Adams, the founder of what is now Art Center College of Design, where La Gatta soon became an instructor.

A demanding teacher, he taught with an "old school" rigor, emphasizing that emotion and perfection must be brought to the process, and that one must give one's all to the work. Many of his pupils went on to careers in illustration, including Bob Peak, Bart Forbes, Mark English, Charles McVicker, and Don Shaeffer, head of the famous Charles E. Cooper Studio.

McVicker recalled La Gatta as "a dapper man, always in a jacket and tie. He'd have the models pose twice—the first week she'd be nude, the second week clothed. The thinking was we'd do better if we knew the figure beneath the clothes. He wanted us to do it like he did: get the substructure in quickly and accurately." Greatly influenced by La Gatta, Mark English said "he did such beautiful women, his line was so sensitive, sensual." His approach was to set up a clothed figure and put a red light on one side and a blue light on the other, making one side warm, the other cool. English continued, "Light is a subtle thing. La Gatta made it obvious."

La Gatta enjoyed his association with the eager young adults in his classes. He liked their intelligence, their "point blank" questions. Metaphorically, he saw them as newly stretched canvases, to be developed into "worthy achievements." After graduation, many wrote letters of praise and admiration.

He taught his last class in 1968, and was soon awarded the Honorary Degree of Doctor of Fine Arts. Deeply honored, the artist expressed his appreciation of his happy years as a faculty member. He continued to paint for galleries until his death in 1977. In 1984 the Society of Illustrators inducted John La Gatta into its Illustrators Hall of Fame.

JILL BOSSERT
author *John La Gatta, An Artist's Life*

GIL ASHBY

When illustrator and teacher Gil Ashby came to Detroit more than a decade ago, he did it for love. For the love of his wife, Maura, who was living in the Metro area when he met her, and also for the love of teaching art and helping young people realize their dreams.

In his role as chair of illustration at College for Creative Study, Ashby made an extraordinary impact on the school and his students. In ten years, he transformed the department, upped enrollment, and raised standards. "The experiences I've had and what they bring to the classroom probably have more to do with my belief in myself," he says, "and my ability to transfer that confidence and that faith to another person, because we all develop and grow by idea exchange. We're all minds; we're all spirits."

As he speaks, in his gentle and thoughtful way, Ashby sounds like he's spent a lot of time considering what it means to be an artist and how that fits into the bigger picture of being a human being. Giving back, contributing, and having a mission are recurring themes in conversation with him. "I think I've just always taken it for granted that people can sense and see truth. And that's the basic premise and the source of my ability to communicate with my students. Because my belief is, 'If I can do it—as imperfect as I am—then you have a chance.'"

Because of his own experience and success, Ashby gives a lot of credence to the idea of intention, preparing oneself for opportunity by working with faith and a sense of purpose. These philosophies have carried him through a very interesting and rewarding career. He grew up in Harlem and graduated from the School of Visual Arts. For years, he worked as a freelance artist and teacher in New York and Georgia. By the mid-1990s he had done everything from courtroom drawings to illustrating the popular children's book, *Rosa Parks* by Eloise Greenfield, which helped fulfill Ashby's wish to create and publish positive images of African Americans. "I grew up in the '60s," he says. "When I was in elementary school, I didn't see many positive images. I wanted to be part of that change."

In order to put more of his energies into teaching and his own work, Ashby recently made the transition from chair to instructor at CCS. The move means a culmination for him, and it coincides with this prestigious award in recognition of the mark he's made in the world of art and illustration.   **NORENE SMITH**

CORINNE REID
Wounded Knee
Digital media
Montserrat College of Art
Fred Lynch, Instructor
$5000 in Memory of Arthur Zankel

JooHee Yoon
Elephant
Screen print and mixed media
Rhode Island School of Design
Susan Doyle and Fred Lynch, Instructors
$5000 in Memory of Joyce Rogers Kitchell

JOHNNY DOMBROWSKI
Passerby
Ink and digital
School of Visual Arts
Tomer Hanuka, Instructor
$4000 Nancy Lee Rhodes Roberts Scholarship Award
Call for Entries Poster

CAMERON SAYADI
Void Reflection
Pen, ink and digital
Academy of Art University
David Ball, Instructor
$4000 Nancy Lee Rhodes Roberts Scholarship Award

PRISCILLA WONG
Part-time Indian
Digital
San Jose State University
Bunny Carter and Courtney
Granner, Instructors
$3000 in Memory of Albert Dorne
The Art Department Scholarship

ARMANDO VEVE
Mysteries that Howl and Hunt
Pen and ink and digital
Rhode Island School of Design
Chris Buzelli, Instructor
$2500 Nancy Lee Rhodes
Roberts Scholarship

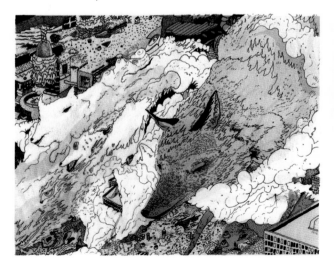

KRISTINA WAYTE
Night Scene
Digital
San Jose State University
David Chai, Instructor
$2500 MicroVisions Award

DADU DAVID SHIN
Lost Dog
Mixed media and digital
Rhode Island School of Design
Chris Buzelli, Instructor
$2500 Nancy Lee Rhodes Roberts
Scholarship Award

TRAN NGUYEN
Our Fluttersome Ordeal
Mixed Media
Savannah College of Art and Design
Allan Drummond, Instructor
$2000 Nancy Lee Rhodes Roberts Scholarship Award
Master Class Program Scholarship

CAROLYN JAO
Lower East Side
Monotype on paper
School of Visual Arts
Frances Jetter, Instructor
$2000 in Memory of Verdon Flory

KEVIN LAUGHLIN
Minotaur
Acrylic
Rhode Island School of Design
Lenny Long, Instructor
$2000 MicroVisions Award

NICK ILUZADA
After Life
Graphite, ink and digital
Maryland Institute College of Art
Dave Plunkert, Instructor
$2000 The Weinstein Foundation Award

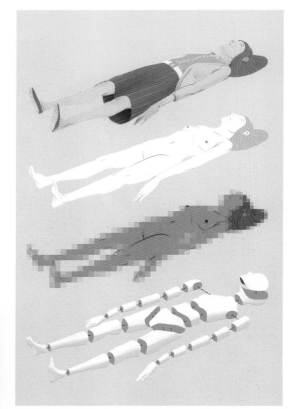

BUSTER BROADWAY
Goodbye For Now
Acrylic on board
School of Visual Arts
Tomer Hanuka, Instructor
$1500 in Memory of Derek Bovay
The Art Department Scholarship

SOEY MILK
Cali
Oil on wood
Art Center College of Design
Sean Cheetham, Instructor
$1500 In Memory of Helen Wohlberg
Lambert and Herman Lambert

MARY NELSON
Snow Geese and Smoke Stacks
Mixed media
Minneapolis College of Art and Design
Linda Frichtel, Instructor
$1000 John Klammer Award

KELSEY GARRITY-RILEY
Humane Society
Mixed Media
Savannah College of Art and Design
Julie Lieberman, Instructor
$1000 The Betsy and Alan Cohn
Foundation Award

AMANDA LANZONE
Sloth
Pen and digital color
School of Visual Arts
Chris Buzelli, Instructor
$1000 in Memory of Effie Bowie

NICOLE GERVACIO
Untitled
Etching, watercolor
California College of the Arts
Caitlin Kuhwald, Instructor
$1000 The Shrunkenheadman Scholarship

SAM WOLFE CONNELLY
Countries
Digital
Savannah College of Art and Design
Kurt Vargo, Instructor
$1000 in Memory of Lila Dryer

KELLAN STOVER
Hurdy Gurdy Gus
Mixed media
Savannah College of Art and Design
Mohamed Danawi, Instructor
$1000 In Honor of The Normandia Family

IVY TAI
Extreme Tourism
Digital
Rhode Island School of Design
David Porter, Instructor
$1000 in Memory of Barbara Carr

DARION McCOY
Lilith and Samael
Mixed media
Savannah College of Art and Design
Daniel Powers, Instructor
$1000 in Memory of Harry Rosenbaum

CALEB WOOD
Little Wild
Rhode Island School of Design
Amy Kravitz
First Place

TED WIGGIN
Terra Firma
Rhode Island School of Design
Amy Kravitz and Daniel Sousa
Second Place

TYLER CARTER
DreamGiver
Brigham Young University
Robert Barrett and Richard Hull, Instructors
Honorable Mention

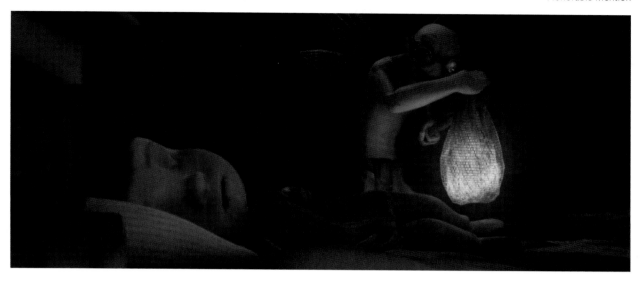

KENNETH ONULAK
Paper Dreams
Rhode Island School of Design
Amy Kravitz, Instructor
Third Place

INDEX

STEVE ADAMS
10108 Galeries d'Anjou Blvd.
Montreal H1J 2Y4 Quebec, Canada
514-352-6655
steve@adamsillustration.com
www.adamsillustration.com

P. 300
ART DIRECTOR:
Martine Combréas
CLIENT:
La Grande Ourse
Theater (France)
MEDIUM: Acrylic

DANIEL ADEL
292 Main St.
Cold Spring, NY 10516
646-250-3206
danieladel@mindspring.com
www.danieladel.com

P. 49
ART DIRECTOR:
Riva Schwartz
CLIENT: Golf Digest
MEDIUM:
Oil on canvas

P. 50
ART DIRECTOR:
Marshall McKinney
CLIENT:
Garden & Gun
MEDIUM:
Oil on canvas

P. 51
ART DIRECTOR:
Jana Roberts
CLIENT: German GQ
MEDIUM:
Oil on canvas

LINCOLN AGNEW
602-2520 Palliser Dr. SW
Calgary T2V4S9 Alberta, Canada
403-719-9465
info@lincolnagnew.com
www.lincolnagnew.com

P. 377
ART DIRECTOR:
Dana Fritts
CLIENT: HarperCollins
MEDIUM:
Pen, ink, digital

P. 378
ART DIRECTOR:
Dana Fritts
CLIENT: HarperCollins
MEDIUM:
Pen, ink, digital

NISHAN AKGULIAN
505 E. 79th St. #18E
New York, NY 10075
917-670-5361
nishan.akgulian@verizon.net
www.nishanakgulian.com

P. 453
MEDIUM:
ink, watercolor, color
pencil, pastel, collage

A. RICHARD ALLEN
31 Ridley Rd.
Bournemouth, BH9 1LD Dorset
England
44 1202525181
info@arichardallen.com
www.arichardallen.com

P. 528
ART DIRECTOR:
Sheri Gee
CLIENT:
The Folio Society
MEDIUM:
Pencil, acrylic, digital

SCOTT BAKAL
PO Box 320638
West Roxbury, MA 02132
631-525-2309
info@scottbakal.com
www.scottbakal.com

P. 301
CLIENT:
Society of Illustrators
MEDIUM: Acrylic, ink

P. 454
MEDIUM:
Charcoal, ink

**ANNA AND ELANA
BALBUSSO**
via Ciro Menotti 15
Milano 20129 Italy
00390270108739
balbusso.twins@gmail.com
www.balbusso.com

GOLD
P. 368
ART DIRECTOR:
Nadia Maestri
CLIENT:
Black Cat Publishing
MEDIUM:
Acrylic, digital

P. 379
ART DIRECTOR:
Sabine Rousselet
CLIENT:
Éditions Milan
MEDIUM:
Acrylic, digital

JOHN-PAUL BALMET
23 Duane St. #3
Redwood City, CA 94062
408-202-3204
jpbalmet@yahoo.com

P. 455
MEDIUM: Digital

JONATHAN BARTLETT
336-345-0369
jb@seejbdraw.com
www.seejbdraw.com

P. 52
ART DIRECTOR:
Nicholas Blechman
CLIENT: The New York
Times Book Review
MEDIUM: Mixed

P. 53
ART DIRECTOR:
Jason Treat
CLIENT:
Atlantic Magazine
MEDIUM: Mixed

P. 54
ART DIRECTOR:
Camille Neilson
CLIENT: MacUser UK
MEDIUM: Mixed

P. 55
ART DIRECTOR:
Emily Kimbro
CLIENT:
Spirit Magazine
MEDIUM: Mixed

P. 56
ART DIRECTOR:
SooJin Buzelli
CLIENT: Assett
International
MEDIUM: Mixed

LOU BEACH
900 South Tremaine Ave.
Los Angeles, CA 90019
323-934-7335
lou@loubeach.com
www.loubeach.com

P. 57
ART DIRECTOR:
Monte Beauchamp
CLIENT:
Blabworld Magazine
MEDIUM: Collage

P. 220
CLIENT:
Tommy McCutchon
MEDIUM: Collage

P. 380
CLIENT:
Diane Sherry Case
MEDIUM:
Collage, digital

P. 456
MEDIUM: Collage

ANA BENAROYA
20 Livingston Ave. #801
New Brunswick, NJ 08901
732-407-4113
ana.benaroya@gmail.com
www.anabenaroya.com

P. 304
ART DIRECTOR:
Ken Macy
CLIENT: Ashi Dashi
MEDIUM: Socks

RICK BERRY
93 Warren St.
Arlington, MA 02474
781-648-6375
berry@braid.com
www.rickberrystudio.com

SILVER
P. 217
MEDIUM: Oil

P. 302
MEDIUM: Oil

P. 303
MEDIUM: Oil

LOUISA BERTMAN
11 Bigelow St.
Cambridge, MA 02139
617-549-0080
louisa@louisabertman.com
www.louisabertman.com

P. 58
ART DIRECTOR:
Jessica Moats
CLIENT:
KONG Magazine
MEDIUM: Pen, ink,
watercolor, digital

P. 59
ART DIRECTOR:
Jessica Moats
CLIENT:
KONG Magazine
MEDIUM: Pen, ink,
watercolor, digital

GUY BILLOUT
274 Shoreham Village Dr.
Fairfield, CT 06824-6229
917-691-9672
guy@guybillout.com
www.guybillout.com

P. 60
ART DIRECTOR:
Deborah Lawrence
CLIENT: The Rotarian
MEDIUM: Digital

P. 305
ART DIRECTOR:
Gary Callahan
CLIENT: Boston
Consulting Group
MEDIUM: Digital

P. 529
ART DIRECTOR:
Andy Frank
CLIENT: UCLA
MEDIUM: Digital

P. 530
Art Directors:
Lora Morgenstern
Chris Malec
CLIENT:
Massachusetts
General Hospital
MEDIUM:
Pencil, ink, digital

CHI BIRMINGHAM
610 6th St. #3R
Brooklyn, NY 11215
831-238-2355
chibirmingham@gmail.com
www.chibirmingham.com

P. 531
MEDIUM: Digital

THOMAS BLACKSHEAR II
1735 North Lynn St.
Arlington, VA 22209
703-292-3815
info@photoassist.com

P. 308
ART DIRECTOR:
Derry Noyes
CLIENT:
U.S. Postal Service
MEDIUM:
Acrylic on board

CATHIE BLECK
2270 Chatfield Dr.
Cleveland Heights, OH 44106
cb@cathiebleck.com
www.cathiebleck.com

P. 457
MEDIUM: Inks, kaolin
clay on clayboard

SERGE BLOCH
c/o Marlena Agency Inc.
322 Ewing St.
Princeton, NJ 08540
609-252-9405
marlena@marlenaagency.com
www.marlenaagency.com

P. 61
ART DIRECTOR:
Jennifer McManus
CLIENT:
More Magazine
MEDIUM: Mixed

P. 306
MEDIUM: Mixed

P. 307
CLIENT:
Emmanuelle Rouiller
MEDIUM: Mixed

P. 381
CLIENT: Bayard
MEDIUM: Mixed

P. 458
MEDIUM: Mixed

RICHARD BORGE
130 Jackson St. #1D
Brooklyn, NY 11211
917-494-4567
stuff@richardborge.com
www.richardborge.com

P. 62
ART DIRECTOR:
Orlie Kraus
CLIENT: The Wall
Street Journal
MEDIUM: Mixed

P. 63
ART DIRECTOR:
Angela Moore
CLIENT: Santa Fe
Reporter
MEDIUM: Mixed

SAM BOSMA
1205 Saint Paul St. #2B
Baltimore, MD 21202
610-322-2923
sambosma@gmail.com
www.sbosma.com

P. 64
ART DIRECTOR:
John Sandford
CLIENT:
Muse Magazine

P. 65
ART DIRECTOR:
SooJin Buzelli
CLIENT:
PlanSponsor Europe
MEDIUM: Digital

P. 459
MEDIUM: Digital

VINCENT BOURGEAU
c/o French Touch Agency
1366 21st Ave
San Francisco, CA 94122
415-823-5019
bonjour@frenchtouchagency.net
http://frenchtouchagency.net

P. 382
ART DIRECTOR:
Gregoire Solotareff
CLIENT:
Ecoles des Loisirs
MEDIUM: Digital

STEVE BRODNER
100 Cooper St. #6G
New York, NY 10034
917-596-2938
stevebrodner@earthlink.net
www.stevebrodner.com

GOLD
P. 40
Art Directors:
Caroline Maihot
Christine Curry
CLIENT:
The New Yorker
MEDIUM:
Watercolor, ink

P. 66
Illustration Editor:
Christine Curry
CLIENT:
The New Yorker
MEDIUM:
Watercolor, ink

P. 67
ART DIRECTOR:
Stacey Clarkson
CLIENT:
Harper's Magazine
MEDIUM:
Watercolor, ink

P. 68
ART DIRECTOR:
Tim J. Luddy
CLIENT: Mother Jones
MEDIUM:
Watercolor, ink

P. 69
ART DIRECTOR:
Jason Treat
CLIENT:
The Atlantic
MEDIUM:
Watercolor, ink

P. 221
Art Directors:
Amy Frith
Paul Yokota
CLIENT: Infor
MEDIUM: Mixed

P. 460
Art Directors:
Christine Curry
Caroline Mailhot
MEDIUM:
Watercolor, ink

CALEF BROWN
136 Maine St. #6
Brunswick, ME 04011
207-373-0500
calef@calefbrown.com
www.calefbrown.com

P. 309
ART DIRECTOR:
Mary Brigid Barrett
CLIENT:
The Library of Congress
MEDIUM:
Acrylic on paper

P. 383
ART DIRECTOR:
Sheila Smallwood
CLIENT: Houghton
Harcourt Books
MEDIUM:
Acrylic on paper

STEVE BRODNER

NIGEL BUCHANAN
51/61 Marlborough St.
Surry Hills, Sydney NSW 2010
Australia
612 9699 3694
nigel@nigelbuchanan
www.nigelbuchanan.com

P. 310
CLIENT:
Screen Australia
MEDIUM: Digital

DANIEL BUENO
rua São Vicente de Paula, 199, #111
São Paulo 01229-010 Brazil
55-11-3881-8418
bu_eno@yahoo.com.br

P. 384
ART DIRECTOR: Maria
Caolina Sampaio
CLIENT: Cosac Naify
MEDIUM:
Digital, collage

MARC BURCKHARDT
1111 W. 7th St.
Austin, TX 78703
512-458-1690
marc@marcart.net
www.marcart.net

P. 70
ART DIRECTOR:
T.J. Tucker
CLIENT:
Texas Monthly
MEDIUM:
Acrylic, oil, wood
carving on board

P. 71
ART DIRECTOR:
T.J. Tucker
CLIENT: Texas
Monthly
MEDIUM:
Acrylic, oil on board

P. 222
Art Directors:
DJ Stout
Julie Savasky
CLIENT:
Advanced Nutrients
MEDIUM:
Acrylic, oil on board

P. 223
ART DIRECTOR:
DJ Stout
Julie Savasky
CLIENT:
Advanced Nutrients
MEDIUM:
Acrylic, oil on board

P. 224
ART DIRECTOR:
Elizabeth Morrow
McKenzie
CLIENT:
Bridgeport Brewing
MEDIUM:
Acrylic, oil on board

P. 385
ART DIRECTOR:
Patrick Barry
CLIENT: Houghton
Mifflin Harcourt
MEDIUM:
Acrylic, oil on board

GOLD
P. 444
MEDIUM:
Acrylic, oil on board

P. 461
MEDIUM:
Acrylic, oil on board

PHILIP BURKE
1948 Juron Dr.
Niagara Falls, NY 14304
716-478-5915
burke.philipburke@gmail.com

P. 72
ART DIRECTOR:
Nancy Butkus
CLIENT: The New York
Observer
MEDIUM:
Oil on canvas

P. 73
ART DIRECTOR:
Nancy Butkus
CLIENT: The New York
Observer
MEDIUM:
Oil on canvas

P. 74
ART DIRECTOR:
Steve Charny
CLIENT: Rolling Stone
MEDIUM:
Oil on canvas

P. 75
ART DIRECTOR:
Nancy Butkus
CLIENT: The New York
Observer
MEDIUM:
Oil on canvas

P. 76
ART DIRECTOR:
Nancy Butkus
CLIENT: The New York
Observer
MEDIUM:
Oil on canvas

CASEY BURNS
215 SE Morrison #2014
Portland, OR 97214
503-753-4291
casey@caseyburns.com
www.caseyburns.com

P. 225
CLIENT: Spoon
MEDIUM: Pen, brush,
ink, silkscreen on
paper

CHRIS BUZELLI
125 E. 4th St. #22
New York, NY 10003
212-614-8111
chris@chrisbuzelli.com
www.chrisbuzelli.com

P. 77
ART DIRECTOR:
SooJin Buzelli
CLIENT: ai5000
Magazine
MEDIUM:
Oil on panel

P. 78
ART DIRECTOR:
Irene Gallo
CLIENT: Tor.com
MEDIUM:
Oil on paper

P. 79
ART DIRECTOR:
Angela Moore
CLIENT: The Santa Fe
Reporter
MEDIUM:
Oil on panel

GOLD
P. 204
ART DIRECTOR:
Paul Mark
CLIENT: Paul Mark
MEDIUM:
Oil on panel

P. 226
ART DIRECTOR:
Gregory DiBisceglie
CLIENT: Macy's
MEDIUM:
Oil on panel

P. 227
ART DIRECTOR:
Elisa Bauch
CLIENT: MGM
Resorts, VIVA
Festival
MEDIUM: Oil on
paper

P. 386
ART DIRECTOR:
Kate Gartner
CLIENT:
Random House

P. 462
MEDIUM:
Oil on panel

MICHAEL BYERS
78B Dublin St. North
Guelph N1H 4N1 Ontario, Canada
519-588-2307
mike.byers@rogers.com

P. 80
ART DIRECTOR: Kristin
K. Lipman
CLIENT: Honolulu
Magazine
MEDIUM: Ink and
digital

P. 228
ART DIRECTOR:
Gregory Pepper
CLIENT: Kazoo
MEDIUM:
Ink and digital

HARRY CAMPBELL
6302 Pinehurst Rd.
Baltimore, MD 21212
410-371-0270
harry@harrycampbell.net
www.harrycampbell.net

P. 81
ART DIRECTOR:
Joe Heroun
CLIENT: The New
Republic
MEDIUM: Digital

P. 463
MEDIUM: Digital

P. 464
MEDIUM: Digital,
screen print

BILL CARMAN
4230 E. Trekker Rim Rd.
Boise, ID 83716
208-426-1610
bcarman@boisestate.edu

P. 311
MEDIUM:
Acrylic on copper

P. 312
MEDIUM:
Acrylic on panel

P. 465: Acrylic, ink

ANDRÉ CARRILHO

P. 82
ART DIRECTOR:
David Harris
CLIENT: Vanity Fair
MEDIUM: Mixed

Q. CASSETTI
Two Camp St.
Trumansburg, NY 14886
607-387-5424
q@theluckystone.com
www.qcassetti.com

P. 229
CLIENT:
Atwater Winery
MEDIUM: Digital

P. 466
MEDIUM: Pen & ink

EFI CHALIKOPOULOU
345 W. 30th St.
New York, NY 10001
646-704-9799
efi@efichaliko.com
http://efichaliko.com

P. 467
MEDIUM:
Pencil, acrylic

DANIEL CHANG
c/o Frank Sturges
142 W. Winter St.
Delaware, OH 43015
740-369-9702
frank@sturgesreps.com
www.sturgesreps.com

P. 83
ART DIRECTOR:
Kevin Fisher
CLIENT:
Audubon Magazine
MEDIUM: Mixed

DOUG CHAYKA
113 W. Gaston St.
Savannah, GA 31401
646-525-9740
doug@dougchayka.com
www.dougchayka.com

P. 84
ART DIRECTOR:
John Pallattela
CLIENT: The Nation
MEDIUM:
Digital, collage

ANGY CHE
3239 Estado St.
Pasadena, CA 91107
626-376-1196
angylche@gmail.com
angyche@blogspot.com

P. 468
MEDIUM: Acrylic on
wood panel

PHILIP CHEANEY
680 Humboldt St. #2
Brooklyn, NY 11222
503-816-2031
mail@philipcheaney.com
www.philipcheaney.com

P. 469
MEDIUM: Mixed

MARCOS CHIN
16 Manhattan Ave. #4H
Brooklyn, NY 11206
646-416-0936
marcos@marcoschin.com
www.marcoschin.com

P. 85
ART DIRECTOR:
Melissa Bluey
CLIENT:
The Atlantic
MEDIUM: Digital

P. 86
ART DIRECTOR:
Cody Tilson
CLIENT: Playboy
MEDIUM: Digital

P. 87
ART DIRECTOR:
Annette Keller
CLIENT: Annabelle
Magazine
MEDIUM:
Digital, mixed

P. 88
ART DIRECTOR:
Angela Tieri
CLIENT: MIT
Technology Review
MEDIUM:
Digital, mixed

P. 230
CLIENT: Diesel,
Buenos Aires
MEDIUM:
Digital, mixed

DAVID CHRISTIANA
13990 N. Sutherland Trail
Tucson, AZ 85739
520-825-4043
david@davidchristiana.com
www.davidchristiana.com

P. 470
MEDIUM:
Egg tempera

JOSEPH CIARDIELLO
35 Little York
Mt. Pleasant Rd.
Milford, NJ 08848
908-996-4392
joe@joeciardiello.com
www.joeciardiello.com

P. 90
ART DIRECTOR:
Nicholas Blechman
CLIENT: The New York
Times Book Review
MEDIUM: Pen & ink

P. 91
ART DIRECTOR:
Nicholas Blechman
CLIENT: The New York
Times Book Review
MEDIUM: Pen & ink

TAVIS COBURN
www.taviscoburn.com

P. 89
Art Directors:
Mark Montgomery
Michael Solita
CLIENT:
IEEE Spectrum
MEDIUM: Digital

JOSH COCHRAN
61 Greenpoint Ave. #515
Brooklyn, NY 11222
626-354-7407
mail@joshcochran.net
www.joshcochran.net

P. 231
ART DIRECTOR:
Zac Boswell
CLIENT:
Founders Council
MEDIUM: Digital

P. 232
ART DIRECTOR:
Matt Dobson
CLIENT:
Humana Festival
MEDIUM: Digital

P. 233
ART DIRECTOR:
Zac Boswell
CLIENT:
Founders Council
MEDIUM: Digital

SILVER
P. 374
Art Directors:
Lauren Rille
Sonia Chaghatzbanian
CLIENT:
Simon & Schuster
MEDIUM: Digital

P. 387
ART DIRECTOR:
Paul Buckley
CLIENT:
Penguin Group
MEDIUM: Digital

RAÚL COLÓN

P. 388
ART DIRECTOR:
Jeanne Hogle
CLIENT: HarperCollins
MEDIUM: Watercolor,
prismacolor pencils,
scratching on water-
color paper

TIMOTHY COOK
10701 Drumm Ave.
Kensington, MD 20895
301-949-5002
tim@timothycook.com
www.timothycook.com

P. 234
CLIENT: Gus Ramsey
MEDIUM: Ink, digital

P. 471
MEDIUM: Ink, digital

JOHN CUNEO
69 Speare Rd.
Woodstock, NY 12498
845-679-7973
john@johncuneo.com
www.johncuneo.com

P. 92
ART DIRECTOR:
David Curcurito
CLIENT: Esquire
MEDIUM: Ink, water-
color on paper

P. 93
ART DIRECTOR:
Marshal McKinney
CLIENT: Garden &
Gun Magazine
MEDIUM: Ink, water-
color on paper

P. 235
ART DIRECTOR:
Martin Colyer
CLIENT: The Great
American Songbook
Project
MEDIUM: Ink, water-
color on paper

P. 313
Art Directors:
Greg Manchess
Jack Unruh
CLIENT:
Earth: Fragile Planet
MEDIUM: Ink, water-
color on paper

P. 472
MEDIUM: Ink, water-
color on paper

HUGH D'ANDRADE
2498 Harrison St.
San Francisco, CA 94110
415-513-3444
hugh@hughillustration.com
www.hughillustration.com

P. 238
CLIENT: Joey Cain
MEDIUM:
Pencil, digital

ANDRÉ DA LOBA
402 19th St.
Brooklyn, NY 11215
646-520-9762
andre@andredaloba.com
www.andredaloba.com

P. 389
ART DIRECTOR:
Margarida Noronha
CLIENT:
Kalandraka Editora
MEDIUM:
Transfer print

P. 390
ART DIRECTOR:
Margarida Noronha
CLIENT:
Kalandraka Editora
MEDIUM:
Transfer print

JOHN D. DAWSON
1735 N. Lynn St.
Arlington, VA 22209
703-292-3815
info@photoassist.com

P. 316
ART DIRECTOR:
Ethel Kessler
CLIENT:
U.S. Postal Service
MEDIUM:
Acrylic on board

GIANNI DE CONNO

GOLD
P. 208
CLIENT: Emergency
MEDIUM:
Digital acrylic

JEFFREY DECOSTER
137 N. Chester Ave.
Pasadena, CA 91106
626-222-5789
jeddysemail@gmail.com
www.jeffreydecoster.com

P. 94
ART DIRECTOR:
Kory Kennedy
CLIENT: Runner's
World Magazine
MEDIUM: Ink, acrylic,
gouache, digital

P. 95
ART DIRECTOR:
Wesley Bausmith
CLIENT: LA Times
MEDIUM: Ink, acrylic,
gouache, digital

P. 96
ART DIRECTOR: Chris-
tine Bower-Wright
CLIENT: Hemisphere's
Magazine
MEDIUM: Acrylic,
gouache, digital

P. 97
ART DIRECTOR:
Kory Kennedy
CLIENT: Runner's
World Magazine
MEDIUM: Ink, acrylic,
gouache, digital

P. 98
ART DIRECTOR:
Rob Hewitt
CLIENT: Hemispheres
Magazine
MEDIUM: Ink, acrylic,
gouache, digital

NICK DEWAR

P. 99
ART DIRECTOR:
Charles Hively
CLIENT: 3x3, The
Magazine of Contem-
porary Illustration

PETER DIAMOND
Lambrechtgase 6/7
Vienna 1040 Austria
+43 680 315 8579
peter@peterdiamond.ca
www.peterdiamond.ca

P. 473
MEDIUM: India ink,
alcohol markers,
digital color

JOHNNY DOMBROWSKI
20-42 42nd St. #2F
Astoria, NY 11105
860-918-4951
johnny@johnnydombrowksi.com
www.johnnydombrowski.com

P. 474
MEDIUM: Ink, digital

P. 475
MEDIUM: Ink, digital

BIL DONOVAN
58 St. Marks Pl.
New York, NY 10003
212-228-3754
dukedonovan@earthlink.net
www.bildonovan.com

P. 236
CLIENT:
Chado Ralph Rucci
MEDIUM:
Brush, ink, digital

P. 237
CLIENT:
Chado Ralph Rucci
MEDIUM:
Brush, ink, digital

P. 476
MEDIUM: Gouache
on BFK paper

P. 477
MEDIUM: Ink, pastel

MATT DORFMAN
474 Henry St. 4th Fl.
Brooklyn, NY 11231
917-613-5596
matt@metalmother.com
www.metalmother.com

P. 532
ART DIRECTOR:
Kelly Doe
CLIENT:
The New York Times
Week In Review
MEDIUM: Collage,
mixed media, digital

RICHARD DOWNS
15394 Wet Hill Rd.
Nevada City, CA 95959
530-470-0435
r_downs@sbcglobal.net
www.downs-art.com

P. 314
ART DIRECTOR:
Erica Heimberg
MEDIUM: Monotype
on Japanese paper

P. 315
ART DIRECTOR:
Erica Heimberg
MEDIUM: Monotype
on Japanese paper

GÉRARD DUBOIS
525 Green St.
Saint-Lambert J4P 1V4 France
450-465-8040
dubois@netaxis.ca

GOLD
P. 42
Art Directors:
Emily Crawford
Andrée Kahlmorgan
CLIENT: TIME
MEDIUM:
Acrylic, digital

P. 391
ART DIRECTOR:
Louis Gagnon
CLIENT: Les Allusifs
MEDIUM: Acrylic

BYRON EGGENSCHWILER
129 Braden Crescent NW
Calgary T2L 1N2 Alberta, Canada
403-998-4962
byron@byronegg.com
www.byronegg.com

P. 100
ART DIRECTOR:
Kelly Carter
CLIENT:
Delaware Today
MEDIUM: Watercolor,
acrylic, digital

P. 239
CLIENT: Scott Shpeley
MEDIUM:
Acrylic, ink, digital

THOMAS EHRETSMANN
29, rue Wimpheling
Strasbourg 67000 France
0033.3.88.24.05.31
thomas.ehretsmann@wanadoo.fr
thomasehretsmann.canalblog.com

GOLD
P. 370
CLIENT:
Éditions Delcourt
MEDIUM:
Acrylic on paper

GÜRBÜZ DOĞAN EKŞIOĞLU
198 6th St. #1
Jersey City, NJ 07302
914-439-0232
doganaslan@yahoo.com
www.gurbuz-de.com

P. 101
ART DIRECTOR:
Filiz Aygunduz
CLIENT: Milliyet
Newspaper
MEDIUM: Mixed

P. 240
ART DIRECTOR:
Vahit Tuna
CLIENT:
Masa Reklam Ajans
MEDIUM: Mixed

DAVID ERCOLINI
461 Sackett St. #2
Brooklyn, NY 11231
508-801-6878
davidercolini@gmail.com
www.davidercolini.com

P. 392
ART DIRECTOR:
Elizabeth Parisi
CLIENT: Scholastic
MEDIUM:
Pen & ink, digital

LEO ESPINOSA
11 Wright St.
Cambridge, MA 01238
617-441-7773
leo@studioespinosa.com
www.studioespinosa.com

P. 241
ART DIRECTOR:
Lucho Correa
CLIENT:
WOK Restaurant
MEDIUM: Digital

P. 317
Art Directors:
Matias Vigliano
Leo Espinosa
CLIENT: DOMA
MEDIUM:
Silkscreen, digital

P. 318
Art Directors:
Matias Vigliano
Leo Espinosa
CLIENT: DOMA
MEDIUM: Acrylic,
watercolor pencil on
masonite

P. 393
ART DIRECTOR:
Nobara Hayakawa
Jorge Restrepo
MEDIUM:
Digital, letterpress

SAMUEL FARINATO
5083 Warm Springs Rd.
Glen Ellen, CA 95442
707-696-3003
contact@farinatoart.com
www.farinatoart.com

P. 478
MEDIUM: Digital

JOSEPH FIEDLER
12632 Pinewoods Rd.
Nevada City, CA 95959
313-804-7047
fiedler@scaryjoey.com
www.scaryjoey.com

P. 102
ART DIRECTOR:
Michiko Toki
CLIENT:
California Magazine
MEDIUM:
Digital, sketches

PETER FIORE
1168 Delaware Dr.
Matamoras, PA 18336
570-491-2610
peter@peterfiore.com
www.peterfiore.com

P. 479
MEDIUM:
Oil on panel

JEFFREY FISHER
c/o Riley Illustration
PO Box 92
New Paltz, NY 12561
845-255-3309
teresa@rileyillustration.com
www.rileyillustration.com

SILVER
P. 214
CLIENT:
Festa Literaria Inter-
nacionale de Paraty
MEDIUM:
Acrylic on paper

P. 394
ART DIRECTOR:
Gavin Morris
CLIENT:
The Folio Society
MEDIUM:
Acrylic on paper

VIVIENNE FLESHER
630 Pennsylvania Ave.
San Francisco, CA 94107
415-648-3794
vivienne@warddraw.com
www.warddraw.com

P. 103
ART DIRECTOR:
Aviva Michaelov
CLIENT:
The New York Times
MEDIUM: Digital

P. 104
ART DIRECTOR:
Leanne Shapton
CLIENT:
The New York Times
MEDIUM: Digital

P. 319
ART DIRECTOR:
Leanne Shapton
CLIENT:
The New York Times
MEDIUM: Digital

BRENDON FLYNN
5004 Woodside Rd.
Fayetteville, NY 13066
215-870-7006
brendontflynn@yahoo.com
www.brendonflynn.net

P. 242
CLIENT:
Freya, Victory
Records
MEDIUM: Acrylic

BART J. FORBES
3017 Green Hill Dr.
Plano, TX 75093
972-306-9753
bart@bartforbes.com
www.bartforbes.com

P. 243
ART DIRECTOR:
Brian Boyd
CLIENT:
Plains Capital Bank
MEDIUM:
Oil on canvas

P. 244
ART DIRECTOR:
Hollis King
CLIENT:
Verve Music
MEDIUM:
Oil on canvas

P. 245
ART DIRECTOR:
Hollis King
CLIENT:
Verve Music
MEDIUM: Oil on
canvas

ANTHONY FREDA
515-6 Hight St.
Port Jefferson, NY 18210
631-828-4497
ambant@earthlink.net
www.anthonyfreda.com

P. 105
ART DIRECTOR:
Roanna Williams
CLIENT:
Migrate Magazine
MEDIUM:
Mixed on wood

SHANNON FRESHWATER
1653 Amberwood Dr. #23
South Pasadena, CA 91030
323-496-7311
sfreshwater1@gmail.com
www.shannonfreshwater.com

P. 395
ART DIRECTOR:
Keith Hayes
CLIENT: Little, Brown
and Company
MEDIUM: Watercolor,
cut paper, digital

JAMES FRYER
160 Lower Farnham Rd.
Aldershot GU12 4EL England
+44 (0)1252 6712377
james_fryer72@ntlworld.com

P. 108
ART DIRECTOR:
Chris Barber
CLIENT: Times Higher
Educational
MEDIUM: Acrylic

THOMAS FUCHS
320 W. 37th St. #9D
New York, NY 10018
212-904-1255
mail@thomasfuchs.com
www.thomasfuchs.com

P. 106
ART DIRECTOR:
Rodrigo Honeywell
CLIENT:
The Atlantic
MEDIUM: Digital

P. 107
ART DIRECTOR:
Riva Schwartz
CLIENT: Golf Digest
MEDIUM: Acrylic

P. 246
ART DIRECTOR:
Christian Schwarm
CLIENT: Dorten
MEDIUM: Sharpie

P. 247
ART DIRECTOR:
Christian Schwarm
CLIENT: Dorten
MEDIUM: Sharpie

P. 248
ART DIRECTOR:
Christian Schwarm
CLIENT: Dorten
MEDIUM: Sharpie

P. 533
ART DIRECTOR:
Christian Schwarm
CLIENT: Dorten
MEDIUM: Sharpie

CHRIS GALL
4421 N. Camino del Santo
Tucson, AZ 85718
520-299-4454
chris@chrisgall.com
www.chrisgall.com

P. 396
ART DIRECTOR:
Chris Thompson
MEDIUM: Mixed

P. 397
ART DIRECTOR:
Chris Thompson
MEDIUM: Mixed

BEPPE GIACOBBE
Via Filippo de Filippi 4
Milano 20129 Italy
+39258303031
bgiacobbe@me.com
www.beppegiacobbe.com

P. 109
CLIENT:
Corriere Della Sera

P. 320
CLIENT: Augusto
Bianchi
MEDIUM: Digital

CARLO GIAMBARRESI
Carrer Sant Paciá 11 4°·1°
Barcelona 08001 Spain
0034 697312663
beef_art@hotmail.com
www.beefart.carbonmade.com

P. 480
MEDIUM:
China ink, digital

DONATO GIANCOLA
397 Pacific St.
Brooklyn, NY 11217
718-797-2438
donato@donatoart.com
www.donatoart.com

P. 249
ART DIRECTOR:
Aaron Fagerstrom
MEDIUM:
Oil on panel

MICHAEL GIBBS
2344 N. Taylor St.
Arlington, VA 22207
703-502-3400
mike@michaelgibbs.com
www.michaelgibbs.com

P. 321
ART DIRECTOR:
Gary Callahan
CLIENT: Boston Con-
sulting Company
MEDIUM: Digital

MICHAEL GLENWOOD
2344 N. Taylor St.
Arlington, VA 22207
888-818-9811
michael@mglenwood.com
www.mglenwood.com

P. 112
ART DIRECTOR:
Scott Seymour
CLIENT: Chronicle of
Higher Education
MEDIUM: Digital

P. 322
ART DIRECTOR:
Lillian Iversen
CLIENT: National
Cherry Blossom
Festival
MEDIUM: Digital

PETER GOOD
3 North Main St., PO Box 570
Chester, CT 06412
860-526-9597
pg@cummings-good.com

P. 250
ART DIRECTOR:
Peter Good
CLIENT:
Dinners at the Farm
MEDIUM: Fabric,
thread (applique)

ALESSANDRO GOTTARDO
Corso Magenta 96
Milan 20123 Italy
+39 3357049862
conceptualillustration@gmail.com
www.alessandrogottardo.com

P. 110
ART DIRECTOR:
Annette Keller
CLIENT:
Internazionale
MEDIUM: Digital

P. 111
ART DIRECTOR:
Fernada Cohen
CLIENT: Terrorismo
Grafico
MEDIUM: Digitial

SILVER
P. 215
ART DIRECTOR:
Antonella Bandoli
CLIENT: Seac
MEDIUM: Digital

SILVER
P. 218
ART DIRECTOR:
Monique Gamache
CLIENT:
Victoria Symphony
MEDIUM: Digital

P. 323
ART DIRECTOR:
Monique Gamache
CLIENT:
Victoria Symphony
MEDIUM: Digital

SILVER
P. 375
ART DIRECTOR:
Riccardo Falcinelli
CLIENT: Minimum Fax
MEDIUM: Digital

P. 398
ART DIRECTOR:
Riccardo Falcinelli
CLIENT: Minimum Fax
MEDIUM: Digital

P. 534
ART DIRECTOR:
Giovanni de Mauro
CLIENT:
Internazionale
MEDIUM: Digital

DONNA GRETHEN
2312 Roosevelt Ave.
Berkeley, CA 94703
510-644-0596
dmgrethen@att.net
www.donnagrethen.com

P. 324
ART DIRECTOR:
Sung Hee Kim
CLIENT: Art Directors
Club of Metropolitan
Washington
MEDIUM: Ink drawings,
gouache, digital

**CHERYL GRIESBACH AND
STANLEY MARTUCCI**
34 Twinlight Ter.
Highlands, NJ 07732
732-291-5945
griesbachmartucci@earthlink.net
www.cherylgriesbach.com

P. 325
ART DIRECTOR:
Stanley Martucci
CLIENT:
Beacon Fine Arts
MEDIUM:
Oil on panel

CHAD GROHMAN
188 Heritage Rd.
Tonawanda, NY 14150
716-319-0555
contact@chadgrohman.com
www.chadgrohman.com

P. 481
MEDIUM: Digital

STEVEN GUARNACCIA
208 Lefferts Ave.
Brooklyn, NY 11225
973-342-2369
sguarnaccia@hotmail.com
www.stevenguarnaccia.com

P. 251
ART DIRECTOR:
Alain Lachartre
CLIENT:
Vue sur la Ville
MEDIUM:
Pen & ink, watercolor

P. 535
ART DIRECTOR:
Monte Beauchamp
CLIENT: BLAB!
MEDIUM:
Pen & ink, watercolor

REBECCA GUAY
45 Spaulding St.
Amherst, MA 01002
413-548-4097
rebeccaguay@yahoo.com
www.rebeccaguay.com

P. 482
MEDIUM: Mixed

EDDIE GUY
309 Racetrack Rd.
Ho-Ho-Kus, NJ 07423
201-251-7660
eddie.guy@verizon.net
www.eddieguyillustration.com

GOLD
P. 44
ART DIRECTOR:
Debra Bishop
CLIENT:
More Magazine
MEDIUM:
3D rendering

P. 113
ART DIRECTOR:
Joe Heroun
CLIENT:
The New Republic
MEDIUM:
Photo collage

P. 114
ART DIRECTOR:
Jana Meier-Roberts
CLIENT: GQ Germany
MEDIUM:
Photo collage

P. 115
ART DIRECTOR:
Debra Bishop
CLIENT:
More Magazine
MEDIUM:
3D rendering

ASAF HANUKA
8 Maharal St. #7
Tel Aviv 62481 Israel
972506709639
asafhanuka@gmail.com
www.asafhanuka.com

GOLD
P. 520
ART DIRECTOR:
Amir Ziv
CLIENT:
Calcalist weekend
edition (Israel)
MEDIUM: Ink, digital

TOMER HANUKA
156 2nd Ave. #5F
New York, NY 10003
917-749-6267
tomer@thanuka
www.thanuka.com

SILVER
P. 46
Art Directors:
Steven Charny
Joe Hutchinson
CLIENT: Rolling Stone
MEDIUM: Mixed

P. 252
ART DIRECTOR:
Mitch Putnam
CLIENT: The Alamo
Drafthouse Theater
MEDIUM: Mixed

Copyright © by Paramount Pictures

GREG HARLIN
Wood Ronsaville Harlin
17 Pinewood St.
Annapolis, MD 21401
410-266-6550
studio@wrh-illustration.com

P. 326
ART DIRECTOR:
Mark Johnson
CLIENT:
Saratoga National
Battlefield Park
MEDIUM: Watercolor

JESSIE HARTLAND
165 William St. 9th Fl.
New York, NY 10038
212-233-1413
jessiehartland@hotmail.com
www.jessiehartland.com

P. 399
ART DIRECTOR:
Eliot Kreloff
CLIENT:
Blue Apple Books
MEDIUM: Gouache

DAVID HENDERSON
21 James Rd.
Boonton Township, NJ 07005
973-402-1461
njartist@optonline.net

P. 483
MEDIUM: Oil on
gessoed board

JOHN HENDRIX
1145 Ursula Ave.
St. Louis, MO 63130
917-597-6310
mail@johnhendrix.com
www.johnhendrix.com

P. 400
ART DIRECTOR:
Chad Beckerman
CLIENT: Abrams
Books for Young
Readers
MEDIUM: Pen & ink,
acrylic washes

P. 401
ART DIRECTOR:
Chad Beckerman
CLIENT: Abrams
Books for Young
Readers
MEDIUM: Pen & ink,
acrylic washes

LESLIE HERMAN
14105 Waters Edge Cr.
Midlothian, VA 23112
804-690-2917
les@leslieherman.com
www.leslieherman.com

P. 253
CLIENT:
The Acme Thunderer
MEDIUM:
Ink, gouache

JODY HEWGILL
260 Brunswick Ave.
Toronto M5S 2M7 Ontario, Canada
416-924-4200
jody@jodyhewgill.com
www.jodyhewgill.com

P. 116
ART DIRECTOR:
Steve Charny
CLIENT: Rolling Stone
Magazine
MEDIUM: Acrylic,
graphite on gessoed
masonite

P. 117
ART DIRECTOR:
Steven Banks
CLIENT: Los Angeles
Magazine
MEDIUM: Acrylic on
gessoed board

P. 254
ART DIRECTOR:
Nicki Lindeman
CLIENT: Arena Stage
MEDIUM: Acrylic on
gessoed board

P. 327
ART DIRECTOR:
Diane Woolverton
CLIENT: Bureau of
International Informa-
tion Programs, U.S.
State Department

P. 484
MEDIUM: Acrylic on
gessoed board

JAKOB HINRICHS
Friedelstr. 40
Berlin 12047 Germany
+49 176 96 36 55 32
mail@jakobhinrichs.com
www.jakobhinrichs.com

P. 536
ART DIRECTOR:
Jens Ehrenreich
CLIENT: DB Mobil,
Deutsche Bahn,
German Railways
MEDIUM:
Digital, woodprint

JESSICA HISCHE
c/o Frank Sturges
142 W. Winter St.
Delaware, OH 43015
740-369-9702
frank@sturgesreps.com
www.sturgesreps.com

P. 328
CLIENT:
Beautiful/Decay
MEDIUM: Digital

JEREMY HOLMES
616 Roberts Ave.
Glenside, PA 19038
215-450-0886
jholmes@muttink.com

P. 122
ART DIRECTOR:
Scott Davies
CLIENT: AARP
MEDIUM: Digital

P. 255
ART DIRECTOR:
Jason Roberson
CLIENT: Sierra Nevada
Brewing Company
MEDIUM: Pencil,
collage, digital

P. 402
ART DIRECTOR:
Josh Dennis
CLIENT:
Crossway Publishing
MEDIUM: Pencil,
collage, digital

HADLEY HOOPER
2111 W. 31st Ave.
Denver, CO 80211
303-2096-5583
hadleyhooper@earthlink.net
www.hadleyhooper.com

P. 256
ART DIRECTOR:
Jeff Savage
CLIENT: Tulsa Opera
MEDIUM: Water
media, toner, digital

P. 485
MEDIUM:
Water media, toner
on paper

PAUL HOPPE
212 Monitor St.
Brooklyn, NY 11222
917-774-5455
info@paulhoppe.com
www.paulhoppe.com

P. 257
CLIENT: Rabid Rabbit
MEDIUM: Ink, digital

STERLING HUNDLEY
14361 Old Bond St.
Chesterfield, VA 23832
804-306-9536
sterling@sterlinghundley.com
www.sterlinghundley.com

P. 118
ART DIRECTOR:
Tyler Darden
CLIENT: Virginia
Living Magazine
MEDIUM: Mixed

P. 119
ART DIRECTOR:
Sonda Pappan
CLIENT: Virginia
Living Magazine
MEDIUM: Mixed

P. 120
ART DIRECTOR:
Tyler Darden
CLIENT: Virginia
Living Magazine
MEDIUM: Mixed

P. 121
ART DIRECTOR:
Tyler Darden
CLIENT: Virginia
Living Magazine
MEDIUM: Mixed

ROBERT HUNT
107 Crescent Road
San Anselmo, CA 94960
415-459-6882
r@roberthuntstudio.com
www.roberthuntstudio.com

P. 123
Art Directors:
Christine Car
Joe Heroun
CLIENT:
The New Republic
MEDIUM: Oil

ROD HUNT
Rod Hunt Ltd
36 Combedale Rd.
London SE10 0LG England
+44 (0)7931 588 750
rod@rodhunt.com
www.rodhunt.com

P. 403
ART DIRECTOR:
Michael Saul
CLIENT:
Random House
MEDIUM: Digital

IC4DESIGN
1-5 Takayama Building #3F
Komachi, Naka-Ku
Hiroshima 7300041 Japan
+81(0)82-243-1999
info@ic4design.com
www.ic4design.com

P. 258
Art Directors:
Pierpaolo Marconcini
Giordano Curreri
CLIENT: ANCMA
MEDIUM: Press

NICK ILUZADA
1 Matthew Ct.
Randolph, NJ 07869
817-602-7632
nickdraws@gmail.com

SILVER

P. 450
MEDIUM:
Graphite, ink, digital

P. 486
MEDIUM: Graphite,
ink, digital

JOEL ISKOWITZ
297 Ohayo Mountain Rd.
Woodstock, NY 12498
845-679-6742
iskart@hvc.rr.com

P. 329
ART DIRECTOR:
Mark Schlepphorst
CLIENT:
Signature Art Medals
MEDIUM: Color pencil,
aquarelle

HIROMICHI ITO
Pen Still Writes
3-6-8 3rd Floor Takaban
Meguro-Ku, Tokyo 152-0004 Japan
81-3-3710-5634
hello@hiromichiito.com
www.hiromichiito.com

P. 404
ART DIRECTOR:
Kenichi Sato
CLIENT: Pelican
MEDIUM: Digital

TARA JACOBY
751 Manhattan Ave. #3R
Brooklyn, NY 11222
609-805-2050
tarajacoby@gmail.com
www.tarajacoby.com

P. 487
MEDIUM:
Gouache, digital

TOM JELLETT
64 Heighway Ave.
Croydon 2132 Sydney, Australia
61-2-9798-4909
mrtom@bigpond.com

P. 126
ART DIRECTOR:
Chris Topp
CLIENT: News Limited
MEDIUM: Ink, digital

ERIK T JOHNSON
PO Box 582061
Minneapolis, MN 55458-2061
612-743-1989
erik@eriktjohnson.us
www.eriktjohnson.us

P. 537
ART DIRECTOR:
Erik Johnson
MEDIUM: Brush, ink,
digital coloring

VICTOR JUHASZ
515 Horse Heaven Rd.
Averill Park, NY 12018
518-794-0881
juhaszillustration@gmail.com
www.juhaszillustration.com

P. 124
ART DIRECTOR:
Damian Wilkinson
CLIENT: Men's Journal
MEDIUM: Pen, ink,
watercolor

P. 125
ART DIRECTOR:
Damian Wilkinson
CLIENT: Men's Journal
MEDIUM: Pencil,
watercolor

GWENDA KACZOR
4309 Yates St.
Denver, CO 80212
303-477-3484
gkaczor@gwenda.com
www.gwenda.com

P. 259
ART DIRECTOR:
Deborah Brown
CLIENT:
Big Island Bees
MEDIUM: Digital

KAKO
Rua Augusta 66 apo9 Consolacao
São Paulo 01304000 Brazil
55 11 2158 0965
kako@kakofonia.com
www.kakofonia.com

P. 127
ART DIRECTOR:
Rob Wilson
CLIENT: Playboy
MEDIUM: Digital

P. 538
ART DIRECTOR:
Sidney Gusman
CLIENT: Mauricio de
Souza Produções
MEDIUM: Digital

LEW KEILAR
Studio 51 61 Marlborough St.
Surry Hills, NSW 2038 Australia
+61 409042174
lewkeilar@iinet.net.au

P. 488
MEDIUM: Ink, digital

EDWARD KINSELLA
2036 Park Ave. #B
Richmond, VA 23220
314-583-6481
info@edwardkinsellaillustration.com
www.edwardkinsellaillustration.com

P. 128
ART DIRECTOR:
Joannah Ralston
CLIENT: The Milken
Institute Review

P. 129
ART DIRECTOR:
Joannah Ralston
CLIENT: The Milken
Institute Review
MEDIUM:
Ink, gouache

PAT KINSELLA
573 Lafayette Ave. #3
Brooklyn, NY 11205
484-947-3117
ptkinsella@gmail.com

P. 406
ART DIRECTOR:
Nathan Gassman
CLIENT: Capstone
Publishers
MEDIUM:
Ink, mylar, digital

TATSURO KIUCHI
Pen Still Writes
3-6-8 3rd Floor Takaban
Meguro-ku, Tokyo 152-0004 Japan
81-3-3710-5634
info@tatsurokiuchi.com
www.tatsurokiuchi.com

GOLD
P. 210
CLIENT:
Society of Illustrators
MEDIUM: Digital

P. 407
CLIENT:
Bookwall/Shueisha
MEDIUM: Digital

JON KRAUSE
2924 Disston St.
Philadelphia, PA 19149
215-338-1531
jk@jonkrause.com
www.jonkrause.com

P. 130
ART DIRECTOR:
Jason Treat
CLIENT:
The Atlantic
MEDIUM:
Acrylic on pine

P. 131
ART DIRECTOR:
Cecelia Wong
CLIENT: TIME Asia
MEDIUM:
Acrylic on wood

P. 132
ART DIRECTOR:
Jason Treat
CLIENT:
The Atlantic
MEDIUM:
Acrylic on paper

P. 133
ART DIRECTOR:
Jason Treat
CLIENT:
The Atlantic
MEDIUM: Acrylic on
masonite

NORA KRUG
c/o Riley Illustration
PO Box 92
New Paltz, NY 12561
845-255-3309
teresa@rileyillustration.com
www.rileyillustration.com

P. 134
ART DIRECTOR:
Larry Gendron
CLIENT:
The Deal Magazine
MEDIUM:
Pencil, digital

GOLD
P. 522
CLIENT:
Spring Magazine
MEDIUM:
Pencil, digital

P. 539
ART DIRECTOR:
Ria Schulpen
CLIENT: Bries Editions
MEDIUM: Pen, digital

CAITLIN KUHWALD
2126 Encinal Ave. #A
Alameda, CA 94501
510-547-1135
caitlin@caitlinkuhwald.com
www.caitlinkuhwald.com

P. 135
ART DIRECTOR:
Stephanie Glaros
CLIENT:
Utne Magazine
MEDIUM: Ink, digital

ANITA KUNZ
218 Ontario St.
Toronto M5A 2V5 Ontario, Canada
416-364-3846
akunz@anitakunz.com

P. 136
ART DIRECTOR:
Carolyn Perot
CLIENT: Mother Jones
MEDIUM: Acrylic

P. 137
ART DIRECTOR:
Steve Charny
CLIENT: Rolling Stone
MEDIUM: Acrylic

P. 260
ART DIRECTOR:
Thomas Knopf
CLIENT:
Ogilvy Frankfurt
MEDIUM: Acrylic

P. 489
MEDIUM: Acrylic

PETER KUPER
235 West 102nd St. #11J
New York, NY 10025
646-875-9360
pkuperart@gmail.com
SILVER
P. 376
ART DIRECTOR:
Michelle Ishay-Cohen
CLIENT: Abrams
MEDIUM: Colored
pencil, watercolors

P. 540
ART DIRECTOR:
Nicholas Blechman
CLIENT: The New York
Times Book Review
MEDIUM: Pen & ink
on scratchboard,
digital coloring

TRAVIS LAMPE
225 S. Catherine Ave.
Lagrange, IL 60525
312-735-2077
travislampe@yahoo.com

P. 261
CLIENT: Jason Kupfer
MEDIUM: Acrylic

ROBBIE LAWRENCE
1621 Chapman Ct.
Aledo, TX 76008
817-368-5003
robbiedraws@gmail.com
http://www.robbiedraws.com

P. 490
MEDIUM:
Graphite, digital

ZOHAR LAZAR
c/o Riley Illustration
PO Box 92
New Paltz, NY 12561
845-255-3309
teresa@rileyillustration.com
www.rileyillustration.com

P. 138
ART DIRECTOR:
John Dixon
CLIENT:
The Village Voice
MEDIUM: Ink, digital

P. 139
ART DIRECTOR:
Anton Ioukhnovets
CLIENT: GQ Magazine
MEDIUM: Gouache

BRENDAN LEACH
91 Jewel St. #2L
Brooklyn, NY 11222
732-921-8975
brendan@iknowashortcut.com
www.iknowashortcut.com

P. 330
CLIENT: SVA Annual
Report 2010
MEDIUM: Ink wash
on paper

PATRICK LEGER
410 Guilford Ave. #2
Greensboro, NC 27401
336-510-8731
patricklegerart@hotmail.com

P. 408
ART DIRECTOR:
Gavin Morris
MEDIUM: Ink, digital

P. 409
ART DIRECTOR:
Gavin Morris
MEDIUM: Ink, digital

PIOTR LESNIAK

P. 140
ART DIRECTOR:
David Harris
CLIENT: Vanity Fair
MEDIUM: Mixed

MARK LEWIS
165 Hudson St.
Denver, CO 80220
303-377-4413
marklewisdesign.co@gmail.com

P. 262
ART DIRECTOR:
Mark Lewis
CLIENT: Pragmatic
Management
MEDIUM: Digital

MICAH LIDBERG

P. 141
ART DIRECTOR:
Chris Malec
CLIENT: TIME
MEDIUM: Digital

FRANK LIN
705 Midcrest Way
El Cerrito, CA 94530
510-326-8127
contact@ftongl.com
www.ftongl.com

P. 491
MEDIUM: Digital

MARIA EUGENIA LONGO
rua tucuma 141ap208
São Paulo 01455010 Brazil
55 11 30320755
maria@mariaeugenia.com
www.mariaeugeniaillustration.com

P. 331
ART DIRECTOR: Tece
Leopoldo E Silva
CLIENT:
Teca Paper Products
MEDIUM: Watercolor

JASON LYNCH
216 Dean St.
Brooklyn, NY 11217
646-250-4837
jason@jasonlynch.org
www.jasonlynch.org

P. 332
Art Directors:
Deroy Peraza
Julia Vakser
CLIENT: Hyperakt
Design Group
MEDIUM: 2-color
silkscreen

ROSS MACDONALD
56 Castle Meadow Rd.
Newtown, CT 06470
203-270-6438
brightwork@earthlink.net

P. 372
ART DIRECTOR:
David Cashion
CLIENT:
Abrams Images
MEDIUM: Watercolor

P. 410
ART DIRECTOR:
David Cashion
CLIENT:
Abrams Images
MEDIUM: Watercolor

P. 411
ART DIRECTOR:
David Cashion
CLIENT:
Abrams Images
MEDIUM: Watercolor

P. 412
ART DIRECTOR:
David Cashion
CLIENT:
Abrams Images
MEDIUM: Watercolor

MATT MAHURIN
20 Makamah Beach Rd.
Northport, NY 11768
631-754-2068
mattmahurin@earthlink.net

P. 142
ART DIRECTOR:
Dan Revitte
CLIENT:
The Boston Globe
MEDIUM: Oil

P. 143
ART DIRECTOR:
Joe Ferrara
CLIENT: Rolling Stone
Australia
MEDIUM: Digital

KAM MAK
1735 N. Lynn St.
Arlington, VA 22209
703-292-3815
info@photoassist.com

P. 333
ART DIRECTOR:
Ethel Kessler
CLIENT:
U.S. Postal Service
MEDIUM: Oil on
fiberboard

NIMIT MALAVIA
30 Chartwell Ave.
Ottawa K2G 6L6 Ontario, Canada
905-483-1631
nimit@nimitmalavia.com
www.nimitmalavia.com

P. 451
MEDIUM:
Mixed, digital

P. 492
MEDIUM:
Mixed, digital

GREGORY MANCHESS
15235 S.W. Teal Blvd. #D
Beaverton, OR 97007
503-590-5447
manchess@mac.com

P. 334
CLIENT: Concept Art
MEDIUM: Oil on linen

P. 335
ART DIRECTOR:
Maritta Tapanainen
CLIENT: Rand
MEDIUM: Oil on linen

JOSÉE MASSE
387, Évangéline
Saint-Jean-sur-Richelieu J2Y 1C7
Quebec, Canada
514-937-2363
joseemasse@videotron.ca

P. 263
CLIENT: Communica-
tion-Jeunesse
MEDIUM: Acrylic on
Strathmore Bristol
paper, digital

P. 413
ART DIRECTOR:
Sara Reynolds
CLIENT: Dutton
Children's Books
MEDIUM:
Acrylic on Strathmore
Bristol paper

P. 414
ART DIRECTOR:
Sara Reynolds
CLIENT: Dutton
Children's Books
MEDIUM:
Acrylic on Strathmore
Bristol paper

BILL MAYER
240 Forkner Dr.
Decatur, GA 30030
404-378-0686
bill@thebillmayer.com
www.thebillmayer.com

P. 144
ART DIRECTOR:
SooJin Buzelli
CLIENT: Plansponsor
MEDIUM:
Airbrush, digital

P. 264
ART DIRECTOR:
Joe Pompeo
CLIENT:
Saatchi & Saatchi
MEDIUM:
Airbrush, digital

P. 336
ART DIRECTOR:
Jim Burke
CLIENT:
Dellas Graphics
MEDIUM: Airbrush,
gouache, digital

P. 337
ART DIRECTOR:
Jim Burke
CLIENT: Dellas
Graphics
MEDIUM: Ink,
gouache, digital

P. 493
MEDIUM: Gouache
on cardboard

MARION MCCALLY
PO Box 3007
South Pasadena, CA 91031
310-519-7559
marionmccally@yahoo.com

P. 494
MEDIUM: Oil

ADAM MCCAULEY
1081 Treat Ave.
San Francisco, CA 94110
415-826-5668
adam@adammcauley.com
www.adammcauley.com

P. 145
ART DIRECTOR:
Alex Knowlton
CLIENT:
Poetry Magazine
MEDIUM:
Pen & ink, digital

P. 265
MEDIUM: Digital

P. 266
ART DIRECTOR:
Lori Lachmann
CLIENT:
Alpine Green Living
MEDIUM: Digital

P. 415
ART DIRECTOR:
Ellice Lee
CLIENT: Random
House
MEDIUM: Digital

P. 541
ART DIRECTOR:
Manuel Velez
CLIENT: The Wall
Street Journal
MEDIUM: Digital

GRADY MCFERRIN
280 Ocean Pkwy. #5T
Brooklyn, NY 11218
917-495-7268
grady@gmillustration.com
www.gmillustration.com

P. 416
ART DIRECTOR:
Michael McCartney
CLIENT:
Simon & Schuster
MEDIUM: Digital

MARK MCGINNIS
165 Court St. #155
Brooklyn, NY 11201
773-368-4045
mistermcginnis@gmail.com

P. 146
ART DIRECTOR:
Catherine Halley
CLIENT:
Poetry Foundation
MEDIUM: Conte, ink,
digital

SCOTT MCKOWEN
428 Downie St.
Stratford N54 1X7 Ontario, Canada
519-271-3049
mckowen@sympatico.ca

P. 267
CLIENT:
Punch & Judy
MEDIUM:
Scratchboard

P. 268
CLIENT: Margot
Harley
MEDIUM:
Scratchboard

P. 417
ART DIRECTOR:
Jeffrey C. Batzli
CLIENT:
Sterling Publishing
MEDIUM:
Scratchboard

WILSON MCLEAN

P. 147
ART DIRECTOR:
Stefan Kiefer
CLIENT:
Der Spiegel for Kids
MEDIUM: Oil

NICHOLAS MCNALLY
44 Riverview St.
Springfield, MA 01108
413-313-1527
ntmcnally@gmail.com

P. 495
MEDIUM: Acrylic

LUC MELANSON
71, Avenue Parissi
Laval H7N 3S4 Quebec, Canada
450-975-7836
luc@lucmelanson.com
www.lucmelanson.com

P. 542
MEDIUM:
Pencil on vellum

RENÉ MILOT
49 Thorncliffe Pk. Dr. #1604
Toronto M4H 1J6 Ontario, Canada
416-425-7726
renemilot@renemilot.com
www.renemilot.com

P. 269
ART DIRECTOR:
Kristi Flango
CLIENT:
Secret Sherry Project
MEDIUM: Digital

TONY MONTAÑO
1001 W. Verbena Dr.
Meridian, ID 83642
208-631-0036
tony@tmontano.com
www.tmontano.com

P. 496
MEDIUM: Digital

GONI MONTES
125-3 Northern Ave.
Decatur, GA 30030
678-860-6934
goni@goniart.com
www.goniart.com

P. 148
ART DIRECTOR:
John Dixon
CLIENT:
The Village Voice
MEDIUM:
Watercolor, digital

CHRIS B. MURRAY
156 Roxborough Ave.
Philadelphia, PA 19127
215-756-3226
contact@chrisbmurray.com
www.chrisbmurray.com

P. 497
MEDIUM: Acrylic

ALEX NABAUM
795 Shadow Rock Ct.
Heber City, UT 84032
alex@alexnabaum.com
www.alexnabaum.com

P. 149
ART DIRECTOR:
Grant Staublin
CLIENT:
The Boston Globe
MEDIUM: Gouache

CHRIS SILAS NEAL
61 Greenpoint Ave. #410
Brooklyn, NY 11222
917-538-3884
chris@redsilas.com
www.redsilas.com

P. 270
CLIENT: Wildbirds and
Peacedrums
MEDIUM: 2-color
screen print

P. 271
CLIENT:
Shout Out Louds
MEDIUM: 2-color
screen print

P. 418
ART DIRECTOR:
Julia Connolly
CLIENT: Penguin UK
MEDIUM: Mixed

BILL NELSON
111 Algonkian Dr., PO Box 579
Manteo, NC 27954
252-473-6181
nelson_studios@hotmail.com

P. 150
ART DIRECTOR:
Bill Nelson
MEDIUM: Mixed

KADIR NELSON
6977 Navajo Rd. #124
San Diego, CA 92119
knelson@kadirnelson.com
www.kadirnelson.com
GOLD

P. 212
ART DIRECTOR:
Howard Paine
CLIENT:
U.S. Postal Service
MEDIUM:
Oil on wood

P. 272
ART DIRECTOR:
Reggie Know
CLIENT: AD-ITIVE
MEDIUM: Oil

P. 419
ART DIRECTOR:
Lizzy Bromley
CLIENT:
Simon & Schuster
MEDIUM: Oil, fabric

P. 420
ART DIRECTOR:
Lizzy Bromley
CLIENT:
Simon & Schuster
MEDIUM: Oil, fabric

P. 421
ART DIRECTOR:
Lizzy Bromley
CLIENT:
Simon & Schuster
MEDIUM: Oil, fabric

ROBERT NEUBECKER
2432 Iron Mountain Rd.
Park City, UT 84060-6559
435-729-0049
robert@neubecker.com
www.neubecker.com

P. 151
ART DIRECTOR:
Payl D. Gonzales
CLIENT: LA Times
MEDIUM: Ink, digital

VICTO NGAI
1623 81st St. #2F
Brooklyn, NY 11214
401-808-2506
victo@victo-ngai.com
www.victo-ngai.com

P. 152
ART DIRECTOR:
SooJin Buzelli
CLIENT: aiCIO
MEDIUM: Mixed

CLIFF NIELSEN
674 South Ave. 21
Los Angeles, CA 90031
323-223-4100
cliffnielsen@earthlink.net

P. 273
ART DIRECTOR:
Eric Panke
CLIENT:
Sparta Insurance
MEDIUM: Digital

CHRISTOPHER NIELSEN
Studio 51/61 Marlborough St.
Surry Hills 2010 Sydney, Australia
+61 412-563-024
chris@christophernielsenillustration.com
www.christophernielsenillustration.com

P. 338
MEDIUM: Acrylic

TAO NYEU

P. 422
ART DIRECTOR:
Jennifer Kelly
CLIENT: Dial Books
for Young Readers
MEDIUM: Cotton
thread on muslin

TIM O'BRIEN
310 Marlborough Rd.
Brooklyn, NY 11226
718-282-2821
tonka1964@aol.com
www.obrienillustration.com
SILVER

P. 47
ART DIRECTOR:
Stefan Kiefer
CLIENT: Der Spiegel
MEDIUM: Oil, mixed

P. 153
ART DIRECTOR:
D.W. Pine
CLIENT: TIME
MEDIUM:
Oil on panel

P. 154
ART DIRECTOR:
Kory Kennedy
CLIENT:
Runner's World
MEDIUM: Oil, mixed

P. 155
ART DIRECTOR:
Steve Charny
CLIENT: Rolling Stone
MEDIUM:
Oil on board

P. 339
ART DIRECTOR:
Nicky Lindeman
CLIENT: Arena Stage
MEDIUM: Oil, mixed

P. 423
ART DIRECTOR:
Anthony Ramondo
CLIENT: Penguin
MEDIUM:
Oil on board

P. 498
MEDIUM: Mixed

P. 499
MEDIUM: Oil, mixed

RAFAL OLBINSKI
212-532-4328
olbinskiart@yahoo.com

SILVER
P. 216
CLIENT: Allegro
MEDIUM: Acrylic, oil

P. 274
ART DIRECTOR:
CLIENT: Allegro
MEDIUM: Acrylic, oil

P. 340
ART DIRECTOR:
CLIENT: Patinae,
MEDIUM: Acrylic, oil

YUTA ONODA
407 Drewry Ave.
North York M2R 2K3 Ontario, Canada
905-467-8101
yuta@yutaonoda.com
www.yutaonoda.com

P. 156
ART DIRECTOR:
Peter Herbert
CLIENT:
Popular Mechanics
MEDIUM:
Mixed, digital

P. 157
ART DIRECTOR:
Jennifer Nosek
CLIENT: Modern
Dog Magazine
MEDIUM:
Mixed, digital

KEN ORVIDAS
16724 NE 138th Ct.
Woodinville, WA 98072
425-867-3072
ken@orvidas.com
www.orvidas.com

P. 158
ART DIRECTOR:
Peter Morance
CLIENT: The New York
Times Science Times
MEDIUM: Pencil,
acrylic, digital

MICHAEL OSBORNE
Michael Osborne Design
444 De Haro St. #207
San Francisco, CA 94107
415-255-0125
info@modsf.com
www.modsf.com

P. 275

RYAN PANCOAST
184 Brookside Pkwy.
Medford, MA 02155
203-513-1025
ryanpancoast@gmail.com

P. 424
ART DIRECTOR:
David Palumbo
CLIENT:
Night Shade Books
MEDIUM: Oil on canvas, digital color

HYEJEONG PARK
3278 35th St. #B1
Astoria, NY 11106
347-846-9247
hyegallery@hotmail.com

P. 341
ART DIRECTOR:
Ki Tae Ryu
CLIENT: KT&G
MEDIUM:
Acrylic on board

P. 425
ART DIRECTOR:
Seung Hee Lee
CLIENT:
Viche Publishers
MEDIUM: Digital

GUY PARKHOMENKO
115 N. 1st St. #206
Richmond, VA 23219
202-657-7423
guy@guyparkhomenko.com
www.guyparkhomenko.com

P. 500
MEDIUM: Ink, acrylic

LEIF PARSONS
223 Monitor St.
Brooklyn, NY 11222
718-349-0302
leif@leifparsons.com
www.leifparsons.com

P. 543
MEDIUM: Drawing
printed on newsprint

C.F. PAYNE
3600 Sherbrooke Dr.
Cincinnati, OH 45241
513-769-1172
cfoxpayne@yahoo.com

P. 426
ART DIRECTOR:
Anne Twomey
CLIENT: Grand Central
Publishing

PHILIPPE PETIT-ROULET
c/o Riley Illustration
PO Box 92
New Paltz, NY 12561
845-255-3309
teresa@rileyillustration.com
www.rileyillustration.com

GOLD
P. 524
ART DIRECTOR:
Alain Beaulet
CLIENT:
Alain Beaulet Éditeur
MEDIUM: Pen & ink

P. 544
ART DIRECTOR:
Katie Long
CLIENT:
The New Yorker
MEDIUM: Pencil, ink,
digital grey tones

P. 545
Illustrations Editor:
Christine Curry
CLIENT:
The New Yorker
MEDIUM: Pencil, ink,
digital grey tones

CRAIG PHILLIPS
3 Young St.
Coledale 2515 NSW Australia
61242684930
phillips@spin.net.au

P. 427
ART DIRECTOR:
Liz Casal
CLIENT:
Hachette Books
MEDIUM: Ink, brush,
digital

JEFFREY PIKE
6145 McPherson Ave.
St. Louis, MO 63112
314 5172939
jpike@wustl.edu

P. 428
CLIENT: Virginia Arts
of the Book Center
MEDIUM: Micron pen,
watercolor

DAVID PLUNKERT
3504 Ash St.
Baltimore, MD 21211
410-235-7803
info@spurdesign.com
www.spurdesign.com

P. 159
CLIENT:
The New York Times
MEDIUM:
Digital, mixed

P. 276
ART DIRECTOR:
David Plunkert
CLIENT: Film Shack
MEDIUM:
Digital, mixed

P. 277
ART DIRECTOR:
David Plunkert
CLIENT:
AIGA Baltimore
MEDIUM:
Digital, mixed

P. 278
ART DIRECTOR:
David Plunkert
CLIENT: The New York
Times Gallery 7
MEDIUM:
Digital collage

P. 279
ART DIRECTOR:
David Plunkert
CLIENT:
Maryland Institute
College of Art
MEDIUM:
Digital, mixed

EMILIANO PONZI
c/o Magnet Reps
1783 S. Crescent Heights Blvd.
Los Angeles, CA 90035
866-390-5656
cora@magnetreps.com
www.magnetreps.com

P. 160
ART DIRECTOR:
Aviva Michaelov
CLIENT:
The New York Times
MEDIUM: Digital

P. 161
ART DIRECTOR:
Nicholas Blechman
CLIENT:
The New York Times
MEDIUM: Digital

P. 162
ART DIRECTOR:
Angelo Rinaldi
CLIENT: La Repubblica
MEDIUM: Digital

P. 163
ART DIRECTOR:
Angelo Rinaldi
CLIENT: La Repubblica
MEDIUM: Digital

P. 164
ART DIRECTOR:
Pam Fogg
CLIENT: Middlebury
Magazine
MEDIUM: Digital

GEORGE PRATT
2515 Loma Linda St.
Sarasota, FL 34239
941 266 0427
gpratt1@ix.netcom.com

P. 501
MEDIUM:
Oil on panel

ANDY RASH
145 Diamond St.
Brooklyn, NY 11222
718-486-7820
mail@rashworks.com
http://www.rashworks.com

P. 502
CLIENT:
The Rashworks
MEDIUM: Digital

P. 546
ART DIRECTOR:
Suzanne LaGasa
CLIENT:
Chronicle Books
MEDIUM: Gouache

OMAR RAYYAN
PO Box 958
West Tisbury, MA 02575
508-693-909
omar@studiorayyan.com
www.studiorayyan.com

P. 503
MEDIUM:
Watercolor

BRIAN REA
4311 1/2 Kingswell Ave.
Los Angeles, CA 90027
646-408-5539
brianarea@gmail.com
brian-rea.org

P. 342
ART DIRECTOR:
Chris Malek
CLIENT:
Proto Magazine
MEDIUM: Pen, pencil,
ink, digital

SILVER
P. 526
ART DIRECTOR:
Corinne Myller
CLIENT:
The New York Times
MEDIUM: Pencil, ink,
pen, digital

RED NOSE STUDIO
c/o Magnet Reps
1783 S. Crescent Heights Blvd.
Los Angeles, CA 90035
866-390-5656
cora@magnetreps.com
www.magnetreps.com

P. 165
ART DIRECTOR:
Tanja Pohl
CLIENT: Angie's List
MEDIUM: 3D

P. 166
ART DIRECTOR:
Brigid McCarren
CLIENT:
HOW Magazine
MEDIUM: 3D

JON REINFURT
268 South Barret Ave.
Audubon, NJ 08106
973-271-9608
jon@reinfurt.com
www.reinfurt.com

P. 343
ART DIRECTOR:
Tripp Underwood
CLIENT: Children's
Hospital Boston
MEDIUM: Mixed

P. 344
ART DIRECTOR:
Beth Lower
CLIENT: Associations
of Now Magazine
MEDIUM: Mixed

**ANTOINE REVOY AND
KELLY MURPHY**
75 Willow St.
Providence, RI 02909
508-215-6219
antoine@revoy.net
www.revoy.net

P. 429
ART DIRECTOR:
Kelly Murphy
CLIENT: Christy
Ottaviano Books
MEDIUM: Crow quill
drawing, ink wash
painting

CLAY RODERY
183 31st St. #2
Brooklyn, NY 11232
281-615-8169
clay@clayrodery.com
www.clayrodery.com

SILVER
P. 48
ART DIRECTOR:
Rob Wilson
CLIENT: Playboy
MEDIUM: Charcoal,
pastel, digital

SATTU RODRIGUES
Rua Tornoplex, 182- Jardim Leonor
Cotia 06700-245 São Paulo, Brazil
4703-0300
sattu.rodrigues@gmail.com

P. 280
CLIENT:
Moma Propaganda

EDEL RODRIGUEZ
16 Ridgewood Ave.
PO Box 102
Mt. Tabor, NJ 07878
973-983-7776
edelrodgiguez@aol.com

P. 167
ART DIRECTOR:
Nicholas Blechman
CLIENT: The New York
Times Book Review
MEDIUM: Mixed

P. 168
ART DIRECTOR:
DJ Stout
CLIENT: Pentagram
MEDIUM: Mixed

P. 169
ART DIRECTOR:
Jordan Awan
CLIENT:
The New Yorker
MEDIUM:
Pastel on paper

P. 281
ART DIRECTOR:
Leo Burnett Agency
CLIENT:
World Wildlife Fund
MEDIUM: Mixed

P. 504
MEDIUM: Acrylic on
canvas

P. 505
MEDIUM:
Coffee on paper

P. 547
ART DIRECTOR:
John Gall
CLIENT:
Random House
MEDIUM:
Acrylic on paper

P. 548
ART DIRECTOR:
Leah Purcel
CLIENT: Newsweek
MEDIUM: Mixed

ROBERT RODRIGUEZ
1735 N. Lynn St.
Arlington, VA 22209
703-292-3815
info@photoassist.com

P. 345
ART DIRECTOR:
Carl T. Herman
CLIENT:
U.S. Postal Service

JUNGYEON ROH
165 E. 89th St. #2C
New York, NY 10128
646-896-4600
jungyeon@jungyeonroh.com
www.jungyeonroh.com

P. 430
ART DIRECTOR:
Marshall Arisman
CLIENT: School of
Visual Arts
MEDIUM: Silkscreen

KIM ROSEN
7 Kary St.
Northampton, MA 01060
845-591-0682
kim@kimrosen.com
www.kimrosen.com

P. 506
MEDIUM: Pastels,
acrylic, digital

MATT ROTA
173 Nostrand Ave.
Brooklyn, NY 11205
410-493-0521
rotamatt@hotmail.com

SILVER
P. 527
ART DIRECTOR:
Joan Brooker
CLIENT:
Midtown Films
MEDIUM:
Ink, watercolor

GRAHAM ROUMIEAU

P. 549
ART DIRECTOR:
Cinders McLeod
CLIENT:
The Globe and Mail
MEDIUM: Mixed

JOHN RUSH
123 Kedzie St. #3E
Evanston, IL 60202
847-869-2078
jd-rush@sbcglobal.net
johnrushillustration.com

P. 285
ART DIRECTOR:
Pat McCaskey
CLIENT: Chicago
Bears Football Club
MEDIUM:
Oil on canvas

PETE RYAN
521 Queen St. W
Toronto N4Z 1G1 Canada
519-393-6796
posixpete@gmail.com

P. 170
ART DIRECTOR:
Ryan Olbrysh
CLIENT:
Las Vegas Weekly
MEDIUM: Acrylic

PHYLLIS SAROFF
503 Tayman Dr.
Annapolis, MD 21403
410-268-1691
phyllis@saroffillustration.com
www.saroffillustration.com

P. 507
MEDIUM: Mixed

KUNIO SATO
3-1-16 Tenma Kita-ku
Osaka 530-0043 Japan
06-6345-9292
info@kunio.biz

P. 346
ART DIRECTOR:
Juriko Kawabata
CLIENT:
Kunio Co., Ltd.

GUIDO SCARABOTTOLO
Via Custodi 16
Milano 20136 Italy
+39-025-810-2263
guido@scarabottolo.com
www.scarabottolo.com
P. 431
CLIENT:
Guanda Publishing
MEDIUM:
Pencil, digital

JASON SEILER
920 W. Wilson
Chicago, IL 60640
773-454-9687
jseiler@jpusa.org

P. 171
ART DIRECTOR:
Pam Shavalier
CLIENT: Miami
New Times
MEDIUM: Digital

KOREN SHADMI
259 Ainslie St. #3R
Brooklyn, NY 11211
917-750-4169
korenshadmi@yahoo.com

P. 172
ART DIRECTOR:
Nick Jehlen
CLIENT:
The Progressive
MEDIUM: Watercolor,
ink, digital

GOLD

P. 446
MEDIUM: Watercolor,
ink, digital

WHITNEY SHERMAN
5101 Whiteford Ave.
Baltimore, MD 21212
410-435-2095
ws@whitneysherman.com
www.whitneysherman.com

P. 347
ART DIRECTOR:
Joannah Ralston
CLIENT: Templeton
Foundation
MEDIUM: Digital

YUKO SHIMIZU
225 W. 36th St. #502
New York, NY 10018
212-760-1171
yuko@yukoart.com
www.yukoart.com

P. 173
ART DIRECTOR:
Rob Wilson
CLIENT: Playboy
MEDIUM: Mixed

P. 282
ART DIRECTOR:
Jason Treat
CLIENT:
The Progressive
MEDIUM: Mixed

P. 283
ART DIRECTOR:
Aida Aguillera
CLIENT: Amarillo
Centro de Diseño
MEDIUM: 3-color sep-
aration silkscreen

P. 284
ART DIRECTOR:
Hansen Smith
CLIENT:
LA Times Magazine
MEDIUM: Mixed

P. 432
ART DIRECTOR:
Pornsak Pichetshote
CLIENT:
DC Comics Vertigo
MEDIUM: Mixed

P. 433
ART DIRECTOR:
Pornsak Pichetshoe
CLIENT:
DC Comics Vertigo
MEDIUM: Mixed

P. 550
ART DIRECTOR:
Albert Tang
CLIENT: W.W. Norton
MEDIUM:
Mixed

P. 551
MEDIUM: Mixed

STEVE SIMPSON
21 Villarea Park
Glenageary, Ireland
+353 (0)87-265-9641
mail@stevesimpson.com
www.stevesimpson.com

P. 286
CLIENT:
Michael Wejchert
MEDIUM:
Pencil, digital

MICHAEL SLOAN
203-887-1243
michaelsloan@earthlink.net
www.michaelsloan.net

P. 552
MEDIUM:
Brush & ink, pencil,
watercolor wash

JEFFREY SMITH
642 Moulton Ave. #E22
Los Angeles, CA 90032
323-224-8317
jjsillustrators@sbcglobal.net

P. 553
ART DIRECTOR:
David Talbot
CLIENT:
Simon & Schuster
MEDIUM: Acrylic inks

LAURA SMITH
6545 Cahuenga Ter.
Hollywood, CA 90068
323-467-1700
laura@laurasmithart.com
www.laurasmithart.com

P. 434
Art Directors:
Simms Taback
Sara Love
CLIENT:
Graphic Artists Guild
MEDIUM: Mixed,
digital, acrylic

MARK SMITH
1 East John Walk
Exeter EX12EW England
07810601878
marksmith71uk@aol.com

P. 287
ART DIRECTOR:
Antony Nelson
CLIENT:
The Economist
MEDIUM:
Mixed, digital

OWEN SMITH
1608 Fernisde Blvd.
Alameda, CA 94501
510-865-1911
owesmithart@att.net

P. 288
ART DIRECTOR:
Sinead McPhillips
CLIENT: Druid Theater
MEDIUM:
Oil on board

P. 348
ART DIRECTOR:
Susan Pontious
CLIENT: Laguna
Honda Hospital
MEDIUM:
Cast concrete

P. 435
ART DIRECTOR:
Erica Sussman
CLIENT: HarperCollins
MEDIUM:
Oil on paper

P. 508
MEDIUM:
Oil on plywood

JOHN SOLTIS
919 California Ave. #2
Santa Monica, CA 90403
310-260-5997
john@adhoccreative.com

P. 289
ART DIRECTOR:
Oleg Zatler
CLIENT: Ignition Print
MEDIUM: Mixed

CARLO STANGA
Via Vigevano 9
Milano 20144 Italy
+39 335 6344062
carlo.stanga@fastwebnet.it
http://www.morgangaynin.com/
stanga

P. 349
Art Directors:
Lydia Bradshaw
Amy Hausmann
CLIENT:
MTA, New York
MEDIUM: Mixed

BRIAN STAUFFER
177 San Marino Dr.
San Rafael, CA 94901
866-220-3142
brian@brianstauffer.com

P. 174
Director of Covers:
Françoise Mouly
CLIENT:
The New Yorker
MEDIUM:
Digital, mixed

P. 175
ART DIRECTOR:
Nicholas Blechman
CLIENT: The New York
Times Book Review
MEDIUM:
Digital, mixed

P. 176
ART DIRECTOR:
Greg Klee
CLIENT:
The Boston Globe
MEDIUM:
Digital, mixed

P. 177
ART DIRECTOR:
Tom Carlson
CLIENT:
Village Voice Media
MEDIUM:
Digital, mixed

P. 178
ART DIRECTOR:
Peter Storch
CLIENT:
Village Voice Media
MEDIUM:
Digital, mixed

P. 290
CLIENT: Various
MEDIUM:
Digital, mixed

P. 291
ART DIRECTOR:
Steve Sage
CLIENT: Video Helper
MEDIUM:
Digital, mixed

JAMES STEINBERG
115 Montague Rd.
Amherst, MA 01002
413-549-1932
jamessteinberg115@comcast.net

P. 350
ART DIRECTOR:
Morteza Majidi
CLIENT: The Green
Party of Iran
MEDIUM:
Acrylic, digital

P. 509
MEDIUM:
Acrylic on paper

OTTO STEININGER
144 W. 27th St. #6F
New York, NY 10001
646-706-6229
ottosteininger@gmail.com
www.ottosteininger.com

P. 179
ART DIRECTOR:
Beth Kamoroff
CLIENT: PC World
MEDIUM: Digital

MARK STUTZMAN
100 G St.
Mt. Lake Park, MD 21550
301-334-3994
mark@eloqui.com
www.eloqui.com

P. 292
ART DIRECTOR:
Gregory Burke
CLIENT:
Atlantic Records
MEDIUM: Watercolor,
gouache, airbrush

STEVEN TABBUTT
527 W. 46th St. #11
New York, NY 10036
917-207-9706
stovetabbutt@nyc.rr.com
http://www.steventabutt.com

P. 436
ART DIRECTOR:
Katie Sears
CLIENT: Katie Sears
MEDIUM: Mixed on
watercolor paper

JILLIAN TAMAKI
573 Leonard St. #3
Brooklyn, NY 11222
917-359-3693
jill@jilliantamaki.com
www.jilliantamaki.com

P. 180
Illustration Editor:
Christine Curry
CLIENT:
The New Yorker
MEDIUM: Ink, digital

GARY TAXALI
1 Wiltshire Ave. #107
Toronto M6N 2V7 Ontario, Canada
416-651-3737
gary@garytaxali.com
www.garytaxali.com

P. 181
ART DIRECTOR:
Tim J. Luddy
CLIENT: Mother Jones
MEDIUM:
Ink on paper

P. 182
ART DIRECTOR:
Nicholas Blechman
CLIENT: The New York
Times Book Review
MEDIUM:
Ink on paper

P. 183
ART DIRECTOR:
Conan Tobias
CLIENT: Taddle Creek
MEDIUM: Mixed

P. 293
ART DIRECTOR:
Doug Engel
MEDIUM: Mixed

P. 351
MEDIUM:
Alkyd oils on masonite

P. 352
ART DIRECTOR:
Declan Fahy
CLIENT:
Aubin and Willis
MEDIUM: Mixed

P. 437
Art Directors:
David Saylor
Phil Falco
CLIENT:
Scholastic Press
MEDIUM: Ink on paper

P. 510
MEDIUM:
Oil on enamels on steel

SACHIN TENG
260 Glen Ave.
New York, NY 10301
917-825-4981
sachinteng@gmail.com

GOLD
P. 448
MEDIUM:
Graphite, digital

P. 511
MEDIUM:
Graphite, digital

THE HEADS OF STATE
c/o Frank Sturges
142 W. Winter St.
Delaware, OH 43015
740-369-9702
frank@sturgesreps.com
www.sturgesreps.com

P. 184
ART DIRECTOR:
Nicholas Blechman
CLIENT:
The New York Times
MEDIUM: Digital

P. 185
ART DIRECTOR:
Nicholas Blechman
CLIENT:
The New York Times
MEDIUM: Digital

P. 186
ART DIRECTOR: DJ Stout
CLIENT:
LMU Magazine
MEDIUM: Digital

P. 187
ART DIRECTOR:
Kory Kennedy
CLIENT:
Runner's World
MEDIUM: Digital

P. 354
CLIENT: National Public
Radio
MEDIUM: Digital

P. 355
MEDIUM: Digital

P. 438
ART DIRECTOR:
Martha Kennedy
CLIENT:
Houghton Mifflin
MEDIUM: Digital

P. 554
ART DIRECTOR:
Jessica Weit
CLIENT:
Real Simple Magazine
MEDIUM: Digital

JACOB THOMAS
215 Calyer St.
Brooklyn, NY 11222
718-795-7447
jthomasillustration@gmail.com

P. 188
ART DIRECTOR:
Paul Gonzales
CLIENT: LA Times
MEDIUM: Ink, digital

P. 189
ART DIRECTOR:
Judy Pryor
CLIENT: LA Times
MEDIUM: Ink, digital

JOHN THOMPSON
109 Euclid Ter.
Syracuse, NY 13210
315-256-8201
jmthom01@syr.edu
www.johnthompsonpaintings.com
P. 512
MEDIUM: Acrylic

MARK TODD
325 Adams St.
Sierra Madre, CA 91024
626-836-2210
marktoddart@gmail.com
marktoddillustration.com

P. 555
Art Directors:
Dave Eggers
Brian McMullen
CLIENT:
McSweeney's Issue 33
MEDIUM: Ink and digital

DAISUKE TSUTSUMI
917-887-1527
dice@simplestroke.com
www.simplestroke.com

P. 513
MEDIUM:
Oil on canvas

POL TURGEON
5187 Jeanne-Mance #3
Montreal H2V 4K2 Canada
514-273-8329
pol@polturgeon.com
www.polturgeon.com

P. 190
ART DIRECTOR:
Erin Benner
CLIENT:
Bicycling Magazine
MEDIUM: Mixed

P. 294
ART DIRECTOR:
Joanne Filion
CLIENT:
Cirque du Soleil
MEDIUM: Gouache,
varnish

MARK ULRIKSEN
841 Shrader St.
San Francisco, CA 94117
415-387-0170
mark@markulriksen.com
www.markulriksen.com

P. 191
ART DIRECTOR:
Jordan Awan
CLIENT:
The New Yorker
MEDIUM:
Acrylic on board

JACK UNRUH
8138 Santa Clara Dr.
Dallas, TX 75218
214-324-2720
jack@jackunruh.com
www.jackunruh.com

P. 192
ART DIRECTOR:
Carolyn Perot
CLIENT: Mother Jones
MEDIUM:
Ink, watercolor

P. 193
Art Directors:
Mike Ley
Neil Jamison
CLIENT:
Field & Stream
MEDIUM: Ink, watercolor

P. 194
ART DIRECTOR:
Nathan Sinclair
CLIENT: AR Absolute
Return+Alpha
MEDIUM:
Ink, watercolor

P. 195
ART DIRECTOR:
Macon York
CLIENT:
New York Magazine
MEDIUM:
Ink, watercolor

P. 196
Art Directors:
Julie Savasky
DJ Stout
CLIENT: Pentagram
MEDIUM:
Ink, watercolor

P. 356
ART DIRECTOR:
Brian Boyd
CLIENT:
RBMM Design
MEDIUM:
Ink, watercolor

DAVID VOGIN
7 E. Patrick St. #1
Frederick, MD 21701
202-607-3286
david@davidvogin.com
www.davidvogin.com

SILVER
P. 219
ART DIRECTOR:
David Vogin
CLIENT: TEDxOil Spill
Conference
MEDIUM:
Digital collage

STEVE WACKSMAN
160 Saint James Pl.
Brooklyn, NY 11238
718-789-0609
wax@houseowax.com

P. 295
ART DIRECTOR:
Lily Smith-Kirkley
CLIENT:
Matchbox Studio
MEDIUM: Ink, digital

P. 556
MEDIUM: Ink, digital

BRUCE WALDMAN
18 Westbrook Rd.
Westfield, NJ 07090
908-232-2840
swgraphics@comcast.net

P. 296
ART DIRECTOR:
Christine Morrison
CLIENT: Technical
Analysis of Stocks
and Commodities
MEDIUM: Monoprint

SAM WEBER
573 Leonard St. #3
Brooklyn, NY 11222
917-374 3373
sam@sampaints.com
www.sampaints.com

P. 197
ART DIRECTOR:
Jason Treat
CLIENT:
The Atlantic
MEDIUM: Watercolor,
acrylic, digital

P. 198
ART DIRECTOR:
Irene Gallo
CLIENT: Tor.com
MEDIUM:
Acrylic, digital

P. 297
ART DIRECTOR:
Jim Burke
CLIENT:
Dellas Graphics
MEDIUM: Watercolor,
acrylic, digital

P. 358
ART DIRECTOR:
Edel Rodriguez
CLIENT: The Society of
Illustrators
MEDIUM: Watercolor,
acrylic, digital

P. 359
ART DIRECTOR:
Rodrigo Corral
CLIENT: American
Illustration
MEDIUM: Watercolor,
acrylic, digital

P. 439
ART DIRECTOR:
Debra Sfetsios
CLIENT:
Simon & Schuster
MEDIUM: Watercolor,
acrylic, digital

ELLEN WEINSTEIN
475 FDR Drive #2107
New York, NY 10002
917-653-4097
ellen@ellenweinstein.com
www.ellenweinstein.com

P. 357
ART DIRECTOR:
Becca Hadzor
CLIENT: The Nashville
Symphony
MEDIUM: Collage

OLIVER WEISS
Brandstaett 10
Grassau 83224 Germany
+49-8641-1465
info@oweiss.com
www.oweisscom

P. 557
MEDIUM:
Mixed, collage

KYLE WHITE
700 Beverly Hills Rd. #221
Hattiesburg, MI 39401
352-576-2337
kyle@kylewhitedesign.com
www.kylewhitedesign.com

P. 360

CARL WIENS
11 Queen St.
Picton KOK 2TO Ontario, Canada
613-476-2500
wiens@kos.net

P. 514
MEDIUM:
Digital assemblage

NATE WILLIAMS
c/o Magnet Reps
1783 S. Crescent Heights Blvd.
Los Angeles, CA 90035
866-390-5656
cora@magnetreps.com
www.magnetreps.com

P. 361
ART DIRECTOR:
Claudia Morales
CLIENT: Hola Amiga
MEDIUM: Mixed

P. 515
MEDIUM: Mixed

MARTIN WITTFOOTH
222 Varet St. #3G
Brooklyn, NY 11206
347-866-3052
info@martinwittfooth.com
www.martinwittfooth.com

SILVER
P. 452
MEDIUM:
Oil on linen

NOAH WOODS
927 Westbourne Rd.
Los Angeles, CA 90069
310-422-2266
noahwoods@mindspring.com

P. 362
ART DIRECTOR:
Katy Fisher
CLIENT:
St. Louis Central
Library
MEDIUM: Mixed

ANDREW WRIGHT
2036 Park Ave. #B
Richmond, VA 23220
773-870-1150
andrew@andrewRwright.com
www.andrewrwright.com

P. 298
ART DIRECTOR:
Sarah Watts
CLIENT: Half Acre
Brewing Company
MEDIUM:
Linoleum print

JAMES YANG
509 12th St. #2D
Brooklyn, NY 11215
347-721-3666
james@jamesyang.com
www.jamesyang.com

P. 299
ART DIRECTOR:
Ken Karlic
CLIENT: A/I/DATA
MEDIUM: Digital

P. 363
ART DIRECTOR:
Deborah Withey
CLIENT:
Society of News-
paper Designers
MEDIUM: Digital

BRAD YEO
602 8th Ave. NE
Calgary T2E 0R6 Alberta, Canada
403-237-5553
bradyeo@bradyeo.com
www.bradyeo.com

GOLD
P. 206
CLIENT:
The Founders' Gallery
MEDIUM: Acrylic

AARP, 122
Abrams, 376
Abrams Books for Young Readers, 400, 401
Abrams Images, 372, 410, 411, 412
Acme Thunderer, 253
AD-ITIVE, 272
Advanced Nutrients, 222, 223
ai5000 Magazine, 77
aiCIO, 152
A/I/DATA, 299
AIGA Baltimore, 277
Alain Beaulet Éditeur, 524
Alamo Drafthouse Theater, 252
Allegro, 216, 274
Alpine Green Living, 266
Amarillo Centro de Diseño, 283
American Illustration, 359
ANCMA, 258
Angie's List, 165
Annabelle Magazine, 87
AR Absolute Return+Alpha, 194
Arena Stage, 254, 339
Art Directors Club of Metropolitan Washington, 324
Ashi Dashi, 304
Assett Internationl, 56
Associations of Now Magazine, 344
Atlantic, 53, 69, 85, 106, 130, 132, 133, 197
Atlantic Records, 292
Atwater Winery, 229
Aubin and Willis, 352
Audubon Magazine, 83
Augusto Bianchi, 320
Bayard, 381
Beacon Fine Arts, 325
Beautiful/Decay, 328
Bicycling Magazine, 190
Big Island Bees, 259
BLAB!, 535
Blabworld Magazine, 57
Black Cat Publishing, 168
Blue Apple Books, 399
Bookwall/Shueisha, 407
Boston Consulting Group, 305, 321
Boston Globe, 142, 149, 176
Bridgeport Brewing, 224
Bries Editions, 539
Bureau of International Information Programs, U.S. State Department, 327
Calcalist weekend edition (Israel), 520
California Magazine, 102
Capstone Publishers, 406
Chado Ralph Rucci, 236, 237
Chicago Bears Football Club, 285
Children's Hospital Boston, 343
Christy Ottaviano Books, 429
Chronicle Books, 546
Chronicle of Higher Education, 112
Cirque du Soleil, 294
Communication-Jeunesse, 263
Concept Art, 334
Corriere Della Sera, 109
Cosac Naify, 384
Crossway Publishing, 402
David Cashion, 372, 411, 412
DB Mobil, Deutsche Bahn, German Railways, 536
DC Comics Vertigo, 432, 433
Deal Magazine, 134
Delaware Today, 100
Dellas Graphics, 297, 336, 337

Der Spiegel, 47
Der Spiegel for Kids, 147
Dial Books for Young Readers, 422
Diane Sherry Case, 380
Diesel, Buenos Aires, 230
Dinners at the Farm, 250
DOMA, 317, 318
Dorten, 246, 247, 248, 533
Druid Theater, 288
Dutton Children's Books, 413, 414
Earth: Fragile Planet, 313
Ecoles des Loisirs, 382
Economist, 287
Éditions Delcourt, 379
Éditions Milan, 370
Emergency, 208
Emmanuelle Rouiller, 307
Esquire, 92
Festa Literaria Internacionale de Paraty, 214
Field & Stream, 193
Film Shack, 276
Folio Society, 394, 528
Founders Council, 231, 233
Founders' Gallery, 206
Freya, Victory Records, 242
Garden & Gun, 50, 93
Globe and Mail, 549
Golf Digest, 49, 107
GQ, 139
GQ Germany, 51, 114
Grand Central Publishing, 426
Graphic Artists Guild, 434
Great American Songbook Project, 235
Green Party of Iran, 350
Guanda, 431
Gus Ramsey, 234
Hachette Books, 427
Half Acre Brewing Company, 298
HarperCollins, 377, 378, 388, 435
Harper's Magazine, 67
Hemisphere's Magazine, 96, 98
Hola Amiga, 361
Honolulu Magazine, 80
Houghton Mifflin Harcourt, 383, 385, 438
HOW Magazine, 166
Humana Festival, 232
Hyperakt Design Group, 332
IEEE Spectrum, 89
Ignition Print, 289
Infor, 221
Internazionale, 110, 534
Jason Kupfer, 261
Joey Cain, 238
Kalandraka Editora, 389, 390
Katie Sears, 436
Kazoo, 228
KONG Magazine, 58, 59
KT&G, 341
Kunio Co. Ltd., 346
L.A. Times, 95, 151, 188, 189, 284
La Grande Ourse Theater (France), 300
La Repubblica, 162, 163
Laguna Honda Hospital, 348
Las Vegas Weekly, 170
Les Allusifs, 391
Library of Congress, 309
Little, Brown and Company, 395

LMU Magazine, 186
Los Angeles Magazine, 117
MacUser UK, 54
Macy's, 226
Margot Harley, 268
Maryland Institute College of Art, 279
Masa Reklam Ajans, 240
Massachusetts General Hospital, 530
Matchbox Studio, 295
Mauricio de Souza Produções, 538
McSweeney's, 555
Men's Journal, 124, 125
MGM Resorts, VIVA Festival, 227
Miami New Times, 171
Michael Wejchert, 286
Middlebury Magazine, 164
Midtown Films, 527
Migrate Magazine, 105
Milken Institute Review, 128, 129
Milliyet Newspaper, 101
Minimum Fax, 375, 398
MIT Technology Review, 88
Modern Dog Magazine, 157
MoMA Propaganda, 280
More Magazine, 44, 61, 115
Mother Jones, 68, 136, 181, 192
MTA, New York, 349
Muse Magazine, 64
Nashville Symphony, 357
Nation, 84
National Cherry Blossom Festival, 322
National Public Radio, 354
New Republic, 81, 113, 123
News Limited, 126
Newsweek, 548
New York Observer, 72, 73, 75, 76
New York Magazine, 195
New York Times, 103, 104, 159, 160, 161, 184, 185, 319, 526
New York Times Book Review, 52, 90, 91, 167, 175, 182, 540
New York Times Gallery 7, 278
New York Times Science Times, 158
New York Times Week In Review, 532
Night Shade Books, 424
Ogilvy Frankfurt, 260
Patinae, 340
Paul Mark, 204
PC World, 179
Pelican, 404
Penguin, 387, 423
Penguin UK, 418
Pentagram, 168, 196
Plains Capital Bank, 243
Plansponsor, 144
Plansponsor Europe, 65
Playboy, 48, 86, 127, 173
Poetry Foundation, 146
Poetry Magazine, 145
Popular Mechanics, 156
Pragmatic Management, 262
Progressive, 172, 282
Proto Magazine, 342
Punch & Judy, 267
Rabid Rabbit, 257
RAND, 335
Random House, 386, 403, 415, 547
Rashworks, 502
RBMM Design, 356
Real Simple Magazine, 554
Richard Solomon, 150

Rolling Stone, 46, 74, 137, 155
Rolling Stone Australia, 143
Rotarian, 60
Runner's World, 94, 97, 154, 187
Saatchi & Saatchi, 264
Santa Fe Reporter, 63, 79
Saratoga National Battlefield Park, 326
Scholastic, 392, 437
School of Visual Arts, 430
School of Visual Arts 2010 Annual Report, 330
Scott Shpeley, 239
Screen Australia, 310
SEAC, 215
Secret Sherry Project, 269
Shout Out Louds, 271
Sierra Nevada Brewing Company, 255
Signature Art Medals, 329
Simon & Schuster, 374, 416, 419, 420, 421, 439, 553
Society of Illustrators, 210, 301, 358
Society of Newspaper Designers, 363
Sparta Insurance, 273
Spirit Magazine, 55
Spoon, 225
Spring Magazine, 522
St. Louis Central Library, 362
Sterling Publishing, 417
Taddle Creek, 183
Teca Paper Products, 331
Technical Analysis of Stocks and Commodities, 296
TEDxOil Spill Conference, 219
Templeton Foundation, 347
Terrorismo Grafico, 111
Texas Monthly, 70
3x3, The Magazine of Contemporary Illustration, 99
TIME, 42, 141, 153
TIME Asia, 131
Times Higher Educational, 108
Tommy McCutchon, 220
Tor.com, 78, 198
Tulsa Opera, 256
U. S. Postal Service, 212, 308, 316, 333, 345
UCLA, 529
Utne Magazine, 135
Vanity Fair, 82, 14
Verve Music, 244, 245
Viche Publishers, 425
Victoria Symphony, 218, 323
Video Helper, 291
Village Voice, 138, 148
Village Voice Media, 177, 178
Virginia Arts of the Book Center, 428
Virginia Living Magazine, 118, 119, 120, 121
Vue sur la Ville, 251
Wall Street Journal, 62, 541
Wildbirds and Peacedrums, 270
WOK restaurant, 241
World Wildlife Fund, 281
W.W. Norton, 550

ART DIRECTORS

AIDA AGUILLERA, 283
MARSHALL ARISMAN, 430
JORDAN AWAN, 169, 191
FILIZ AYGUNDUZ, 101
ANTONELLA BANDOLI, 215
STEVEN BANKS, 117
CHRIS BARBER, 108
MARY BRIGID BARRETT, 309
PATRICK BARRY, 385
JEFFREY C. BATZLI, 417
ELISA BAUCH, 227
WESLEY BAUSMITH, 95
MONTE BEAUCHAMP, 57, 535
ALAIN BEAULET, 524
CHAD BECKERMAN, 400, 401
ERIN BENNER, 190
DEBRA BISHOP, 44, 115
NICHOLAS BLECHMAN, 52, 90, 91, 161,
    167, 175, 182, 184, 185, 540
MELISSA BLUEY, 85
ZAC BOSWELL, 231, 233
CHRISTINE BOWER-WRIGHT, 96
BRIAN BOYD, 243, 356
LYDIA BRADSHAW, 349
LIZZY BROMLEY, 419, 420, 421
JOAN BROOKER, 527
DEBORAH BROWN, 259
PAUL BUCKLEY, 387
GREGORY BURKE, 292
JIM BURKE, 297, 336, 337
NANCY BUTKUS, 72, 73, 75, 76
SOOJIN BUZELLI, 56, 65, 77, 144, 152
GARY CALLAHAN, 305, 321
CHRISTINE CAR, 123
TOM CARLSON, 177
KELLY CARTER, 100
LIZ CASAL, 427
DAVID CASHION, 410
SONIA CHAGHATZBANIAN, 374
STEVEN CHARNY, 46, 74, 116, 137, 155
STACEY CLARKSON, 67
FERNADA COHEN, 111
MARTIN COLYER, 235
MARTINE COMBRÉAS, 300
JULIA CONNOLLY, 418
RODRIGO CORRAL, 359
LUCHO CORREA, 241
EMILY CRAWFORD, 42
DAVID CURCURITO, 92
GIORDANO CURRERI, 258
CHRISTINE CURRY, 40, 66, 180, 460, 545
TYLER DARDEN, 118, 120, 121
SCOTT DAVIES, 122
GIOVANNI DE MAURO, 534
JOSH DENNIS, 402
GREGORY DIBISCEGLIE, 138, 226
JOHN DIXON, 148
MATT DOBSON, 232
KELLY DOE, 532
DAVE EGGERS, 555
JENS EHRENREICH, 536
DOUG ENGEL, 293
LEO ESPINOSA, 317
AARON FAGERSTROM, 249
DECLAN FAHY, 352
RICCARDO FALCINELLI, 375, 398
PHIL FALCO, 437
JOE FERRARA, 143
JOANNE FILION, 294
KATY FISHER, 362
KEVIN FISHER, 83
KRISTI FLANGO, 269
PAM FOGG, 164
ANDY FRANK, 529

AMY FRITH, 221
DANA FRITTS, 377, 378
LOUIS GAGNON, 391
JOHN GALL, 547
IRENE GALLO, 78, 198
MONIQUE GAMACHE, 218, 323
KATE GARTNER, 386
NATHAN GASSMAN, 406
SHERI GEE, 528
LARRY GENDRON, 134
STEPHANIE GLAROS, 135
PAUL GONZALES, 188
PAYL D. GONZALES, 151
PETER GOOD, 250
SIDNEY GUSMAN, 538
BECCA HADZOR, 357
CATHERINE HALLEY, 146
DAVID HARRIS, 82, 140
AMY HAUSMANN, 349
NOBARA HAYAKAWA, 393
KEITH HAYES, 395
ERICA HEIMBERG, 314, 315
PETER HERBERT, 156
CARL T. HERMAN, 345
JOE HEROUN, 81, 113, 123
ROB HEWITT, 98
CHARLES HIVELY, 99
JEANNE HOGLE, 388
RODRIGO HONEYWELL, 106
JOE HUTCHINSON, 46
ANTON IOUKHNOVETS, 139
MICHELLE ISHAY-COHEN, 376
LILLIAN IVERSEN, 322
NEIL JAMISON, 193
NICK JEHLEN, 172
ERIK JOHNSON, 537
MARK JOHNSON, 326
ANDRÉE KAHLMORGAN, 42
BETH KAMOROFF, 179
KEN KARLIC, 299
JURIKO KAWABATA, 346
ANNETTE KELLER, 87, 110
JENNIFER KELLY, 422
KORY KENNEDY, 94, 97, 154, 187
MARTHA KENNEDY, 438
ETHEL KESSLER, 316, 333
STEFAN KIEFER, 47, 147
SUNG HEE KIM, 324
EMILY KIMBRO, 55
HOLLIS KING, 244, 245
GREG KLEE, 176
THOMAS KNOPF, 260
REGGIE KNOW, 272
ALEX KNOWLTON, 145
ORLIE KRAUS, 62
ELIOT KRELOFF, 399
ALAIN LACHARTRE, 251
LORI LACHMANN, 266
SUZANNE LAGASA, 546
DEBORAH LAWRENCE, 60
ELLICE LEE, 415
SEUNG HEE LEE, 425

MARK LEWIS, 262
MIKE LEY, 193
NICKI LINDEMAN, 254, 339
KRISTIN K. LIPMAN, 80
KATIE LONG, 544
SARA LOVE, 434
BETH LOWER, 344
TIM J. LUDDY, 68, 181
KEN MACY, 304
NADIA MAESTRI, 68
CAROLINE MAIHOT, 40, 460
MORTEZA MAJIDI, 350
CHRIS MALEC, 141, 342, 530
GREG MANCHESS, 313
PIERPAOLO MARCONCINI, 258
PAUL MARK, 204
STANLEY MARTUCCI, 325
BRIGID MCCARREN, 166
MICHAEL MCCARTNEY, 416
PAT MCCASKEY, 285
MARSHAL MCKINNEY, 50, 93
CINDERS MCLEOD, 549
JENNIFER MCMANUS, 61
BRIAN MCMULLEN, 555
SINEAD MCPHILLIPS, 288
JANA MEIER-ROBERTS, 114
AVIVA MICHAELOV, 103, 160
JESSICA MOATS, 53, 59
MARK MONTGOMERY, 89
ANGELA MOORE, 63, 79
CLAUDIA MORALES, 361
PETER MORANCE, 158
LORA MORGENSTERN, 530
GAVIN MORRIS, 394, 408, 409
CHRISTINE MORRISON, 296
ELIZABETH MORROW MCKENZIE, 224
FRANÇOISE MOULY, 174
KELLY MURPHY, 429
CORINNE MYLLER, 526
CAMILLE NEILSON, 54
ANTONY NELSON, 287
BILL NELSON, 150
MARGARIDA NORONHA, 389, 390
JENNIFER NOSEK, 157
DERRY NOYES, 308
RYAN OLBRYSH, 170
HOWARD PAINE, 212
JOHN PALLATTELA, 84
DAVID PALUMBO, 424
ERIC PANKE, 273
SONDA PAPPAN, 119
ELIZABETH PARISI, 392
GREGORY PEPPER, 228
DEROY PERAZA, 332
CAROLYN PEROT, 136, 192
PORNSAK PICHETSHOE, 432, 433
D.W. PINE, 153
DAVID PLUNKERT, 276, 277, 278, 279
TANJA POHL, 165
JOE POMPEO, 264
SUSAN PONTIOUS, 348
JUDY PRYOR, 189
LEAH PURCEL, 548
MITCH PUTNAM, 252
JOANNAH RALSTON, 128, 129, 347
ANTHONY RAMONDO, 423
JORGE RESTREPO, 393
DAN REVITTE, 142
SARA REYNOLDS, 413, 414
LAUREN RILLE, 374
ANGELO RINALDI, 162, 163
JASON ROBERSON, 255
JANA ROBERTS, 51
EDEL RODRIGUEZ, 358

SABINE ROUSSELET, 379
KI TAE RYU, 341
STEVE SAGE, 291
MARIA CAOLINA SAMPAIO, 384
JOHN SANDFORD, 64
KENICHI SATO, 404
MICHAEL SAUL, 403
JEFF SAVAGE, 256
JULIE SAVASKY, 196, 222, 223
DAVID SAYLOR, 437
MARK SCHLEPPHORST, 329
RIA SCHULPEN, 539
CHRISTIAN SCHWARM, 246, 247, 248, 533
RIVA SCHWARTZ, 49, 107
KATIE SEARS, 436
SCOTT SEYMOUR, 112
DEBRA SFETSIOS, 439
LEANNE SHAPTON, 104, 319
PAM SHAVALIER, 171
TECE LEOPOLDO E SILVA, 33
NATHAN SINCLAIR, 194
SHEILA SMALLWOOD, 383
HANSEN SMITH, 284
LILY SMITH-KIRKLEY, 295
MICHAEL SOLITA, 89
GREGOIRE SOLOTAREFF, 382
GRANT STAUBLIN, 149
PETER STORCH, 178
DJ STOUT, 168, 186, 222, 223
ERICA SUSSMAN, 435
SIMMS TABACK, 434
DAVID TALBOT, 553
ALBERT TANG, 550
MARITTA TAPANAINEN, 335
CHRIS THOMPSON, 396, 397
ANGELA TIERI, 88
CODY TILSON, 86
CONAN TOBIAS, 183
MICHIKO TOKI, 102
CHRIS TOPP, 126
JASON TREAT, 53, 69, 130, 132, 133,
    197, 282
T.J. TUCKER, 70, 71
VAHIT TUNA, 240
ANNE TWOMEY, 426
TRIPP UNDERWOOD, 343
JACK UNRUH, 313
MANUEL VELEZ, 541
MATIAS VIGLIANO, 317, 318
DAVID VOGIN, 219
SARAH WATTS, 298
JESSICA WEIT, 554
DAMIAN WILKINSON, 124, 125
ROANNA WILLIAMS, 105
ROB WILSON, 48, 127, 173
DEBORAH WITHEY, 363
CECELIA WONG, 131
DIANE WOOLVERTON, 327
PAUL YOKOTA, 221
MACON YORK, 195
OLEG ZATLER, 289
AMIR ZIV, 520

Thomas Ehretsmann
Gold Medal, Book

David Vogin
Silver Medal
Institutional

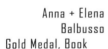
Anna + Elena
Balbusso
Gold Medal, Book

Asaf Hanuka
Gold Medal
Sequential
(detail)

Tim O'Brien
Silver Metal
Editorial

Brad Yeo
Gold Metal
Advertising

Joseph Adolphe
 Brian Ajhar
 Raúl Allén
 Martin Ansin
 Stuart Briers
 David M. Brinley

 Nigel Buchanan
 Lonnie Busch
 Jonathan Carlson
 Stephanie Dalton Cowan
 Robert de Michiell
 John S. Dykes

 Jan Feindt
 Matthieu Forichon
 Phil Foster
 Anthony Freda
 Mark Fredrickson
 Arthur E. Giron

 Asaf Hanuka
 Daniel Hertzberg
 Jakob Hinrichs
 Peter Horjus
 Peter Horvath
 Celia Johnson

 Douglas B. Jones
 James Kaczman
 Laszlo Kubinyi
 PJ Loughran
 Bernard Maisner
 Hal Mayforth

 Sean McCabe
 Richard Mia
 Bruce Morser
 Shaw Nielsen
 James O'Brien
 Yuta Onoda

 Hank Osuna
 Dan Page
 Cara Petrus
 John Pirman
 Jean-Francois Podevin
 Scotty Reifsnyder

 Jon Reinfurt
 Rafael Ricoy
 Marc Rosenthal
 Alison Seiffer
 Seth
 Whitney Sherman

 Jeffrey Smith
 Ryan Snook
 Bob Staake
 James Steinberg
 Elizabeth Traynor
 Eva Vazquez

 Andy Ward
 Anders Wenngren
 Michael Witte
Noah Woods
Phil Wrigglesworth
Brad Yeo

THEN & NOW

1 **Erin McGuire '08** Reel Fx
www.emcguire.net

2 **Mirna Stubbs '08** Hallmark
www.twoheadedbeast.net

3 **Jay Epperson '05** Retro Studios
www.jayepperson.com

4 **Erik Jones '07** Freelance
theirison.com

5 **Christina Ellis '10** Moonbot Studios
skellopia.blogspot.com

6 **Cody Kenworthy '04** THQ/Relic Entertainment
swiftstroke.blogspot.com

Ringling College of Art + Design
Department of Illustration
Destroying the myth of the starving artist.
www.ringling.edu

ERIC FOWLER: Cityscapes

For commissions contact :

epfowler@attglobal.net

or call

studio 212-532-1231
cell 609-658-5924

143 East 37 St. Apt 1R NYC 10016 **www.ericfowlerstudio.com** info@fineartistprints.com

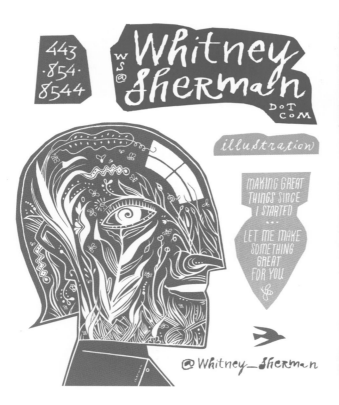

gilpin   kolesova   dave phillips   faricy   kennedy

koelsch   andreasen   bollinger   caparo   keltie

elwell   haya   nielsen   cowdrey   papp

nordstrand   bonatakis   rebenschied   craig phillips   haagensen

morrow   parks   comport   raven   roe

212.333.2551

shannonassociates.com

PARSONS
BFA IN
ILLUSTRATION

A pioneer in the field of illustration since 1898, Parsons
The New School for Design continues to set the pace in the world
of visual communication. Illustration by William Crosby, Class of 2011

www.newschool.edu/illustration
PARSONS THE NEW SCHOOL FOR DESIGN

Rule No. 3

Being visible is essential. You're everywhere.

You want to be seen in as many places as possible. Think of any new product or service that's come out, you see them here and then there and then on the shelf. It seems like they've been around forever and yet they're a brand new product. You're no different.

And like a brand, you'll need to be seen at least three times before you've even made the slightest impression. That could mean mailing three postcards or three email blasts over a short period of time. But definitely one shot is not enough to make any impression; if it does then it's a rarity.

So you want to be seen in as many places as physically and financially possible. And don't just seek out the free spots to be in, spend some cold hard cash advertising and promoting yourself. Successful illustrators spend at least 20 percent of their income on promotion.

By promoting yourself you look successful. Look successful. Be successful.

THIS IS JUST ONE OF MANY TIPS YOU'LL FIND IN *3X3 MAGAZINE*'S LATEST BOOK. WRITTEN BY CHARLES HIVELY, *NUTS & BOLTS* IS A NO-NONSENSE APPROACH TO BUILDING A CAREER AS AN ILLUSTRATOR. PERFECT FOR THOSE NEW TO THE INDUSTRY OR FOR THOSE WHO HAVE BEEN OUT IN THE MARKET JUST A FEW YEARS. INTELLIGENT, PRICELESS ADVICE FROM AN ART DIRECTOR'S POINT OF VIEW.

ISBN 978-0-9819405-4-0
100 PAGES, PERFECT BOUND 7.5X7.5-INCHES
AVAILABLE AT AMAZON.COM AND ONLINE AT 3X3MAG.COM
RETAIL PRICE $13.95 (ALSO AVAILABLE AS AN E-BOOK)
PUBLISHED BY *3X3 MAGAZINE*, A PUBLICATION OF ARTISANAL MEDIA LLC